EVERYDAY LIFE AND POLITICS
IN NINETEENTH CENTURY MEXICO

 DIÁLOGOS

A SERIES OF COURSE-ADOPTION BOOKS ON LATIN AMERICA

Independence in Spanish America: Civil Wars, Revolutions, and Underdevelopment
(revised edition)—Jay Kinsbruner, Queens College

Heroes on Horseback: A Life and Times of the Last Gaucho Caudillos—John Charles Chasteen,
University of North Carolina at Chapel Hill

The Life and Death of Carolina Maria de Jesus—Robert M. Levine, University of Miami, and
José Carlos Sebe Bom Meihy, University of São Paulo

The Countryside in Colonial Latin America—Edited by Louisa Schell Hoberman,
University of Texas at Austin, and Susan Migden Socolow, Emory University

¡Que vivan los tamales! Food and the Making of Mexican Identity—Jeffrey M. Pilcher,
The Citadel

The Faces of Honor: Sex, Shame, and Violence in Colonial Latin America—Edited by
Lyman L. Johnson, University of North Carolina at Charlotte, and
Sonya Lipsett-Rivera, Carleton University

The Century of U.S. Capitalism in Latin America—Thomas F. O'Brien, University of Houston

Tangled Destinies: Latin America and the United States—Don Coerver, Texas Christian University,
and Linda Hall, University of New Mexico

Everyday Life and Politics in Nineteenth Century Mexico: Men, Women, and War—
Mark Wasserman, Rutgers, The State University of New Jersey

Lives of the Bigamists: Marriage, Family, and Community in Colonial Mexico—
Richard Boyer, Simon Fraser University

Andean Worlds: Indigenous History, Culture, and Consciousness Under Spanish Rule, 1532–1825—
Kenneth J. Andrien, Ohio State University

The Mexican Revolution, 1910–1940—Michael J. Gonzales, Northern Illinois University

Quito 1599: City and Colony in Transition—Kris Lane, College of William and Mary

Argentina on the Couch: Psychiatry, State, and Society, 1880 to the Present—Edited by
Mariano Plotkin, CONICET (National Council of Scientific Research, Argentina),
and Universidad Nacional de Tres de Febrero, Buenos Aires, Argentina.

A Pest in the Land: New World Epidemics in a Global Perspective—Suzanne Austin Alchon,
University of Delaware

The Silver King: The Remarkable Life of the Count of Regla in Colonial Mexico—
Edith Boorstein Couturier, Ph.D., Professor Emerita

National Rhythms, African Roots: The Deep History of Latin American Popular Dance—
John Charles Chasteen, University of North Carolina at Chapel Hill

The Great Festivals of Colonial Mexico City: Performing Power and Identity—
Linda A. Curcio-Nagy, University of Nevada at Reno

*The Souls of Purgatory: The Spiritual Diary of a Seventeenth-Century Afro-Peruvian Mystic,
Ursula de Jesús*—Nancy E. van Deusen, Western Washington University

Dutra's World: Wealth and Family in Nineteenth-Century Rio de Janeiro—
Zephyr L. Frank, Stanford University

Death, Dismemberment, and Memory: Body Politics in Latin America—Edited by
Lyman L. Johnson, University of North Carolina at Charlotte

Plaza of Sacrifices: Gender, Power, and Terror in 1968 Mexico—Elaine Carey,
St. John's University

*Women in the Crucible of Conquest: The Gendered Genesis of Spanish American Society,
1500–1600*—Karen Vieira Powers, Arizona State University

Beyond Black and Red: African-Native Relations in Colonial Latin America—
Edited by Matthew Restall, Pennsylvania State University, University Park

Mexico OtherWise: Modern Mexico in the Eyes of Foreign Observers—Edited and translated by
Jürgen Buchenau, University of North Carolina at Charlotte

SERIES ADVISORY EDITOR: LYMAN L. JOHNSON, UNIVERSITY OF NORTH CAROLINA AT CHARLOTTE

EVERYDAY LIFE AND POLITICS IN NINETEENTH CENTURY MEXICO

MEN, WOMEN, AND WAR

Mark Wasserman

ALBUQUERQUE

The University of New Mexico Press

09 08 07 06 05   3 4 5 6 7

LIBRARY OF CONGRESS CATALOGING-IN-PUBLICATION DATA

Wasserman, Mark, 1946–

Everyday life and politics in nineteenth century Mexico : men, women, and war /
Mark Wasserman. — 1st ed.

      p.   cm. — (Diálogos)

Includes bibliographical references and index.

  ISBN 0-8263-2170-4 (alk. paper) — ISBN 0-8263-2171-2 (pbk. : alk. paper)

  1. Mexico—History—19th century.

2. War and society—Mexico—History—19th century.

3.Regionaliam—Mexico—History—19th century.

I. Title. II. Diálogos (Albuquerque, N.M.)

F1232 .W38 2000

972' .04—dc21

                99-006913

This book is dedicated with
love to my siblings Jane Wasserman Newman,
James I. Wasserman, and Lee S. Wasserman,
and to the memory of Faye B. Parker.

CONTENTS

Illustrations, Maps, and Tables ... *ix*

Acknowledgments ... *xi*

Introduction ... 3

Part I. The Age of Troubles ... 15

Antonio López de Santa Anna ... 17

Timeline ... 21

Chapter 1. **Everyday Life, 1821–46: Tradition and Turmoil** ... 22

Chapter 2. **The Politics of Disorder, 1821–45** ... 45

Chapter 3. **The Origins of Underdevelopment** ... 61

Chapter 4. **The Disastrous War** ... 74

Part II. The Age of Civil Wars ... 91

Benito Juárez ... 93

Timeline ... 98

Chapter 5. **Politics and Economy in Civil War, 1848–61** ... 99

Chapter 6. **Foreign Intervention and Reconstruction, 1861–67** ... 112

Chapter 7. **Everyday Life, 1849–76: The Impact of War and Reform** ... 133

Part III. The Age of Order and Progress ... 159

Porfirio Díaz ... 161

Timeline ... 167

Chapter 8. **The Economy of Progress** ... 168

Chapter 9.   **Everyday Life, 1877–1910: The Onslaught of Change**   *182*
Chapter 10. **The Politics of Order, 1877–1910**   *209*

Epilogue   *229*
Selected Bibliography   *233*
Index   *239*

ILLUSTRATIONS

1. Antonio López de Santa Ana   16
2. The Aguador   31
3. Calle de Tacuba   36
4. Vendor carries home artisan production   38
5. A busy marketplace on the outskirts of Mexico City   39
6. Guadalupe Victoria   47
7. Anastasio Bustamante   48
8. Juan Alvarez   49
9. Valentín Gómez Farías   52
10. José Joaquín de Herrera   78
11. Benito Juárez   92
12. Maximilian   118
13. Carlota   119
14. The Battle of San Lorenzo   122
15. Tortilla seller   143
16. A mestiza and a mestizo   145
17. Railroad bridge overlooking rural home   149
18. Wash day   151
19. Going to Mass   155
20. Porfirio Díaz   160
21. Carmen Romero Rubio de Díaz   162
22. Mining camp   194
23. Pachuca, a mining town   197
24. Zocalo or Plaza in Mexico City   201

MAPS

1. Mexico, An Overview   2
2. Mexican Territorial Losses from 1836 to 1853   88
3. Two Major Railroads and Physical Features   173

TABLES

Table 1. Mining Production   176
Table 2. Population, Selected Years, 1803 to 1910   199

ACKNOWLEDGMENTS

This is a work of synthesis and, as such, owes many debts to historians and observers of the times for its insights and descriptions. I have borrowed freely from their interpretations and analyses. Because the book is meant for a general audience, in the interest of space and narrative flow, I have not employed notes. Instead, I will recognize contributions of fact and interpretation in three ways: in these acknowledgments, in notes at the beginning of each chapter, and in select instances in the body of the text. Most historians of Mexico will quickly recognize their own and colleagues' contributions. I have included a select bibliography for those students who wish to read further. (I will furnish a complete bibliography of works cited on request.)

Several generations of historians, including Timothy E. Anna, Silvia Arrom, Jan Bazant, Charles Berry, Wilfrid Callcott, Mario Cerutti, John H. Coatsworth, Roberto Cortés Conde, Daniel Cosío Villegas, Michael P. Costeloe, Egon Caesar Count Corti, Moisés González Navarro, Charles Hale, Richard A. Johnson, Robert J. Knowlton, Laurens Perry, T. G. Powell, Ricardo Rendón, Jaime E. Rodríguez O., Ralph Roeder, Fernando Rosenzweig, Walter V. Scholes, Otis Singletary, William F. Sprague, Barbara Tenenbaum, Paul J. Vanderwood, Stuart F. Voss, and Josefina Zoraida Vázquez were brave pioneers into the nineteenth century. Their work has withstood well the test of time, and furnished the basis of this work.

Other more recent investigators provided keen insights and enlightening information: Ana María Alonso, Rodney D. Anderson, William H. Beezley, Thomas Benjamin, Enrique Cárdenas, Margaret Chowning, Barbara M. Corbett, Harry E. Cross, William A. DePalo, Torcuato DiTella, Don E. Dumond, Michael T. Ducey, John S. D. Eisenhower, Romana Falcón, Will Fowler, William E. French, Stanley C. Green, Richard Griswold del Castillo, Peter F. Guardino, Stephen H. Haber, Brian Hamnett, Charles H. Harris III,

Alicia Hernández Chávez, Ian Jacobs, Michael Johns, Gilbert M. Joseph,
Jonathan Kandell, Friedrich Katz, Alan Knight, Enrique Krauze, Stanley
Langston, John Lear, Florencia E. Mallon, Carlos Marichal, William K.
Meyers, Simon A. Miller, Tony Morgan, Herbert Nickel, María de la Luz
Parcero, Douglas W. Richmond, Piedad Peniche Rivero, Terry Ruggeley,
Heather Fowler Salamini, Richard Salvucci, Elizabeth Salas, Pedro Santoni,
Alex Saragoza, Frederick J. Shaw, Donald F. Stevens, Guy Thomson,
John Tutino, Richard A. Warren, Charles A. Weeks, and Allen Wells.

Special thanks to Barbara Corbett, Michael Ducey, Glen Kuecker, John
Lear, Richard Salvucci, Guy Thomson, and Richard Warren for sharing
their unpublished materials.

Several colleagues took considerable time and expended invaluable
effort toward making the manuscript better. Their comments and suggestions were extraordinarily helpful. William DePalo provided an exceptional
critique of chapter 4. His book on the Mexican army is an outstanding
source. Anne Rubenstein not only gave me her astute ideas on the first six
chapters, but also provided greatly appreciated encouragement that I was
on the right track. Richard Salvucci read chapter 3 and patiently answered
my uninformed questions about economic development. Pedro Santoni
read the early chapters on politics and saved me from a number of egregious errors. His fine book helped clarify Mexican politics at mid-century.
He also furnished me with crucial bibliographic assistance. Donald Stevens
read the first three chapters, urging me to trust students more. His book has
become a classic for the study of the era from 1821 to 1860. Barbara Tenenbaum read the first section of the manuscript and provided her usual
provocative insights and sensible suggestions. She convinced me to rethink
my approaches to Santa Anna and Maximilian. Her book is a must-read for
understanding the period. Tom Benjamin also read the first half of the
manuscript and helped me incorporate a sense of evolving historiography.
John Coatsworth clarified the debates over economic development. Glen
Kuecker supplied astute comments on the introduction. Richard Warren
read the first three chapters and provided helpful suggestions.

The most valuable and careful comments and suggestions came from
Diálogos series editor Lyman Johnson. His dedication to making this a
better book was rather extraordinary. His editing was superb. He kept me
focused. Thanks to David Holtby and Lyman for giving me the opportunity
to write this book. Barbara Kohl improved the book with her editing.

The author and the publisher gratefully acknowledge the General Library at the University of New Mexico and their Donald C. Turpen Mexican Revolution of 1910 Collection as well as the special assistance of the library's Center for Southwest Research in making available the following volumes as sources for the illustrations reproduced in this book:

José Francisco Godoy, *Porfirio Díaz, President of Mexico* (1910)
Brantz Mayer, *Mexico as It Was and as It Is* (1844)
Frederick A. Ober, *Travels in Mexico and Life Among the Mexicans* (1887)
Vicente Riva Palacio, *Mexico a traves de los siglos* (5 vols., 1887–1889)
Nevin O. Winter, *Mexico and Her People of To-day* (1907)

The assistance of Rutgers University Library enabled reproduction of illustrations from one other source:

William Butler, *Mexico in Transition* (1893)

A special thanks to my daughter Danielle, whose cheery return from school in the afternoons provided a welcome respite from the solitude of writing. Marlie Parker Wasserman, as always, provided the love and encouragement that keeps me going.

No one mentioned above incurs any blame for any errors or inelegancies. They are mine alone.

EVERYDAY LIFE AND POLITICS
IN NINETEENTH CENTURY MEXICO

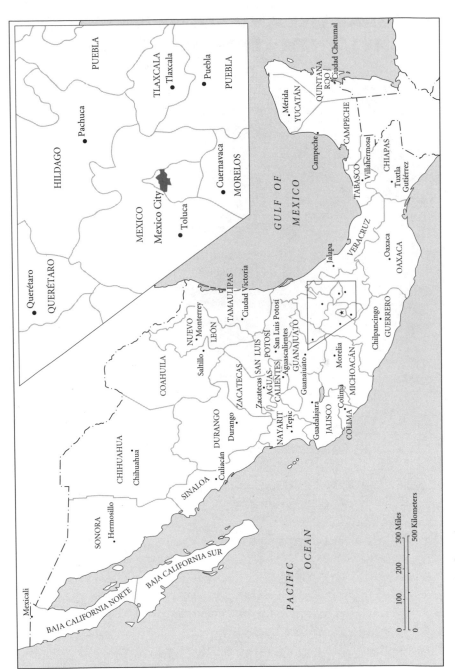

Map 1. Mexico, An Overview

INTRODUCTION

The three great watersheds of modern Mexican history were Independence (1821), the Reform (1855–60), and the Revolution (1910). This book
is an effort to make sense of the century that encompasses all three, and re-
volves around three principal themes. First, the struggle of common people
to retain control over their everyday lives was central to nineteenth-century
politics. These efforts were at the heart of the factional disputes over regionalism, federalism, centralism, and caudilloism. This struggle is the unifying
theme of the book and why I have entitled it *Everyday Life and Politics*. Second, external war, to my mind quite inexplicably overlooked by historians as
an explanatory tool, was *a,* if not *the,* dominant factor in Mexico's economic
development and crucial to its politics during this era. Constant war goes a
long way toward explaining the nation's economic stagnation between 1821
and 1880. Third, the demographic and social aspects of war, the mass migration of women from the countryside to the city, and the industrialization of
urban employment transformed gender relations.

The three themes explain the organization of this book. The three chapters
on everyday life attempt to describe, as well as the documentation available
allows, the lives of Mexicans, and, at the same time, how the concerns of common people about their daily lives affected politics. The struggle of common
people to control access to land, taxes, the draft, and other such matters tied
together the local, regional, and national. In addition, I explore in individual
chapters the three most important wars of the era: the war with the United
States (1846–48), the War of the Reform (1858–60), and the French Intervention (1861–67). Finally, in the chapters on everyday life and wars I examine the
role of women in response to the transformations that take place over the
course of the nineteenth century.

Regionalism plays a prominent part in my analysis, for it underlies any understanding of nineteenth-century Mexico. There were, indeed, "many Mex-
icos." Not only were each of the new nation's states (sometimes called

provinces) quite unique, but they were, in turn, divided into distinct geographic and ethnic areas. Generalizations about political behavior, land tenure systems, and labor are seldom applicable to the entire country. (I will, nonetheless, try to present sensible overviews.) As historians Donald Stevens and Timothy Anna have reminded us, regionalism was perhaps the most important heritage of colonial rule. The era after Independence was not the "disintegration of a formerly cohesive, political, social or 'national' unit," but rather the creation of "something new." Given its colonial tradition of political fragmentation and its involvement in foreign wars, the wonder of newly independent Mexico was that it remained a nation at all.

The book also tries to return to some extent to the days when colorful biography and lively narrative were the common tools of the historian, while not abandoning the best influences of modern social science. When I began my studies of Mexico, historians, at least in the United States, eschewed the personalist approach to history that had so dominated earlier studies. In the interim the prose of social science led the way. I have sought to establish a balance between narrative and analysis.

The Late Colonial Heritage, 1700–1810

The last half of the eighteenth century brought profound changes to the people of New Spain. These transformations led to a massive upheaval in 1810 that initiated the Wars of Independence. Change evolved from two major sources: a remarkable demographic recovery, which greatly increased the population of the colony; and the transfer of the Spanish monarchy from the Hapsburgs to the Bourbons, who after 1714 embarked on a broad program of economic and bureaucratic reform. Each of these developments created enormous stresses and strains in colonial society and contributed to the rebellions that lasted from 1810 until 1821.

At the time when the Spaniards arrived in what is now Mexico in 1519, there were between 6 million and 25 million indigenous inhabitants. (There is a heated controversy over the exact number.) A century of epidemic disease and exploitative European rule brought about a calamitous drop in population to under 1 million, a decline of between 84 and 96 percent, depending on which figure one uses for the original population. Population recovery was slow until the eighteenth century, when a surge brought the number of residents to approximately 6 million, roughly equal to the lowest estimate for 1519. Prior to

European rule, the indigenous city-states of the central plateau and the Valley of Mexico were periodically unable to feed their people or to provide enough arable land. There is considerable evidence that these problems had recurred by the end of the 1700s and formed much of the basis for discontent in the countryside. This, in turn, led to the revolt of Father Miguel Hidalgo in 1810 and the beginning of the movement for independence.

In 1700 the Spanish Hapsburg king Charles II died without an heir. It took more than a decade of European war and diplomacy before a branch of the French Bourbon royal family ascended to the Spanish throne. The new monarch Philip V and his successors set about to renovate and streamline colonial administration in Spain's New World empire. The Bourbon reforms tightened colonial rule, especially at the local level. This disturbed a long-time political equilibrium, for the Hapsburgs had virtually ignored many areas and allowed for considerable local self-rule. In addition, the Bourbon drive to increase revenue flows to Spain from her colonies effectively raised taxes without providing significant new benefits for New Spain (Mexico). When the wars in Europe initiated by the French Revolution weakened Spain and simultaneously intensified its need for revenues, the stage was set for the struggle for independence in Spain's American colonies.

Regions and localities were the core of the colonial heritage. Independent Mexico, as Timothy Anna points out, was actually comprised of three colonial kingdoms—México, Guadalajara, and Guatemala (Central America)—and three major territories that were separately governed—Yucatán, the Internal Provinces (the north), and the South (the hot country south of Mexico City). Twenty-one of the new nation's twenty-eight provinces had not been part of colonial New Spain. There was in 1821, then, no sense of Mexican nationhood. Actual governance during the colonial era occurred on the local level. Local elites, made up of merchants, large landowners, and soldiers, ruled with the cooperation of regional oligarchies.

The political culture was not only local, but personalist. Often family ties formed the basis of political alliances (see in particular the discussion of notable families in chapter 2). The head of the family or group (*patrón*) dispensed favors to his dependents and clients in return for loyalty. Large landowners (*hacendados*) also commonly acted as patrons for their employees. Village leadership required personal relations with constituents. A leader's ability to function, in turn, depended on personal relations with higher-ups, such as district level officials or governors. The military also depended on personal associations. Soldiers most likely followed their family patrón or hacendado to war, rather than enlisting to fight for a particular ideology. It is not surprising, then, that a pyramid of patron-client relations led ultimately to a series of national personalist leaders (*caudillos*) such as Antonio López de Santa Anna, Benito Juárez, and Porfirio Díaz.

The Legacy of War

Mexico's first half-century as an independent country brought virtually continuous strife. Eleven years of mass upheaval from 1810 to 1821 resulted in separation from Spain, while taking an enormous toll politically, psychologically, and financially. The Independence war devastated the colonial economy. Mining, its fulcrum, was in ruins. Consequently, the other central economic institution, the large estate or hacienda, which depended on the mines for its markets, deteriorated badly. A long series of foreign invasions and civil wars followed, consuming immeasurable human and material resources.

In 1829 Mexico defeated Spain's attempt to reconquer its former colony. A serious defeat ensued when Texas fought for and won its independence in 1836. Mexico repulsed a French invasion in 1838. The most disastrous conflict occurred at mid-century, when the United States wrenched away half of Mexico's territory as a result of war in 1846–48. The Caste (race) War erupted in Yucatán in 1847. A vicious civil war, the War of the Reform, devastated the nation between 1857 and 1860. Finally, the French, in an effort to impose a European monarch, invaded and occupied much of the country from 1861 to 1867. Innumerable, shorter-lived rebellions marked the years between these major conflagrations. These seemingly endless armed conflicts exacted a terrible price. Mexico stagnated economically; once the jewel in the crown of the Spanish empire, it fell badly behind the United States and other Latin American nations, such as Argentina and Brazil.

Politics

Politics changed at two major watersheds: Independence in 1821 and the Reform (La Reforma) from 1854 to 1861. Independence opened a half-century-long set of dialogues between opposing political positions: centralism and federalism, conservatism and liberalism, monarchism and republicanism, pro-clericalism (pro-Roman Catholic Church) and anti-clericalism, and dictatorship and democracy. The national economic debate pitted laissez faire (free trade) against protectionism (high tariffs on imports), and collective against individual land ownership.

By the 1840s, the main contestants for power in Mexico were Conservatives and Liberals. Conservatives believed in a civil bureaucracy based on the Spanish colonial model, a powerful military, and the Catholic Church. They sought to preserve the colonial economic and social order with themselves, of course, at the top of the hierarchy. Conservatives generally favored a powerful central government. Liberals supported a series of constitutional freedoms, such as freedom of the press, as well as equality before the law. They were also opposed to a powerful Church. Liberals favored secular rather than church-run education. They believed, furthermore, that the Church, as a large landowner and guardian of enormous funds, was an impediment to economic development.

Liberals, however, were badly split into moderate and radical wings over other crucial issues. Moderate Liberals (*moderados*) did not entirely reject the colonial heritage. Being quite wary of the lower classes' involvement in politics, they were reluctant republicans. Radical Liberals (*puros*) rejected the colonial past. These radicals were insistent republicans who actively sought to destroy the economic power of the Church. Conservatives and moderate Liberals differed over the role of the state. Conservatives wanted a strong central state, while moderates favored a weaker government, relying on laws to facilitate individual private initiative. Liberal ideals changed quite extensively over time to meet the challenges of new circumstances, particularly after 1867, in pursuit of the Liberal goals of political stability and economic development. The Reform era brought the contest to an end by establishing the ascendancy of republican liberal centralism and the appearance of constitutional democracy, but in reality the Liberals set up an authoritarian regime.

As in politics, the Reform marked a major turning point in the nation's economic development, for it brought the triumph of free market capitalism, private property rights, and individual initiative over communal collectivism. The Reform also ended the preeminent role of the Roman Catholic Church in economic affairs. The Liberal government redistributed vast Church properties both in the cities and the countryside. The Reform era brought a halt to the enormous revenues received by the Church via tithes (a mandatory ten percent tax on all income, collected by the colonial government on behalf of the Church) and benefices (bequests to the Church), which had enabled the

Church to function as Mexico's principal banking institution and most important rural landholder and urban landlord. The Liberals also instituted secular education and secularized birth and marriage record keeping.

Mass violence stopped temporarily in the 1880s. This era of relative peace, in fact, lasted three decades. During this era, known as the *Porfiriato,* after the first name of dictator General Porfirio Díaz, who ruled from 1877 to 1911, Mexico pursued and in some ways achieved "order and progress." Díaz, a political genius, built an intricate network of political alliances and checks and balances that depended on his personal credibility, continuous economic growth, and a selective use of coercion. Mexico attained widespread economic development based on the export of minerals and other primary commodities and on foreign investment in transportation, agriculture, and industry. But economic modernization in the form of industrialization, commercialization of agriculture, and internationalization of capital cost the nation dearly. The lower classes, especially the rural poor, endured an unfair system that robbed them of an equitable share of the benefits of new economic development and deprived them of a say in the political decisions that determined the path of national development. Mexico's last and greatest civil war, the Mexican Revolution (1910–20) was essentially a protest against this system.

Everyday Life and Politics

Beneath the national level, other layers of politics, economics, and everyday life were affected by and, in turn, affected the great events of the era. Certainly, the most important task of the average Mexican was, as it was for anyone in the nineteenth-century world, to manage survival for himself and his family. Hard as life was, Mexicans endured, if not with elegance and grace, then with simplicity and dignity. The picture painted on the following pages is not pretty. Everyday existence was often dismal and dangerous. For the majority, sustenance and shelter were minimal. Nonetheless, people struggled on and, perhaps surprisingly, exerted influence on their own environment and helped shape the politics of the times.

Everyday life deeply influenced politics at all levels. Local and regional autonomy were at the heart of the national political debate throughout the century. Therefore, the governance of everyday life was at the center of political discourse. Most important was the demand of Mexicans to rule over their own localities. This meant effective control over access to land, the administration of taxes, the operation of the police and courts, the allocation of labor, and the conduct of their private lives. Local control meant a "fair shake." Although life in Mexico's rural villages was hardly idyllic — they were often deeply divided along class and other lines — rural dwellers closely guarded their autonomy. There was dignity, too, in choosing your own leaders, however bad they might turn out. The right to sustain and control one's own family without government interference also was the foundation of Mexican patriarchy.

The struggle to protect local autonomy drew the residents of villages and towns into broader political events and wider patterns of violence. Political factions required soldiers to fight their battles. The people of the villages comprised the armies of the various competing groups. Because politics for most Mexicans were local, decisions about which side to support depended on local rather than national situations. In search of supporters, national leaders courted the concerns of everyday people. One result of this responsiveness on the part of political elites to the concerns of common folk was that in most regions of the country collective land ownership survived intact for a half-century or more and local autonomy remained extensive until the 1880s.

In Mexico's cities during the nineteenth century everyday concerns were focused on food and shelter, rather than on issues of governance. But for much of the first fifty years after Independence, city dwellers pushed for high tariffs on imported manufactures to protect their employment as artisans and as factory workers. They also occasionally rioted in protest against high staple prices. When allowed to participate in elections in Mexico City during the 1820s, they were very active.

For all Mexicans, but for rural people especially, everyday life and politics meant more than elections, land, and taxes. In many regions, common people resisted the incursions of modernity, such as the efforts to diminish the role of the Church in marriage and education and the effort to expand government oversight in aspects of private life. After mid-century they also resisted the new discipline of the export-oriented workplace. In mines and factories, Mexicans fought employers' efforts to instill the capitalist work ethic.

The struggle over local autonomy (fought out at the national level in the conflict between centralism, which favored a strong national government, and federalism, which sought to keep the national government weak and state governments strong) played out in three stages from 1821 to 1911. In the first era, from 1821 into the 1850s—a period roughly coinciding with the political career of Antonio López de Santa Anna—the widespread disruptions caused by external war and frequent national regime changes provided maneuvering room for villages to assert their autonomy and reshape economic relations in the countryside. In the Yucatán, for example, Maya Indians defended their notions of governance and labor relations so successfully that they nearly forced non-Indians from the peninsula in the late 1840s. The leader who more than any other epitomized federalism was Juan Álvarez, the political boss of southern Mexico. Juan Álvarez briefly became president in 1854 after successfully heading a rebellion that overthrew centralism. The second stage, from the mid-1850s to the early 1890s, much of it the age of Benito Juárez, marked a transition during which the triumphant Liberals abandoned federalism in order to further their program to modernize the Mexican economy. This era of the Reform brought a nationwide assault on local prerogatives.

By 1900, the height of the Porfiriato, centralization and capitalism appeared to have had triumphed. Yet, although seldom noticed by foreigners or even by most members of the elite, Mexico's common people had waged steady resistance to the incursions of government and the inculcation of capitalist labor discipline since 1880. At first they used tried and true methods that had proven successful in the past. In the countryside, they engaged in shrewd political alliances, which played off elite political factions against one another, formulated and sent petitions and appeals to higher authorities, litigated in the courts, bribed local and state officials, and committed limited violence. In the mining camps and factories, they protested through slowdowns and absenteeism. There were occasional, short-lived uprisings, particularly during the early 1890s. By the end of the century, they adopted newer tactics, such as migration and the organization of mutualist societies and labor unions. Increasingly, workers resorted to strikes. Driven by desperate economic circumstances during economic downturns, many rural people rebelled, unsuccessfully during the 1890s and triumphantly in 1910 and 1911.

Race and class tensions were never far beneath the surface in politics. Although centuries of intermarriage led to considerable cultural intermingling and the interchange of social attitudes, status in Mexican society remained closely associated with color. The population growth of the eighteenth century was among indigenous and mixed blood peoples, the *castas*. The Mexican elite reacted to the burgeoning population of color by hardening social barriers. During the early colonial years, a scarcity of white women, a drastic decline in the indigenous population, and practical politics (the need to intermarry for strategic reasons with Indian elites) had combined to blur racial lines. By the end of the colonial period, white parents had become much more strident in limiting the marriage choices of their children in order to safeguard family honor, defined simply in terms of color.

The memories of the Wars for Independence, such as the massacre of Spaniards at the *alhóndiga* (granary) in Guanajuato by Father Hidalgo's hordes, the reverberations of the cries of "Death to the *gachupines*" (a pejorative for Spaniards) shouted by the lower classes, and the picture of 60,000 angry peons (rural dwellers who labored on the large landholdings) and workers poised to attack Mexico City in 1811 did not easily vanish from their minds. When combined with elite concerns about the excesses of the French Revolution and the uprising in Haiti in the 1790s, these experiences formed a view of government and the lower classes that was to inhibit political development for a century. Fear deepened in the aftermath of Independence, because thousands of people displaced by the war roamed in the countryside as bandits. Horror stories of holdups were commonplace in the conversations of wealthy men and women. Neither person nor property seemed secure in the new nation. Occasional riots, provoked by food shortages in the cities, reinforced these middle-class suspicions of the nation's less fortunate.

The late colonial trend toward creation of greater racial barriers apparently lessened with Independence. The new nation's Constitution of 1824 proclaimed that all citizens of any color were equal under the law. Other evidence from the first half of the nineteenth century also indicates a considerable degree of flexibility and flux in racial attitudes. One study found a high degree of intermarriage among ethnic groups, indicating that occupation was more important than race in determining status. Intermarriage rates were twenty-seven percent for Spaniards and forty-four percent for mestizos. The same study found that there was little residential segregation, for people of different color lived side by side on the same streets.

However, Mexicans mostly continued to marry within their own ethnic group. The fact that the overwhelming proportion of high-level positions were held by whites was evidence enough of the relation between race and status.

There seems little doubt that people saw each other in terms of race rather than occupation. Indians, mestizos, and mulattoes filled the lower occupational rungs; few creoles (whites born in Mexico) had these occupations. Whites, however, continued to fear and disdain people of color, Indians (*indios*) and mixed bloods, known as mestizos or castas, whom they saw as dangerous rabble. Nevertheless, endless warfare from 1810 permitted a degree of upward mobility for non-whites. Although in the two decades after 1821 the *hombres de bien*—the so-called "good people," the whites of the upper and middle classes—dominated politics at the national level, they functioned always with a wary eye on the lower classes. The Reform era at mid-century brought to preeminence a generation of mestizo and Indian leaders trained and hardened by the exigencies of decades of war. With a new generation of hombres de bien, who came to be known as *científicos* (technocrats), it would be mestizos who led Mexico into the twentieth century. The emergence of a class of upwardly mobile mestizos, however, did not end racism. "Order and Progress," the motto of the Díaz dictatorship, specifically excluded Mexico's large Indian population from participation in national life.

Everyday life at the end of the imperial age was for most Mexicans "a desperate world" of bare survival. The level of national deprivation and misery remained high throughout the nineteenth century. After Independence the most populous area, the Valley of Mexico and the contiguous central plateau, continued to endure vicious cycles of epidemic diseases, drought, and famine. Tropical regions like Tampico and Veracruz, two of the nation's biggest seaports, were virtually unlivable because of insect-borne disease and unsanitary conditions. For the poor, Mexico City itself was barely livable. Secondary cities, like Puebla, Oaxaca, and Guanajuato were no healthier.

The increase in population that occurred in the last half of the eighteenth century put tremendous pressures on limited resources. Because wealthy whites had long ago taken the preponderance of cultivable land, there was not nearly enough land for the growing population in the countryside. Many people were forced to flee rural poverty to seek better prospects in the cities and mining camps, but many, if not most, found little more than a new form of misery. Unlike in rural areas, where networks of kin could help them through bad times, the urban poor often went hungry. At the same time, Bourbon administrative changes intruded deeply on long-established local prerogatives. Village residents felt they were under siege. Nor were the rich at peace. Popular uprisings in Peru and Haiti in the last decades of the eighteenth century scared elites into a state of almost constant paranoia. The hordes of landless and starving seemed to be continually on the brink of uprising.

Changes in Gender Relations

Mexican gender relations were altered during the nineteenth century. First were the transformations brought on by war. Casualties, of course, fell disproportionately on young males. This resulted in a larger population of single females: those who were widowed and those who were delayed in marriage while eligible males were off at war. War also obviously reduced the birth rate. As a result of these developments, more women spent much of their lives independent of men. They had to earn their own income, make their own decisions, and often raise their children alone. War also sent women out into the wider world. Thousands served as the supply, transportation, and medical corps of Mexican armies (and often foreign armies as well). It was not uncommon for women to fight as soldiers. Many others traveled far beyond and experienced far more than their villages. War did not completely alter gender relations, however, for it remained predominantly a male endeavor, despite participation by women, and as such reinforced patriarchal society.

The turmoil and disruptions war brought to the countryside caused an enormous migration of women, most of whom were young, to the cities. They left their familial support systems (if the fighting had not destroyed them) and set off alone to the cities where they fended for themselves. They had only limited occupational possibilities and employers took advantage of them by paying low wages. The great majority worked as exploited and poorly remunerated domestic servants. Women hated domestic work, for society regarded it as demeaning, but it was often the only way to survive. As the century went on, the transformation from artisan to factory manufacturing created opportunities for women. The work forces of some industries such as textiles and cigarettes were comprised almost entirely of women. Though pay was poor and the work monotonous, most Mexican women found it considerably more attractive than domestic service.

In the countryside export crop production changed women's employment as well, often demanding the labor of entire families. Many women took on the burden of field work, in addition to their endless household and commercial chores. Although much else changed, seldom did women's wages rise in any sector of the economy or region.

It is difficult to analyze the effects of greater mobility, economic independence, and urbanization on women, or to summarize how relations were altered between women and men, because we lack adequate documentation. However, we can offer some reasonable probabilities. First, Mexican women remained without political rights. (Suffrage came only in 1952.) Second, they continued to endure a sexual double standard. And finally, their economic status certainly did not improve and may have, in fact, deteriorated in comparison to men.

During the century between the *Grito de Dolores* (the Cry of Dolores) in 1810, which began the movement for Independence, and the revolution led by Francisco I. Madero in 1910, Mexico struggled unsuccessfully to develop its economy and in nation building. Mexicans did not settle their political disagreements in the ninety years after Independence. The desperate gap between elite modernizers and a recalcitrant people was not appreciably narrowed. Nor did ten more years of brutal civil war from 1910 to 1920 resolve the issues of local autonomy and social and economic justice. Much of the protests that emerged seven decades later during the 1980s and 1990s originated in localities and regions, where citizens once again sought to reestablish control over their own everyday lives.

THE AGE OF TROUBLES

Antonio López de Santa Anna

Antonio López de Santa Anna

S*adly looking back* on his life as he was about to turn eighty years old in 1874, General Antonio López de Santa Anna penned the last lines of his memoirs: "ostracized by my countrymen and in exile." But the old man outlived his harshest critics. With amnesty he returned to Mexico that very same year after an eighteen-year absence. One newspaper exclaimed at the time that "Mexico does not remember the great political errors of the man who so long controlled its destinies." Santa Anna, who had been president of Mexico eleven times, died embittered, " . . . in the midst of the greatest want, abandoned by all except a few of his friends. . . ." And this was the man who had towered over Mexican politics for nearly forty years!

There has been no more controversial figure in Mexican history than Antonio López de Santa Anna Pérez de Lebrón (1794–1876). In a career spanning more than three decades from the Independence wars through the 1850s, Santa Anna was alternately hero and villain, patriot and traitor. Personal strengths and weaknesses aside, Santa Anna's life encapsulated the history of an era in Mexico. The general and sometimes president symbolized the ambiguities, uncertainties, and continuities of politics in the Independence epoch and its aftermath.

In her famous account, *Life in Mexico*, Fanny Calderón de la Barca described Santa Anna as "a gentlemanly, good-looking, quietly dressed, rather melancholy-looking person, with one leg, apparently somewhat of an invalid. . . . He has a sallow complexion, fine dark eyes, soft and penetrating, and an interesting expression of face."

Legend swirled around him. Some said he had "a way with women," siring innumerable illegitimate children. Others claimed he was addicted to cockfighting and opium. Perhaps most famous was the story of the leg he lost in defense of the homeland. In 1838 France landed troops in the port of Veracruz in order to collect claims for damages to the property of its citizens living in Mexico. Santa Anna lost his leg below the knee to a French cannonball while leading a cavalry charge. Although most Mexicans saw him as a hero, his detractors said he was in full retreat when the cannonball hit him. He recovered from his wounds, but the lost leg would later become notorious. In 1842, while serving as president, Santa Anna buried the leg in the Santa Paula cemetery in Mexico City with full military honors, including a parade, before an audience of diplomats and luminaries. In 1845 an angry mob, fed up with his rule, disinterred the leg and dragged it through streets to derisive laughter.

Santa Anna was born February 21, 1794, the son of well-to-do Spanish parents. His father was a minor official in Veracruz province under the Spanish colonial regime, and later was a mortgage broker. From an early age Santa Anna was regarded as "quarrelsome." He chose a military career and saw action as a young officer against the masses led by Father Miguel Hidalgo, who initiated the movement for Mexican independence in 1810.

Antonio was known as "reckless and brave," but had good military sense. Despite quick promotions in rank, the young man showed certain character flaws. After losing heavily in gambling, he forged his superiors' signatures on drafts to repay his debts. He escaped dire consequences when higher-ups discovered his misuse of funds, but emerged from the incident penniless. This early love for gambling remained with him throughout his life. As president he was often found at cockfights betting with the common people.

He joined Agustín de Iturbide in 1821 in betraying the royalist army and reaching agreement with the rebels to establish Mexican independence. Santa Anna emerged from the Independence Wars, in the words of his chief biographer Wilfrid Callcott, as a "... man trained in a ruthless and brutal school where fear was the chief taskmaster, where morality and ethics were largely unknown and where the end was held to justify the means. With such training and an experience far beyond his years, the record of ensuing decades should not be surprising."

Two years later, Santa Anna led the republicans against Iturbide, his former ally, who had established himself as Emperor Agustín I (1822–23). He played an important role in politics during the 1820s, serving two short stints as governor of the state of Veracruz and a brief term as governor of Yucatán, and then acting as an important ally of Presidents Guadalupe Victoria (1824–29), and Vicente Guerrero (1829). In 1829 Santa Anna led Mexican forces that repelled a Spanish invasion seeking to reconquer its former colony. After ousting President Anastasio Bustamante (1830–32), the general took the reins of government himself in 1832. For the next two decades he shuttled in and out of the presidency.

During the early 1820s, Santa Anna began acquiring property in the vicinity of Jalapa in the state of Veracruz, which was strategically located on the main road connecting the port of Veracruz to Mexico City. Eventually, he became one of the region's largest landowners with his showplace, the Hacienda Manga de Clavo (Clove Spike). He was married in 1824 to Doña Ines García. They had two daughters and three sons (one of whom died at five and another who was sickly or disabled). Doña Ines died in 1844 at age 33. After a scandalously short period of mourning, Santa Anna married María Dolores Tosta.

In financial matters Santa Anna was a man of contradictions. On the one hand, the general was infamous for his corruption. There were times, for example, when he had difficulty distinguishing between the national treasury and his own fortune. On the other hand, during the war with the United States he used his own funds, some raised from mortgaging his properties, to outfit an army to fight the invaders.

Santa Anna was at the center of Mexico's disastrous foreign wars. He drove the Spaniards from Veracruz in 1829. He suffered the ignominious defeats that led to the loss of Texas in 1836. Nonetheless, he recovered from his shame and won a hero's plaudits in 1838, when he lost his leg resisting the French.

His greatest defeat lay ahead, for in the midst of the crisis of war in 1846, he took over the defense of Mexico against the invading armies of the United States. Santa Anna fought bravely, if ineptly, and his valiant and bloody resistance temporarily restored his military reputation. But the peace treaty that ended the war cost half of Mexico's territory to the northern colossus.

After years in exile, Santa Anna returned once again in 1853 to establish his harshest regime. Although uncrowned, he insisted on all of the trappings of royalty, including the title of "His Serene Highness." The next year he was overthrown for the last time by a coalition of southern country people and northern Liberals who objected to his centralized rule. The new government not only forced him into exile, but also confiscated his properties. Conservatives restored them a few years later, but in 1866 the Liberal regime of Benito Juárez declared him a traitor.

Santa Anna's career symbolized the complexities of Mexican politics in the post-Independence era. He epitomized the uncertain choices that confronted the people of the new nation. He began as a monarchist, switched sides to become a republican in 1821, and then in his later career took on the trappings of royalty during his dictatorship. Further, he illustrated the dilemma between federalists and centralists. Initially he was a federalist, but soon he recognized the impracticality of regionalism and changed to a centralist position. Nonetheless, Santa Anna was first and foremost a regional political boss. His remarkable ability to rebound from defeat owed in great part to his strong political and military base in Veracruz. In his first presidency he allied with the Liberals, but he abandoned that stance almost at once. Moreover, Santa Anna was proof of the domination of the military in an era of foreign and civil wars.

The general was probably a political genius. Otherwise, how can we account for his longevity and for his many remarkable comebacks? Until the emergence of Benito Juárez (president of Mexico from 1857 to 1872), Santa Anna was the only leader who had the charisma and ability to unite his nation even for a short period. Despite his catastrophic losses, given the poor weapons, training, and leadership of his armies, it is doubtful that anyone could have done more.

Independent Mexico searched for more than half a century for legitimate successors to Iberian colonial rule. Given the geographic, ethnic, and class divisions that separated Mexico, and the daunting economic difficulties that confronted it, the Mexican people turned to military officers who had emerged during the Wars of Independence to obtain badly needed leadership. The burdens of colonial rule—regional fragmentation, the wide gap between law and practice, corruption, and economic stagnation—proved too heavy for even Antonio López de Santa Anna.

TIMELINE

The Age of Troubles

1810	Grito de Dolores
1821	Independence
1822–23	Emperor Agustín I (Iturbide)
1824	Constitution (Federalist)
1824–29	Presidency of Guadalupe Victoria
1828	Parián Riot (Mexico City)
1829	Presidency of Vicente Guerrero
1829	Spain attempts reconquest
1830–32	Presidency of Anastasio Bustamante
1833	First presidency of Antonio López de Santa Anna
1833	Presidency of Valentín Gómez Farías
1836	Constitution (Centralist)
1836	Texas War
1838	Pastry War (France)
1845	Annexation of Texas by the United States
1846–48	War with the United States
1853	Treaty of Mesilla (Gadsden Purchase)

Chapter 1

EVERYDAY LIFE, 1821–46: TRADITION AND TURMOIL

After Independence Mexico experienced a half-century of transition. The country was much changed, especially in the realm of politics and governance, but the core of everyday life retained its essential characteristics. Neither thousands of years of indigenous tradition and culture, nor 300 years of Spanish colonial heritage disappeared. Most Mexicans ate the same foods, resided in the same kind of dwellings, and wore the same kinds of clothes as had their ancestors for decades if not centuries. The constant tension and frequent conflict between elite visions of a modern nation, the reluctance of common people to accede to them, and the transformations that would result do much to explain the often muddled events of the nineteenth century. The conditions of daily life both influenced and were affected by local, regional, and national politics. The major issues of the era, such as local autonomy, access to land, taxes, the military draft, the role of the Catholic Church, and the fair application of laws were deeply interwoven into the fabric of everyday life and were contested at all levels.

In 1800 there were approximately 6 million residents of New Spain (colonial Mexico). Fifty years later, with the population growing at less than one percent a year, there were 7.6 million inhabitants. Incessant wars, periodic epidemics, including a deadly cholera outbreak in 1850, and the expulsion of Spaniards following Independence accounted for the slow population growth. Most Mexicans were Indians or mestizos. The countryside was more Indian

---

Thanks to Silvia Arrom, whose investigations provide almost all the material on Mexico City women and Frederick Shaw, whose dissertation furnishes the material on Mexico City's dismal conditions. I also wish to extend my appreciation to Harry Cross, Charles Harris, Friedrich Katz, Florencia Mallon, Simon Miller, and Richard Warren.

than the cities. At the turn of the nineteenth century, for example, the state of Puebla was 75 percent Indian, 10 percent white, and 15 percent castas (mixed bloods, such as mestizos and mulattoes), but the city of Puebla was 25 percent white, 40 percent casta, and 35 percent Indian. In 1814 the Yucatán peninsula was 75 percent Maya (Indian), 14 percent European, and 11 percent mixed blood.

Typically, nineteenth-century Mexicans resided in one of four categories of communities. Most lived in the countryside either on haciendas (large land-holdings), where they worked for the hacienda or leased its land as tenants or sharecroppers, or in villages, where they cultivated their own individual or communal small plots. A third much smaller group lived in mining camps. Mexico's urban population was concentrated overwhelmingly in Mexico City, whose population from 1820 to 1900 fluctuated between 150,000 and 200,000. In rural areas much of the land was controlled by owners of haciendas, known as hacendados. The majority of the rural population consisted of Indians, who continued to live as in colonial times in relatively autonomous villages (pueblos). The *milpa*—the small, individual plot of land used for family subsistence farming—was the basis of rural life. There were also small properties called *ranchos*. (The term "rancho" had different meanings according to region.) Communally held landholding predominated in many regions, particularly in the Valley of Mexico and its environs.

The Haciendas

Conditions on Mexican haciendas in the nineteenth century are much debated by scholars. Because their operations varied widely according to era, region, size, and crops, it is almost impossible to describe a typical hacienda. Fortunately, records from a number of haciendas survive for the period. It is from these illuminating documents that we can piece together the following descriptions.

Haciendas had a unique hierarchical structure. At the top of hacienda society was the owner, the hacendado, and his family. Beneath the hacendado were the supervisors and administrators, headed by the chief administrator or *mayordomo*. Males typically headed haciendas, but occasionally a widow operated a large property. Hacendados, at least in the early decades of the nineteenth century, hardly lived in opulence on their estates. Fanny Calderón de la Barca, the wife of the minister (now called ambassador) of Spain to Mexico, visited the sugar estate of Anselmo Zurutuza near Cuernavaca in the 1840s, and wrote the following:

> As for the interior of these haciendas, they are all pretty much alike . . . a great stone building, which is neither farm nor country-house . . . , but has a character peculiar to itself—solid enough to stand a siege, with floors of painted brick, large deal tables, wooden benches, painted chairs, and white-washed walls; one or two painted or iron bedsteads, only put up when wanted; numberless empty rooms; kitchen and outhouses; the courtyard a great square round which stand the house for boiling the sugar, whose furnaces burn day and night; the house with machinery for extracting the juice from the cane. . . .

Although many hacendados lived modestly without opulence, the economic boom that came later in the century would change all this. Large landowners who lived near towns and cities often chose to reside away from their estates to enjoy the greater comforts of urban life.

In general there were two broad groups of people employed on the large estate: those who worked permanently on the hacienda and those who were temporary laborers. Permanent inhabitants included resident peons, tenants, and sharecroppers, though the latter two types of workers did not necessarily have to reside on the property. Temporary labor on the haciendas came from neighboring villages. Villagers supplemented their incomes from communally held land or family plots by working seasonally at planting and harvest on the hacienda.

Some hacendados farmed their own land with their own employees. Others rented or sharecropped the land to locals. Depending on the time, place, and crops, tenants paid their rent to the hacendado in the form of cash or a portion of the harvest. Though most tenants leased small plots, there were a few who leased entire haciendas. Sharecroppers paid the landowners a predetermined percentage of the harvest, usually half. Although the hacendado's profit potential was higher when he farmed his own land, the risk was greater. Tenants and sharecroppers assumed the risks of drought and failed harvests. Probably the most common arrangement in this era was a mixture of owner- and renter-cultivated lands. The hacienda's directly farmed land employed permanent and temporary labor, who may or may not have lived on the estate. What is considered to have been a typical arrangement in the central region of Mexico between the hacendado and his employees and tenants is described below.

Resident peons earned wages and a good ration of corn to feed their families and received the use of small plots of land for cultivation. Tenants received a hut, firewood, seeds, and some pasturage, along with their plots, in return for half their crop. Occasionally tenants worked for the hacendado and earned cash. It appears that for peons the crucial part of the arrangement was the corn ration. Hacendados were obligated by custom in some areas to provide peons with the ration regardless of the market price of corn. Because corn comprised an average seventy-five percent of a peon family's diet, this ensured the peon's basic staple even in periods of drought and crop failure and partially insulated him and his family from the effects of inflation. Tenants and sharecroppers had no such security. Their well-being depended on the vagaries of the weather. A good-sized plot with oxen and good rain might turn a profit, but there were no guarantees. We do not know very much about the situations of day laborers other than the fact that agricultural wages remained nominally the same in the central area of Mexico throughout the nineteenth century.

Debt peonage is the most notorious and controversial aspect of hacienda labor. In this system peons would go into debt to the hacienda in order to pay church taxes and fees; expenses for rites of passage, such as marriage and baptism; or ordinary purchases at the hacienda store. Peons would then be obligated to work until they repaid the debt. But the peon, of course, often could not repay it. In some regions multiple generations were tied to the hacienda, since children were expected to repay their parents' debts. Debt peonage in a few areas was nearly indistinguishable from slavery. For example, on the haciendas of the Sánchez Navarro family, whose properties extended through Coahuila and Durango, armed retainers hunted peons who tried to escape their obligations. In other areas, however, debt served as a kind of cash advance or bonus, attracting peons to work on a particular hacienda. In some regions where labor was scarce, the hacienda store, which scholars have long considered to be a villainous institution that overcharged and cheated workers to keep them in insurmountable debt, may have actually subsidized peons. The hacienda store certainly was not always a profit center for the hacienda, nor necessarily an instrument of repression.

Conditions on the haciendas varied according to region, depending on the availability of labor. A relatively dense population concentrated in mestizo or Indian villages, as in the central area of the nation, meant a large pool of potential workers and, therefore, low wages and less favorable terms for tenants and sharecroppers. Labor shortages, as in the far north and the far south, produced one of two outcomes: heavy competition for workers, which raised wages and added benefits, such as advances on wages; or intensification of coercion to retain employees.

The Hacienda del Maguey, a grain and livestock estate in Zacatecas, provides us with an example of a mix of certain elements of both central and northern estates, although its living conditions were a bit more benign than most. The normal workday on this hacienda lasted from 6 A.M. to 6 P.M. There were breaks for breakfast and a traditional midday dinner followed by a resting period (siesta), which lasted for two to three hours. The complete workday was therefore eight to nine hours long. Given the standards experienced by the nineteenth-century industrial workforce in the United States or Western Europe, this was not an arduous day in terms of hours. The work load was fairly light for much of the year, although the few weeks devoted to harvest, sowing, and weeding were certainly more strenuous. Work on livestock haciendas was less demanding. Shepherds, for example, merely followed their flocks of sheep. Their actual hours may have been long, but much of their time was spent sitting and sleeping. Labor was intense only during roundups for slaughter once a week or for shearing in March and August.

A peon on the Hacienda del Maguey, by the calculations of historian Harry Cross, was quite well nourished, more than meeting his daily caloric requirements. The average peon laboring in the fields probably needed 2,150 calories a day. His family, approximately two adults and two children, by extension would require 9,000 calories. The ration of maize provided by his employer contained seventy-five percent of this caloric requirement. The rest of the diet consisted of frijoles (beans), chile peppers, lard, salt, and meat. Meat (pork or beef) was inexpensively purchased by residents of this hacienda. The peon added wheat flour, rice, and sugar purchased at the hacienda store. The typical family would also gather herbs, spices, and cacti from the countryside at no cost. Alcoholic beverages, particularly *pulque*—the fermented juice of the maguey plant—were consumed in large quantities, providing vitamins (in addition to intoxication if taken in excess). The combination of beans and corn provided most of the diet's protein. Cross argues that the combination of the hacienda's rations, their own subsistence plots, and harvesting natural resources furnished country people of the near north with a "remarkably nutritious and diverse diet." By this estimate, families living on the Hacienda del Maguey were able with little financial strain to eat a nutritionally adequate diet.

The Hacienda del Maguey did more than just feed its employees well and treat them fairly. For decades it employed a schoolteacher to educate its children. Moreover, its peons were free to leave at any time. Cross calculates that 9.78 percent of the hacienda population was over 50. In the same era, the proportion of whites over 50 in the United States was slightly higher, which indicates that conditions on the hacienda could not have been too bad.

In Yucatán, located in the far south, the main supply of hacienda labor came from temporary workers called *luneros*. Instead of wages, luneros were granted access to hacienda land and water in return for one day's labor each week on Monday—hence the name lunero from the Spanish word for Monday (*lunes*). This arrangement benefited both parties, for the worker received land for subsistence, while the landowner obtained workers without having to pay high wages, despite relative labor scarcity. During the economic growth that occurred in the nineteenth century, Yucatecan haciendas doubled their labor needs. The lunero system proved insufficient in these new conditions. As a result, a new form of debt peonage evolved in which the hacendado assumed responsibility for paying the peon's church taxes, and, in exchange, the peon was bound to labor on the hacienda until he repaid his debt.

The estate for which we have the most information in this era was that of the Sánchez Navarro family. At its largest, this hacienda's vast holdings encompassed in excess of 15 million acres spread over the states of Coahuila and Durango. Situated in the middle of the war zone with the Comanches and Apaches, working conditions were quite dangerous. The Sánchez Navarros maintained both a resident and temporary labor force by means of indebtedness. They first acquired a substantial number of peons with the purchase of the enormous Marquisate of Aguayo in 1840; the transaction transferred the peons' debts to the new owner. Because of the constant state of war with Comanches and the geographic isolation of the entire Sánchez Navarro estate, there was an ongoing, acute shortage of labor. To complicate matters, the estate's need for workers was highly seasonal, with the most intense demands for planting, harvest, and sheep shearing. Temporary agricultural labor was paid in cash and sometimes a ration in addition. A passer-by noted the conditions for resident peons in 1846:

The poor peon lives in a miserable mud hovel or reed hut (sometimes built of cornstalks, thatched with grass). He is allowed a peck of corn a week for his subsistence, and a small monthly pay for his clothes. . . .

Shepherds and cowboys (*vaqueros*) earned more than common laborers: five pesos a month and two pecks of corn (a peck equals a quarter bushel or eight quarts) a week. Peons generally earned two or three pesos a month and one or two pecks of corn a week. These modest wages hardly covered an average family's necessities. However, peons incurred much of their debt because of religious fees for baptisms, marriages, and burials rather than through the purchase of necessities. As a general practice, the local cleric billed the estate for these services and the hacendado then added this sum to a peon's account. Employees lost part of their pay when they missed a day's work and when they lost or broke a tool. As a result of these cumulative charges, many peons fell hopelessly in debt. The hacienda, for the most part, limited individual indebtedness to no more than fifty pesos or ten months' wages. The highest amount owed by a peon on the books was 137 pesos (more than two years' salary).

Corporal punishment was an ongoing part of hacienda culture (though obviously not accepted by the victims) and abuses were not uncommon. One of the Sánchez Navarros' mayordomos, Atanacio Muñoz, was particularly brutal, employing a club (whipping was illegal) to discipline miscreants. Peons who fled the hacienda for whatever reason were hunted down. The pursuit was sometimes relentless. One hapless peon avoided capture for seven years until he foolishly returned to the hacienda to visit his wife one night and was captured. Another unfortunate, Dionisio Beltrán, evaded his creditors for more than six years, only to be apprehended in Zacatecas, more than 200 miles away.

It seems that no one on the Sánchez Navarro estates starved and examples of mistreatment of peons were probably limited, but conditions were nonetheless harsh. The climate was inhospitable—temperatures often went to extremes of hot and cold and sometimes years went by without rain. The danger from raids by Apaches and Comanches was considerable; a number of residents lost their lives every year.

Although we know little about the lives of most country women, we do have some pictures of women's lives among the middle-class. In the big house (*casco*) women dressed in linen or silk. They spent much of the morning, be-

ginning around nine, doing needlework together in the drawing room and
working in what was called "virtuous silence." After the midday meal every female family member carried out routine chores before retiring for a siesta
(nap). During the mid-afternoon the women gathered again to continue their
needlework. Males and females gathered at eight in the evening to say prayers
and eat the evening meal. Another hour of needlework followed while one
of the men read aloud to the family. Daily life for both men and women therefore focused on work and meals.

Women administered the domestic sphere and, at times, may have taken
over as family heads when husbands were away. Girls stayed at home while the
boys went (sometimes far away) to school. The young women learned needlework and enough reading competency to carry out religious observances. One
of the more curious relationships was that between wealthy families and their
household servants, who were at once part of and separate from the family.
A hacienda's rich and poor children grew up together, even shared confi-
dences, but friendship was never a possibility, because the social barriers between classes were too great.

The Villages

We know substantially less about daily life in the pueblos than on the haciendas, for the villages did not leave the kinds of documentation generated
by the estates. Villages certainly existed in both symbiotic and conflictual relationship with haciendas. Villagers relied on the estates for work to supplement their earnings from working their own lands. Haciendas, in turn,
depended on village residents for temporary labor and tenants. Not infre-
quently, however, haciendas and pueblos clashed over land and water rights.
Because the hacienda owners were the political elite, they of course dominated
the countryside for most of the era. But the relationship between villages and
haciendas was, perhaps, most equal in the 1821–85 period, when haciendas
were severely weakened by shrinking markets for their products and uncertain political conditions.

The villages had their own forms of social stratification with *caciques* (local
bosses), municipal officeholders, and lay leaders of religious organizations
comprising the upper level. At times, small traders, muleteers, and some of the
larger tenants (in terms of quantity of rented land) joined the top group. At

the bottom were poorer residents who worked permanently or temporarily as hacienda peons and tenants with small holdings. Those who left the pueblos to work on the haciendas were called variously *naborios, laborios,* or *gañanes.*

There is probably no model that would adequately describe village politics throughout nineteenth-century Mexico. In the highlands of Puebla, historian Florencia Mallon found villages in "a constant process of change, negotiation, and adaptation. . . ." Ethnic and class conflicts abounded. "A civil-religious hierarchy" emerged, which combined municipal and *cofradía* (an organization set up to support the local church and prepare for local saints days) office holding. Generally, pueblo leadership came from older men, known in Puebla as *pasados.* The pasados nominated people for local offices, made decisions in times of crisis, and oversaw all dealings by local officeholders with the wider society. Elders attained their elevated status, according to Mallon, not necessarily because of "economic or ethnic prestige," but rather through "service and sacrifice." Those who worked hard for their community became elders. In times of potential conflict communal assemblies were called to resolve them. The good leader was bound to "guard the peace by acting justly." As the century wore on, the ability of the pasados to act fairly and to reach community consensus declined, because of the intrusions of state and national governments on their autonomy.

During the colonial era, Indian villages, which fell under jurisdictions known as *repúblicas de indios,* operated with considerable autonomy. As long as their leadership supplied local Spanish authorities with prescribed tax revenues and neighboring haciendas with requisite labor, the pueblos remained as separate, virtually self-governing, entities. Village leaders often acted as intermediaries between Europeans and Indians. Village autonomy, as discussed in greater detail in chapters 2, 5, and 10, was at the heart of political discourse throughout the nineteenth century.

Politically, all village residents concerned themselves primarily with the protection of individual and collective landholding and with minimizing taxes, both of which required local autonomy, the right to govern their everyday affairs without interference from state or national governments. Taxes oppressed country people and throughout the nineteenth century were a never-ending source of friction between indigenous people and the various levels of government. The Maya, for example, deeply resented having to pay annual taxes and fill labor rosters for state projects. Country people were also subject to military conscription.

For most rural dwellers like the Maya life revolved around their individual plots of land (milpas) and their families. Country people lived in two worlds: the first was the subsistence economy wherein ancient practices were retained, and the second was the money and wage economy, the boundaries of which country people carefully limited. The Maya participated in the money economy by working for others at various trades, including carrying the mail for the government. By no means, however, did they adopt the discipline and values of the industrial workplace (to the unending disappointment and irritation of Mexican elites and foreigners). North American John Lloyd Stephens, who traveled extensively in the peninsula in the 1840s, reported that "The Indians worked . . . , as if they had a lifetime for the job." Working slowly, moreover, was only one strategy for resisting the demands of overbearing hacendados. The Maya had longstanding expectations about what they were to be paid. Any attempt to alter existing custom or wages was met with resistance in the form of strikes or mass migrations. The Maya and other rural dwellers expected a wide variety of privileges and protested coercive measures like beatings. For example, protest sometimes took the form of demanding to return home to their own plots at crucial times during plant-

The Aguador

ing and harvest seasons. The Maya might also protest and avert any and all obligations through flight to the forests of neighboring (what was later called) Quintana Roo or Campeche, where they were out of the hacendados' and government authorities' reach.

Despite Maya recalcitrance, Yucatecan landowners and clergy conspired to inculcate labor discipline among them. The Maya owed church taxes, fees for incidental church services, taxes to subsidize periodic church inspections, and taxes to subsidize mandatory catechism for their children, which they could not or would not pay. A landowner had only to pay these delinquent taxes (debts) to the priest, whereupon a local judge would assign the unlucky Maya to the landowner to work off the debt in tasks such as weeding or cane cutting. In effect, the priests in Yucatán, as was also the case in Coahuila, allowed hacendados to use uncollected debts to compel Maya people to work. The priest received cash, while the landowner got labor below market cost. Most of the Maya, tied to their homes by family and tradition, were unwilling to flee and thus suffered. Local and state governments also oppressed the Maya by arbitrarily pressing them into military service.

The Maya considered family life and milpa to be intertwined. For the Maya marriage was a necessary condition of adulthood and they looked for a spouse as soon as they reached the age of responsible labor, usually in their mid-teens. All rural Mexicans utilized the family as an economic unit, both on their own milpas and on the haciendas. Families, including men and women, worked together in the fields, especially during planting and harvest. The men worked eight- to nine-hour days at the hacienda, or perhaps longer on their own milpa, or in helping neighbors at planting and harvest times. But women's responsibilities went far beyond. They had to rise early, well before dawn, to prepare the family's food. The work of making tortillas took hours: the corn had to be soaked for hours, and then ground in a *metate* (stone bowl). Since the men required both breakfast and lunch to take along to the fields, the women had to prepare enough for both meals early in the day. Long, luxurious lunches were only for the rich in the cities, not for rural dwellers. Chores around their modest home, caring for children, tending to the garden and, perhaps, fowl or livestock, and weaving or sewing filled out an active day. Opportunities for women in rural areas were limited and, consequently, a large number of young women migrated to the cities, where most entered domestic service.

Families planted land watered only by erratic rainfall. Often the plots were cultivated by slash and burn, whereby a field was cleared from forest or scrub, the debris burned for ash fertilizer, and the land tilled with a wooden digging stick. Crops quickly exhausted the land after only two or three years, whereupon the farmer abandoned it. Seven years were typically necessary for the land to restore itself for cultivation. This process, therefore, required enormous amounts of land. The Spaniards had introduced the steel plow, commonly drawn by oxen or horses, but generally Indians could afford neither the equipment nor the livestock.

Though the rural routine was humdrum, it was not without camaraderie and fun. G. F. Lyon, an Englishman on tour in the 1820s, described a scene of two young Indian women grinding maize and slapping tortillas, all the time singing, gossiping, and laughing. The work may have been hard, but it did not preclude a good time.

Religion occupied a central place in rural life as it permeated popular culture. Literate people read devotional pamphlets or books. Devotional artwork decorated the houses of the rich, while altars with candles, flowers, and a likeness of a saint, often occupied a corner of a poor family's hut. Local priests, called *curas,* lived only in the larger villages or towns, but periodically traveled through the villages in their districts to perform masses (Catholic religious services) and sacraments (baptism, marriage, burial). Most country people, however, rarely encountered a priest. As a result, the folk Catholicism practiced in the countryside retained many indigenous customs from pre-Christian times. Perhaps the most important religious institution was the cofradía, the village organization that maintained the church and financed religious celebrations.

The Mining Camps

Mining camps were in constant flux, due to the continuous movement back and forth between the large number of small mining settlements and agricultural villages. Mine owners had great difficulty attracting labor, because of the geographic isolation of most mining regions and the difficulty of the work. Labor scarcity kept wages relatively high and working conditions relatively favorable. Competition for labor forced employers to offer workers better conditions than existed in the countryside.

The economic and social hierarchy in the mining camps shifted according to good and bad times. Big operators, who might have employed hundreds of men and dug out millions of pesos worth of silver and gold, occupied precarious positions, for theirs was a boom and bust business. One never knew how long a bonanza (rich ore strike) would last. Small operators were numerous, since it was not hard to make a claim for a mine and only a minimal level of activity legally maintained it. Scavengers worked some older flooded mines that guerrilla bands had ruined and looted.

There were two categories of workers: skilled and unskilled. Skilled miners, such as *barreteros* or drillers, who often headed their own work gangs in the mine shafts, earned significantly higher pay. Workers who dug in the deep shafts earned more than those who worked aboveground, for their jobs required more skill and were more dangerous. Sometimes miners could smuggle ore from the shafts and sell it. Regardless of the skills they possessed or where they worked, all miners functioned in a high risk occupation. Accidents were frequent and there were occasional catastrophic cave-ins. The injured could not work and employers left them to their own devices. Overseers stood between the mine owners and miners. Rounding out the transient population of the camps were traders, moneylenders, and ore buyers.

Mexico City

The city was laid out in a grid with an enormous central plaza, called the Zocalo, which still exists today. The great cathedral stood at the north end, with the palace of government on the east, and the municipality offices on the south. Ninety-seven smaller plazas dotted the rest of the city. Five causeways furnished access to the city over the lake beds. As a legacy from Aztec times, the city was divided into distinct sections, known as barrios. One barrio housed predominantly women cigar makers, another muleteers and highwaymen. A third held the *populacho* or *léperos,* as the city's poor were known. Although rich and poor lived near one another, the outer margins of the city were left to the poor while the affluent lived in the central area.

Most residents lived in apartments or modest houses. A small minority, perhaps fifteen percent, resided in the *casas grandes,* the palatial homes of the rich. In the poor-dominated periphery, people lived in rooms rented in crowded tenements known as *vecindades.* According to Frederick Shaw, the interiors of the houses were generally filthy, with trash scattered everywhere. Because the city endured periodic flooding, ground floor rooms were constantly damp. During the rainy season the floods dumped a "foul concoction of mud, garbage, and human feces" in the houses. Badly ventilated, filthy, and crowded, the vecindades were breeding grounds for disease. Apartments lacked cooking facilities, which meant most of the poor took all their meals from street vendors. Lacking garden plots, people who prepared their own meals bought food from farms on the city's outskirts in local markets. Bread and tortillas were purchased from street vendors or neighborhood stores. Not everyone was fortunate enough to have a roof over their heads. In 1824 Joel Poinsett, the U.S. Minister, estimated that 20,000 people slept in the streets.

The Spaniards built the city on the ruins of the great Aztec capital Tenochtitlán and surrounding dry lake beds, which flooded during the rainy season. As a result, flooding was a serious problem. It was not uncommon in the rainy season for the Zocalo to be knee deep in water and for outlying districts to be transformed into lakes. At times canoes were needed for urban transport. When the floods came, raw sewage floated everywhere.

Mexico City never had enough potable water or sufficient waste disposal (nor does it today). The air smelled horribly from the sewage flowing alongside the roads and the garbage littering the streets. Piles of trash were everywhere, sometimes large enough to block street traffic. Walking the thoroughfares of the city was dangerous to one's health. The city council eventually decided to dump the trash into Lake Texcoco, which was unfortunately one of the most important sources of municipal drinking water. Unsanitary conditions had an enormous cost. Infant mortality rates were very high: more than one-third of all deaths in the city were children under three years of age. Diseases like smallpox, scarlet fever, measles, typhoid, and cholera were endemic. Periodically epidemics erupted: smallpox killed more than 2,000 children in 1840; and cholera killed almost 6,000 in 1833, and 9,000 in 1850. These diseases and others, such as diarrhea and dysentery, undoubtedly were closely associated with the wretched living conditions. The poor, suffering from malnutrition and living in filth, were particularly susceptible. Street noise was appalling. Above all was the din of the church bells, which rang on the hour to call good Catholics to mass.

If the periodic floods, bad smells, unsanitary conditions, and unending noise were not sufficient misery for city residents, earthquakes struck with unsettling frequency. Fanny Calderón de la Barca experienced at least one earthquake:

> Suddenly, the room, the walls, all began to move, and the floor to heave like waves of the sea! At first, I imagined that I was giddy, but almost immediately saw that it was an earthquake. We all ran, or rather staggered as well as we could, into the gallery, where the servants were already arranged on their knees, praying, and crossing themselves with all their might. The shock lasted above a minute and a half, and I believe has done no injury, except

frightening the whole population, and cracking a few old walls. All Mexico was on its knees while it lasted.

The city was not only difficult to inhabit, but enormously busy as well. Fanny Calderón de la Barca described the hustle and bustle of urban life in the 1840s.

> The number of carts, the innumerable Indians loaded like beasts of burden, their women with baskets of vegetables in their hands and children on their backs, the long strings of *arrieros* and their loaded mules, the droves of cattle, the flocks of sheep, the herds of pigs, render it a work of some difficulty to make one's way on horseback out of the gates of Mexico. . . .

Curiously, she noted that "the whole scene is lively and cheerful enough to make one forget that there is such thing as a care in the world."

If all this was not enough, political turmoil at times disrupted the daily routine and presented no little danger as well. Calderón de la Barca was jolted by a rebellion in mid-summer 1840:

Calle de Tacuba

The state of things is very bad. Cannon planted all along the streets, and soldiers firing indiscriminately on all who pass. . . . There is a great scarcity of provisions in the centre of the city, as the Indians, who bring in everything from the country, are stopped. . . . While I am writing, the cannon are roaring almost without interruption. . . . [A] shell has just fallen in her [a neighbor's] garden. . . .

In the biggest cities high civil government and ecclesiastical officials, merchants, and wealthy mine owners and landowners and their families comprised the upper-classes. The mine owners and large landowners often chose to live the more comfortable urban life away from their holdings. Next in the hierarchy came professionals, such as doctors and lawyers, prosperous merchants, civil servants, industrialists, and other businesspeople, who comprised an upper middle class closely associated in outlook with the elites. Together these upper-classes accounted for roughly twenty percent of the population. The middle social sectors consisted of small shopkeepers, tradespeople, artisans, and the better-off skilled workers. At the bottom were unskilled workers, peddlers, artisans of low prestige trades, and others who lived at the margins of society, such as prostitutes and beggars (the latter often called léperos as well). It is likely that in the smaller cities the middle class was smaller than in Mexico City. Moreover, the middle sectors were closer to the lower classes in income and status than to the elites. Mexican society in this period could be described as a two-class construct with subtle, important gradations within each class.

By 1800 Mexico City was battered and bruised from rapid growth in population and urbanization. The city always appeared to be bursting its seams. With 137,000 people in 1800 and 168,846 in 1811, Mexico City was the largest city in the western hemisphere and the fifth largest city in the Western world. Half of its population was of Spanish descent, with the rest comprised of Indians, mixed bloods, and African Mexicans. During the next three decades through the 1850s the population of the city fluctuated between 160,000 and 205,000, as epidemics periodically caused precipitous drops in the population from which recovery was slow. Because of high mortality rates, migration from the countryside, rather than natural increase, continued to account for net population growth.

The population of the city increased by one-third during the second half of the eighteenth century as 40,000 people migrated from neighboring areas as a result of crop failures in the 1784–1787 and 1808–10 periods. Migration accelerated with the encroachments of the haciendas on village lands in some regions. Growth continued at the rate of 1.4 percent a year after Independence, when the dislocations of war in the countryside sent more migrants to the city in search of shelter and employment.

Peons sometimes fled to the city to escape their debts. Bernardino Pérez, for example, was an agricultural laborer who fled Monte Alto, when a 7-peso debt swelled to 25. On his arrival in the capital he found work in a textile factory (*obraje*). After his former employer hunted him down, he borrowed enough money from his new boss to repay the old debt. Bernardino was happily free from one burden, but, of course, he still owed a considerable sum.

Vendor carries home artisan production

Women accounted for between 57 and 59 percent of Mexico City's inhabitants throughout the first half of the nineteenth century. They also made up the majority of migrants from the countryside. As with the men, almost all were castas or Indians who came from the densely populated regions around the capital. These women left their rural birthplaces in search of employment in industry or services. Most women migrants were single in the 15 to 29 age group.

Eighty percent of urban dwellers were either artisans or unskilled laborers and their families. Most capital residents were poor, and struggled mightily every day to survive. Wages were generally barely sufficient for subsistence and there was never enough steady employment. Only thirty percent had full-time jobs. Most of the employed were able to find only part-time work. The poor, as a result, lived wretched lives. They were always hungry, dressed in tatters, and resided in unsanitary dwellings. A third of their children died before

A busy marketplace on the
outskirts of Mexico City

age three, and epidemics killed urban people in huge numbers. Petty crime was a way of life.

The most common occupations were domestic service, manual labor, and artisan. Of the skilled workers, shoemakers, carpenters, and tailors were most common. Among the unskilled, the most numerous were bricklayers, domestics, and street peddlers. The average daily salary was 0.5 to 1.0 peso (the peso was equal to the U.S. dollar until late in the century) for skilled workers and 0.25 to 0.50 for unskilled workers, while the minimum daily cost of subsistence was 0.75 to 1.0 peso. Because of the stagnant economy and a labor surplus, wages did not significantly rise throughout the 1830s. A large number of tiny businesses supplied consumer goods; many conducted their commerce on blankets in the filthy main market. Most of the urban poor were outside the wage economy. Only 1.4 percent of city residents owned property.

Working conditions were sometimes horrendous, and working children often suffered mistreatment. Historian Frederick Shaw relates the plight of Loreto Flores's sixteen-year-old son during the 1850s. The young man worked long hours in a bakery in Mexico City. One evening he collapsed from exhaustion, only to have his foreman force him back to his tasks by hitting him. The lad made up his mind to quit, only to be tricked by the administrator, who accused him of helping another boy to escape, and then docked him for the escapee's debts. Flores was jailed in the bakery and beaten. Another sad case in the 1820s was that of Cosmo Damián. At five his drunken father sold him to an obraje, where he worked endless hours for crusts of bread. His one day off a year was expensive, for he and the other workers paid for the celebration from their wages. Eventually he was set free by local authorities.

Income and wealth inequities were reflected in the social structure. One way to measure status in Mexico was to count the number of household servants. Historian Silvia Arrom defines the upper-classes as people of independent wealth, such as prosperous merchants and miners, and top-level bureaucrats and clergy. This top four percent had on average three or four household servants. The middle class included intellectuals, professionals, merchants and businesspeople of modest means, government and private clerks, middle ranking militia officers and lower clergy, some independent artisans, and small shopkeepers. The middle class accounted for about eighteen percent of all households and employed one or two servants per household.

Artisans, who comprised the upper echelons of the urban poor, struggled increasingly after Independence, because Mexico's newly established government disbanded the protective associations, known as guilds, and opened up the domestic market to the competition of foreign manufactures. Many textile trades, for example, suffered near collapse as a result of competition from large domestic clothing and fabric factories and foreign imports.

Cofradías provided some comfort for artisans in time of need. They originated in the guilds' obligation to develop the spiritual welfare of their members. Each one was dedicated to the performance of a specific religious function, usually the veneration of a saint. Their principal usefulness was in times of sickness or death. The cofradía would pay for the administration of sacraments, funeral and burial expenses, and certain widow and orphan benefits. Membership dues financed these functions. Unfortunately, only a minority of artisans and no laborers belonged.

Because of competition from foreign manufacturers, lack of an adequate domestic market, and insufficient local investment capital, Mexico City did not industrialize until late in the nineteenth century. Consequently, industrial jobs were scarce. There were thousands of small workshops, but these were mainly one-person operations, such as independent carpenters or masons.

There were some unusual jobs peculiar to the requirements of Mexico City. One such occupation was water carrier (*aguador*). The only available water in the city came from fountains, each of which had its aguadores who supplied neighborhoods that lacked fountains. From 6 A.M. to 11 P.M., the aguador carried huge jugs of water suspended from his head by rope, his hands holding two large ladles. Because he was illiterate, the aguador used colored beans to signify the amount of water each customer consumed. The aguador was often a beloved figure, because he treated the children to free drinks, dispensed local gossip, delivered letters, and acted as a jobs information center. He also drowned unwanted cats.

Thanks to the research of historian Silvia Arrom, we have a clearer picture of the plight of Mexico City's female residents during the three decades after Independence. A quarter of all women worked, comprising one-third of the workforce in the capital. Few upper-class women participated in the workforce. (Wealthy women had some economic influence, however, for at the time of Independence women owned about one-fourth of all privately held property in the capital.) Over a third of casta woman and almost half of all Indian women worked. Nearly sixty percent of these women worked as domestic servants. Twenty percent sold food from their homes, on the street, or in the markets. Other occupations ran the gamut from midwives and healers to peddlers and waitresses. For about a decade, there was increased access to artisan trades. Opportunities for women to work as artisans declined again by mid-century.

Women fared no better than men in the conditions and remuneration of employment. Most were underemployed, and women were concentrated in the worst-paying occupations. Domestic service jobs were regarded by many women as humiliating. For the many who swallowed their pride, conditions varied drastically. Some servants were treated well, and a few like family members. Servants as a general rule owed "submission, obedience, and respect" to employers. They were on call twenty-four hours a day, and were often paid only room and board. There was also a hierarchy among domestic servants. At the top were the housekeepers, then kitchen maids, chambermaids, children's nurses, and laundresses. Because there were so many young women available for domestic service, the labor market precluded any improvement in conditions. Factories paid no better, although work there brought less dishonor than domestic service. Conditions in the textile and tobacco industries, other large employers of women, deteriorated considerably over the course of the 1820s and 1830s. Women were not allowed into the clergy, military, or government bureaucracy, which were, of course, the main paths to upward mobility.

When women arrived in the city they remained surprisingly independent and desperately poor. Slightly less than half were married. Because the census of 1811 indicates a high proportion of single women in the 45 to 54 age group, it is possible that many women never married. Eighty percent of women married at some point in their lives, either in formal or informal unions. But most spent only a small portion of their lives married. If they migrated from the countryside, they delayed marriage. Because of the higher mortality rate among men, it was likely that they would be widowed. Seventy percent of married women between 45 and 54 had outlived their husbands. Rich or poor, women spent much of their lives on their own.

According to Arrom's estimates, high mortality rates among men and children left women with fewer children than one might expect. Many women were widowed before their childbearing days ended. While an average woman in the capital bore approximately five children, with infant mortality (death before age three) estimated at twenty-seven percent, it was likely that she would outlive at least one of them. Although two-thirds of adult women bore children, fewer than half of these women had children at home. One-third of adult women were single or widowed at the time of the censuses in 1811 and 1848.

Because a substantial proportion of Mexico City's women headed their own households as widows for much of their lives, they enjoyed a degree of independence and, perhaps, respect, if they were among the more well-to-do. This independence, of course, should not be exaggerated, for in many cases an adult son or son-in-law controlled the finances and negotiated with the outside world for the woman. Wealthy women were more likely to head their own households. Half of white women headed their own households in 1811, compared to only a third of casta or Indian women. Wealthy widows benefited from inheritance laws that forced the division of an estate among surviving spouse and children. The wife in these cases would always have at least some control over the estate. Because males commonly married late, the number of offspring was limited, thereby keeping the widow's share of the estate larger. These kinds of calculations, of course, were of no consequence to the poor. Women could barely subsist on their own. They had few alternatives to turning to men for support. Even then survival was uncertain. Children were the only form of old-age insurance; consequently, there were no worries about too many heirs.

Although it was less likely that married women would work because of social convention, economic necessity among the poor made working very likely. Men's incomes alone could not generally support an average family. Families simply would not survive without the woman's earnings. Marriage and motherhood did not end a woman's working career, but often may have led to a change in occupation. Domestic service was not an option, because it required living in a separate residence. In contrast, self-employment allowed women to care for their children while generating income. They could prepare food for sale, sew, operate small retail establishments, or peddle. Women dominated the local markets.

Marriage was an unequal institution. A wife was expected to accept submission to her husband and to "obey him in everything reasonable." Domestic violence was common. The double standard was widely practiced; that is, it was acceptable — to men, at least — that men could engage in extramarital relations, while women could not.

Conclusion

Everyday life in nineteenth-century Mexico was uncertain. The struggles for food and shelter were unending and precarious. Common people, both in the countryside and in the cities, simultaneously fought to assert and maintain control over crucial aspects of their daily subsistence. They could not isolate themselves, however, from either politics or broader social affairs. The next chapter is dedicated to their efforts to establish and maintain control over their own culture, traditions, politics, and economy in the midst of national instability, civil conflict, and foreign wars.

Chapter 2

THE POLITICS OF DISORDER, 1821–45

After eleven years of intermittent civil wars, Mexico gained its inde pendence on September 27, 1821. On that day Agustín de Iturbide, a turncoat Spanish army officer, who forged an arrangement with rebel patriot leaders, led his victorious army into Mexico City. It may be indicative of how Mexicans eventually came to view the event that the nation's Independence Day is celebrated on September 16, the day when Father Miguel Hidalgo proclaimed Mexican independence in his Cry of Dolores (*El Grito de Dolores*) in 1810, rather than the anniversary of Iturbide's triumph. Hidalgo ultimately failed leading a mass popular movement, while Iturbide prevailed in a backroom deal.

The foundation of the new nation was shaky from the beginning. Independence resulted from an arrangement between royalist army officer Iturbide and the surviving rebel leadership, Vicente Guerrero and Guadalupe Victoria. The agreement was based on "The Three Guarantees": Roman Catholicism would be the religion of the country, with no toleration of other faiths; *criollos* (creoles, white Spaniards born in New Spain) and *peninsulares* (white Spaniards born in Spain) would be equal under the law; and the form of government would be a constitutional monarchy. A new army, combining royalist and rebel forces, was to oversee the implementation of the plan.

The deal makers' original intent was for Mexico to obtain a monarch from a European royal family. The first choice was Ferdinand VII of Spain, who had presided over the disastrous loss of his nation's empire. This was a curious preference. Fortunately, Ferdinand was unwilling. When no other European

For this chapter I am deeply indebted to the works of the following: Timothy Anna, Michael Costeloe, Thomas Cotner, Torcuato DiTella, Michael Ducey, Don Dumond, Will Fowler, Stanley Green, Peter Guardino, Terry Ruggeley, Frank Samponaro, Pedro Santoni, William Sprague, Donald Stevens, Barbara Tenenbaum, and Richard Warren.

prince came forth, Iturbide crowned himself Emperor Agustín I on July 21, 1822. His colorful reign lasted less than a year. A revolt led by a then-unknown brigadier general, Antonio López de Santa Anna, forced the floundering emperor to abdicate in March 1823.

If It Was Chaos, Why?

In the first decades of Independence, Mexicans were unable to reach consensus about two crucial questions: what form of government was most suitable for Mexico, and who should rule? As a result, the rebellion against Iturbide initiated a long period of turbulence in national government. Between 1824 and 1857, Mexico had 16 presidents and 33 provisional chief executives, for a total of 49 national administrations. Guadalupe Victoria, the first elected president, was the only president to finish his term (1824–29). Cabinet secretaries proved even more transient. The war ministry changed leaders 53 times, the foreign ministry 57 times, and the justice ministry 61 times. The average tenure for a cabinet officer was only seven months. These figures most certainly point to a high degree of political turmoil. However, the question of what constitutes stability or instability is debatable, for there were several underlying elements of stability.

Throughout this period, the military dominated the highest echelons of the national government. Only six civilians served as president of the nation between 1821 and 1851, while fifteen generals held the highest office. Three of the civilian presidents lasted only a few days. In addition, there was continuity in leadership. Anastasio Bustamante, Antonio López de Santa Anna, Valentín Gómez Farías, Nicolás Bravo, and José Joaquín de Herrera each served in the presidency on three or more separate occasions. Anastasio Bustamante held the position for the longest consecutive period: four and a half years of an eight-year term (called for in the centralist Constitution of 1836) from 1837 to 1841. Santa Anna was chief executive eleven times. Together Bustamante and Santa Anna occupied the presidency for approximately half of the first thirty years. Consequently, there was a measure of stability, despite the fact that terms were abbreviated.

Despite the high turnover in the cabinet, there also may have been a significant degree of continuity in these offices as well. The same people from an elite known as hombres de bien ("good people"; see below) served again and again and provided the underlying stability of politics beneath the surface of revolving governments. In many cases the same men served in various capacities in several different administrations.

Mexican politics were conducted on three levels—national, state, and local—all of which influenced each other, but none of which dominated. At the national level, the hombres de bien, a small group of men from a relatively homogeneous background, mostly well-educated professionals and military officers, contested in "gentlemanly" fashion for control over the central gov-

Guadalupe Victoria

ernment. They plotted, rebelled, legislated, and debated among themselves in Mexico City. They argued incessantly over alternative political and economic systems: federalism or centralism, liberalism or conservatism, free trade or protectionism, and pro-clericalism or anti-clericalism. Working always behind the scenes, the *agiotistas* (moneylenders), who furnished the national government with its operating funds, also exerted considerable influence.

On the second level, state politics were largely in the hands of the *notables*, regionally prominent landowning and merchant families who competed from their geographical power bases in small provincial cities, where they domi-

Anastasio Bustamante

nated the municipal governments. Rivalries among notables were often quite heated. At the local level in the countryside, each village had its own leadership. These rural people, usually of quite modest means, vied for control over tax levies and access to land. At both the state and local levels, rivals fought about what mattered in their everyday lives. The connecting link between the national and local levels was the issue of local and regional (state) autonomy

Juan Álvarez

as opposed to centralized authority. This was manifested in the nationwide debate between federalism and centralism.

None of the three groups was isolated from each other nor from the forces of the outside world. Political elites at all levels sometimes sought alliances with rural people and, on rarer occasions, with the urban poor. These alliances could be crucial in determining national political outcomes, such as when Iturbide found support among Mexico City's urban poor (known as léperos or el populacho, the rabble) during the early 1820s or when the mulatto (mixed African and European ancestry) farmers of the hot country of Guerrero stood with Juan Álvarez, the political boss of southern Mexico, in 1854 to topple Santa Anna. Rural people were the soldiers in all the armies and guerrilla bands that contested national and regional politics.

Country people and lower-class urban dwellers participated actively in Mexican politics during the early nineteenth century. To be sure, Mexican politics, for the most part, did not involve the mass of people and only a small minority of Mexicans engaged in the debates and conspiracies of the era. No revolt attracted widespread adherents, nor did any rebellion require more than a few thousand soldiers. And almost certainly, the vast majority of Mexicans could not do much more than to pay attention to their daily survival. Nonetheless, the popular classes attempted to exert their political will. Their methods and goals varied considerably. Country people sided with factions of notables. Sometimes they took up arms against the notables when they sought to protect or extend their village lands. Mexico City dwellers rioted for cheaper food or in defense of their city against foreign intruders. The first five decades after Independence provided an unprecedented opportunity for the lower classes in some (we do not have documentation for all) regions to exert significant influence over the institutions that helped lay out the pattern of their everyday lives and an even rarer opportunity to determine the path of nation building.

The basis of multi-class political participation was the Constitution of 1824, which reinforced the notion of democracy by proclaiming all Mexicans equal before the law. Although the qualifications for voting were much debated at the time, there were no restrictions on the vote (for males) until 1836, when the Conservative government cut the voting population by sixty percent. The vulnerable consensus that produced Iturbide's coalition and the federalist ascendancy that created the Constitution of 1824 broke down by the end of the decade. Never far beneath the surface was the deeply instilled fear of the masses held by the hombres de bien. The elite's memory of the nightmare of

Father Hidalgo's mob killing Spaniards in 1810 and 1811 tainted nineteenth-century Mexican politics. The Parián riot of 1828, which erupted in Mexico City in support of the presidential candidacy of Vicente Guerrero, added to this distrust, when 5,000 "insolent plebes" assaulted and robbed the exclusive shops in the central square. Though it lasted only twenty-four hours, the uprising shook the city's rich to their core.

Hombres de Bien

The hombres de bien were people of education, property, "virtue," and "honor." Their views encompassed the political spectrum. They commonly believed in their own qualifications to run the nation and almost all mistrusted the masses. Thus, they advocated limiting suffrage by qualification of income. Radical Liberal Valentín Gómez Farías put it this way:

> You would want all the classes in our society represented in congress; in my opinion, that has a serious drawback because the classes are so varied and diverse and very few of them have people of sufficient aptitude and understanding to be able to carry out the arduous and difficult task which has to be entrusted to their care.

Despite the existence of considerable racial prejudice, some men of mixed blood entered the ranks of the hombres de bien, though this was not commonplace. The typical hombre de bien was born at the end of the eighteenth century to a well-to-do family. He went to Roman Catholic Church schools, where he learned theology and law. He earned his living from the practice of his profession and, perhaps, a modest inheritance or rents from rural property. With an income of approximately 1,000 pesos a year, he maintained a comfortable lifestyle. The hombre de bien probably rented an apartment (likely from the Church, for it was the city's largest landlord) in downtown Mexico City, and had three or four household servants. He was well dressed in the latest European fashions. A man about town, he would have frequented trendy cafes and restaurants in the city. Some obtained positions in the national government, which paid little, but added to their personal status.

Most important to the hombre de bien was social standing. Ideology was not nearly as important as class solidarity. He feared unrestricted suffrage more than anything, for in his worldview the poor and illiterate deserved no say in government, nor did they have any inherent right to full citizenship. A government of the people, he believed, would lead only to violence and ruin.

Valentín Gómez Farías

Members of this elite advocated what they thought was best for the masses and did not shy from articulating the will of the people (without consulting them). There were personal ties, as well as political alliances. There were grudges, family rivalries, and friendships. But all was within the bounds of an old boys' network. No matter how bitter the political debate, it was under-laid with class solidarity.

The Military

Almost all Mexican presidents during the nineteenth century were military officers. (The most notable exceptions, as we will see, would be the presidents of the Reform era, Benito Juárez and Sebastián Lerdo de Tejada.) The domi-nant political personalities of the years from 1821 to 1854—Santa Anna, Bus-tamante, and Gómez Farías—were well-respected military officers, each of whom had fought initially against Mexican independence. The military was arguably the most important institution in Mexican society prior to 1880. Be-cause of the constant threat of war, no Mexican politician could easily reduce the military in size or importance. Consequently, the army absorbed an enor-mous portion of the nation's resources.

The military was also a critical social force, because it provided a means for upward mobility for castas since the wars of Independence. This institution was particularly difficult to control due to its special privileges, the most im-portant of which was the *fuero* or right of members of the military to be tried in a court of their peers, which put soldiers beyond the reach of civilian ju-risdiction. From the beginning, the army was conservative and centralist with most of the officer corps coming from the ranks of the royalist army. Throughout the era federalists advocated the formation of popular militias controlled by the states to counterbalance the centralist national military.

In the mid-1820s there were officially 58,000 men in the army. But this army existed only on paper. To meet the Spanish invasion in 1829 the Mexican gov-ernment could muster only 8,000 soldiers. The army was top heavy with of-ficers, expensive, and inefficient. In the mid-1830s there were 13 divisional generals and 18 brigadiers with combined salaries of 159,000 pesos a year. Mil-itary expenditures sometimes surpassed treasury revenues. The Bustamante regime, for example, sought to win over the military by purchasing new equip-ment, and between 1830 and 1832 spent 10 million pesos on the army, even though no foreign invasions threatened. In 1836 the military spent an aver-

age of 600,000 pesos a month, while government revenues amounted to
430,000 pesos a month. The Texas campaign added another 200,000 pesos per
month to the deficit. In 1845 there were at least 535 infantry and cavalry officers, 29 of whom were generals, paid 820,830 pesos by the government, although they were furloughed. Generally speaking, there was little to show for
vast military expenditures, for the Mexican army did not fight well against the
Spanish in 1829, the Texans in 1836, or the French in 1838.

Country People

Country people who lived in villages or owned their own land were the
most likely to have political impact. Villages had their own leadership, sense
of identity, and collected their own taxes and regulated access to land. They
were most powerful in regions where large estates were absent and villages
controlled most of the land. Villages everywhere in Mexico were quite capable of seeking recourse through informal political networks, such as local patrons or intermediaries; through formal government, such as the courts; or
through violence.

From 1820 to 1880 villagers and small landholders held the balance of power
in many areas. They influenced events by joining with regional and national
factions at crucial times. Because they were virtually autonomous in some regions, they rejected and modified laws passed by state and national governments of which they disapproved. Country people fought fiercely to retain and
extend the rights they possessed. Though circumstances varied widely according to region, the early republic was an era of opportunity in the sense
that country people actively competed for control of local governments.

It was no accident that centralists' first target, when they took power in 1836,
was local autonomy. Centralists wanted to limit the influence of country people, so they severely restricted suffrage by raising annual income requirements
for voter eligibility and reduced the number of municipalities. As a result,
taxes increased drastically. Centralists appointed local justices of the peace,
who carried out many of the duties previously the responsibility of town
councils. But the central government was unable to provide a corps of officials sufficiently numerous, educated, and motivated to enforce its will in the
countryside without major concessions to the rural population. Nor could it
afford a bureaucracy and military large enough to enforce centralization.
Thus, village communities persisted with most of their rights and prerogatives
intact until the mid-1880s.

The Hero Presidents: Victoria and Guerrero

The Constitution of 1824 organized the government into executive, legislative, and judicial branches. Presidents were elected for four-year terms and were not eligible for immediate reelection. Rather than through direct vote, presidents were elected by state legislatures; each state had one vote. The candidate with the second highest vote became vice president. Congress had two houses. Each state had two senators elected for four-year terms. Population count determined the number of each state's representatives to the lower house, the Chamber of Deputies, whose members served two-year terms. Towns and cities were governed by town councils (*ayuntamientos*), consisting of a mayor and six councilors.

Three factions, soon reduced to two, dominated the political scene in the 1820s. First, there were the Iturbidistas, followers of the deposed emperor, who were drawn from the old colonial nobility, church officials, army officers, and the rabble of Mexico City (léperos). Second, the centralists (see introduction) favored a strong national government. And third, the federalists envisioned strong states and a weak national government. It is difficult to determine the precise class make-up of the latter two factions, because both had large landowners, merchants, and industrialists among their ranks. The majority of centralists were from large urban centers. Federalists came from the peripheral states, most notably in the north. The federalists initially gained the upper hand after the fall of Iturbide.

After a short interval (1823–24) during which a three-person executive ruled while the new federalist constitution was written, Guadalupe Victoria (1789–1843), one of the heroes of the Independence wars, won election as the first president of Mexico in 1824. Although Victoria was careful not to favor either federalists or centralists, he could not prevent their heated competition. Financial difficulties haunted the Victoria administration, though with the help of loans obtained from Great Britain, Victoria remained in office to the end of his term.

The seemingly natural successor to Victoria was fellow Independence hero Vicente Guerrero (1782–1831). The son of "a poor farm couple, of mixed Spanish, Indian, and probably Negro ancestry," Guerrero had fought under Father José María Morelos and was, by his own claim, a veteran of nearly 500 battles. He had won additional popularity when he defeated an uprising against Victoria in 1828. Guillermo Prieto, an acute observer of the times described him as follows:

He was rather tall in stature . . . had a swarthy complexion, coarse hair heaped on his forehead, and black penetrating eyes with an inexpressible gentleness. His whiskers were well grown, his mouth, contracted and sincere. . . . Although modest, his manners were not retiring. His high and unmusical voice repelled one at first impression. Near him, one felt the goodness of his soul. . . .

Nonetheless, a rival to Guerrero arose in Manuel Gómez Pedraza, with the support of the hombres de bien, who feared having someone they considered part of the rabble as president. After a mudslinging election, Gómez Pedraza emerged the winner by a narrow margin. Santa Anna was unwilling to allow Gómez Pedraza, a personal enemy, to take office and led a small-scale rebellion that overturned the election results. After Victoria completed his term, Guerrero succeeded him in April 1829. Notoriously ill–at ease among the bureaucrats of the capital, the general inherited a bankrupt government badly handicapped by the belief of many Mexicans that it was illegitimate. During less than a year in office, Guerrero abolished slavery in Mexico and defeated Spain's foolhardy attempt to reconquer Mexico in 1829. Despite these accomplishments, his own vice–president, Anastasio Bustamante, ousted Guerrero on the first day of 1830.

The 1820s were a time of unparalleled political participation by the masses. In Mexico City the lower classes voted in elections to an unprecedented extent. Iturbide had built his political base from the urban lower classes and the military. The lower classes of the capital adored him for ridding the nation of the hated Spaniards. The urban poor took to the streets in 1823 in a futile effort to prevent the emperor's overthrow by Santa Anna. Iturbide refused to lead the mob, although it was his only chance to retain his throne. In the end, his class loyalty superseded personal ambition.

The casta Guerrero's rise epitomized the possibilities of upward mobility for the lower classes. And it was during his presidency that the political participation of the urban lower classes reached its peak. Urban workers voted in support of tariffs to protect artisan and manufacturing jobs against inexpensive foreign imports.

Widespread agitation and a heavy voter turnout during the elections of 1828 frightened Moderates and Conservatives to the point that in late 1829 they overthrew Guerrero. The hombres de bien believed in their hearts that Mexican society was on the edge of breaking down.

Anastasio Bustamante (1780–1853)

Historians have generally ignored Anastasio Bustamante despite his having led Mexico for approximately seven years. Born of poor Spanish parents in Michoacán in 1780, he was educated in a seminary and later studied medicine. After a short stint as a doctor (without a degree), he joined the military. Like so many of the early leaders of the republic, he began as a soldier for Spain during the Independence wars who fought against the insurgents, and switched sides with Iturbide in 1821. As a favorite of the emperor, he reached the rank of field marshal. Bustamante ascended to the presidency, when, after serving briefly as vice president under Vicente Guerrero for seven months in 1829, he rebelled and ousted him. Contemporary Guillermo Prieto described Bustamante as of "medium build, plump, round faced with small eyes, with a broad forehead and rather pursed lips, and with a tendency to strut about splay-footed or with the toes pointed outward."

Bustamante professed no political allegiance and therefore drew the enmity of both centralists and federalists. Much like Santa Anna, with whom he alternated as president for a time, Bustamante was most successful as a political survivor. His years in office were turbulent. Almost immediately, he faced a year-long rebellion led by overthrown president Guerrero, which ended only when Guerrero was captured and executed in February 1831.

Juan Álvarez

Juan Álvarez, who ruled unchallenged as the political boss of much of the south and southwest of the nation, was the dominant political figure in Mexico outside the capital in the first half century after Independence. A mestizo, Álvarez had an unlucky youth, for the executor of his father's estate cheated him of his inheritance. After a stint as a cowherd, he fought on the side of the insurgents in the 1810s. Wounded several times, he spent much of the war recuperating. As a result of his injuries, Álvarez needed crutches to walk, but could still ride a horse skillfully. He returned to war, leading insurgents on the southwest coast during the last years of the rebellion, rising in rank to colonel.

Following the Independence wars, he acquired a large estate and expanded his political base among the mulatto militia of the Costa Grande. His true skill was in organizing larger movements. Álvarez represented the concerns of the southern small farmers for local autonomy. By far the most enduring of Mex-

ico's regional bosses, Álvarez held sway in the south until 1868. Though he
never reached the revered national status of his contemporaries like Guerrero,
Victoria, and Nicolás Bravo, his control and influence, though geographically
limited to the south, would last longer.

Álvarez, as much as any political figure of the era from 1821 to 1855, epitomized the regional foundations of Mexican politics. First and foremost, he
guarded his base in Guerrero; the nation was secondary among his concerns.

Liberal Interregnum, 1832–34

Bustamante lasted until the waning days of 1832, when Santa Anna deposed
him. In March 1833 Santa Anna was elected president and Gómez Farías vice
president. Santa Anna left governance to Gómez Farías, preferring to maintain his regional power base and his army in Veracruz. Over the course of a tumultuous year Gómez Farías and the radical Liberals attacked the pillars of
Conservatism: the government bureaucracy, the Church, and the military. The
radicals tried to change the nation's political culture by eliminating thousands
of people from their government posts, reaching down to the municipal level.
They inflicted a major blow on the Church, when in 1833 they abolished the
tithe (which had obligated people to pay one-tenth of their yearly incomes
to the Church), the Church's largest source of revenue. They also tried to limit
the power of the army. The radicals' heyday was short lived, because they
alienated the army and the Church without winning popular support, despite
their concerted efforts to mobilize the lower classes. The radicals lost the crucial support of the hombres de bien, who feared lower-class participation in
politics. Santa Anna ended the radical reforms when he returned to office
in 1834.

The Conservative Ascendancy, 1834–46

Santa Anna met his demise in Texas. The humiliation of his defeat forced
him from the political stage. While Santa Anna was losing vast territories in
the north, centralists in the national congress in 1836 engineered and adopted
a new constitution that became known as the Seven Laws (Siete Leyes), which
limited suffrage, strengthened the executive, and limited local political autonomy. The most important of the new laws restricted voting rights to men
with high incomes, effectively excluding the vast majority of the Mexican people from voting and public office. The new Constitution changed the presi-

dential term to eight years and permitted reelection. The central government was to appoint state governors. Governors were to name prefects to administer the municipalities. The Siete Leyes' limitations on mass participation in politics showed clearly that the fear of the people by the hombres de bien had triumphed.

Anastasio Bustamante was the obvious Conservative choice for president. Taking office in early 1837, again he walked a tightrope while attempting to balance the demands and plots by radical Liberals and Conservatives. A bizarre episode known as the Pastry War further undermined him. Frustrated because its citizens (one of whom was the owner of a bakery in Sonora, hence the Pastry War) were unable to gain restitution for losses suffered in one of Mexico's many revolts, France sent a naval squadron to Veracruz. When the Mexican government ignored the gesture, the angry French blockaded the port. Bustamante, displeased with his military commanders in Veracruz, ordered Santa Anna, then at home near Jalapa only a short march away, to take command. Santa Anna became a hero when he suffered a severe wound in a skirmish with the French and, ever the masterful publicist, turned this escapade to his political advantage. Restored to glory, the hero Santa Anna loomed like a dark shadow over Bustamante.

Over the next year, Mexico appeared on the brink of political and fiscal disintegration. The coalition of the hombres de bien, the Church, and the army, which had supported the centralist regime, came apart. In one wild week in July 1839, radicals staged a coup in Mexico City, turning the Zocalo into a shooting gallery with an artillery battle, while roving bands looted the city. Bustamante survived the incident, but forever lost the confidence of the horrified hombres de bien. Santa Anna sent him into exile in 1841.

Santa Anna's comeback was rather remarkable, given the fact that he was widely regarded as a venal, unprincipled, untrustworthy opportunist. We cannot underestimate Santa Anna's political skills, his charisma, or his enormous energy. The general had won the military's support by carefully courting military leaders over the years with promotions, raises, and praise. Santa Anna was also a master of patronage, using lucrative government concessions to purchase allies. He also benefited from the mistaken belief on the part of the hombres de bien that they could control him. Although the general had proven this a wrong-headed assumption in the past, the good men in their arrogance stuck with their illusion.

The triumphant Santa Anna closed Congress in 1842 and ruled by decree until the end of 1844. He pushed through a new constitution, the Organic

Bases (Bases Orgánicas), which shortened the presidential term to five years, broadened presidential powers, and narrowed the franchise even further. One contemporary called it "constitutional despotism." As always, Santa Anna soon wore out his welcome. He alienated all sectors of society with his outrageous personal behavior, marrying a fifteen-year-old girl only weeks after the death of his wife of nineteen years. In late 1844 Santa Anna's popularity had sunk to a new low, when an angry mob dug up his amputated leg and dragged it through the streets of Mexico City to great laughter. The rioters shouted "Death to the Cripple: long live Congress." By January 1845 Santa Anna was in exile again.

The hombres de bien first turned to one of their own, José Joaquín de Herrera, a moderate Liberal. Herrera subsequently won election to the presidency, only to be overthrown in the days leading to the war with the United States, because he tried to negotiate a peaceful settlement.

During the 1840s Mexico nearly disintegrated. War with the United States (1846–48) and the resultant loss of half the national territory was only the most dramatic of its troubles. Infuriated by the intrusions of the centralized government and the diminution of local autonomy, the countryside erupted. Rural people took up arms to assert control over their everyday lives. When Maya Indians in Yucatán rose in the so-called Caste War in 1847, they nearly forced their white and mestizo tormenters from the peninsula. In areas like Guerrero country people obtained a considerable measure of autonomy.

Seemingly at the height of its power, centralism had broken down. Severely limiting the franchise and cutting the number of municipalities backfired, creating exactly the outcome that the centralist conservatives had feared all along. The war with the United States forced the government to raise taxes, evoking more bitter protests. Country people, upset with local issues, such as land, taxes, and conscription, sought and found allies among the badly fragmented regional and national political factions. Regional notables were ready and willing to take advantage of the weakness of the central government in order to extend their autonomy. Notables and small landowners and villages in some areas thus became allies against the centralists. In Yucatán local leaders, known as *batabs,* led the rebellion that turned into the Caste War. Centralists had left only one road open for the people of the countryside, rich and poor, to influence the political process: violence. Twenty years of mass violence followed.

Chapter 3

THE ORIGINS OF
UNDERDEVELOPMENT

During the six decades after Independence Mexico fell into prolonged economic stagnation. The worst conditions occurred before 1850. Per capita annual income fell more than 50 percent, from 116 pesos in 1800 to 56 pesos in 1845. There were several causes for the new nation's economic difficulties. First, Mexico was almost constantly at war from 1810 to 1877. The Wars of Independence ravaged the nation from 1810 to 1821. There followed four foreign invasions and an unending succession of civil wars. The worst, the War of the Reform, lasted for three bloody years (1857–60). The wars also resulted in the loss of half of the nation's territory, incalculable destruction, and nonproductive consumption of huge quantities of human and capital resources. War disrupted commercial and capital markets, exacerbated uncertainties, and discouraged long-range investment and planning.

Second, Mexico's lack of inexpensive transportation and easy communications added vastly to the cost of production and stymied the creation of national and regional markets. Mexico's topography made it very expensive to construct an extensive road network. Existing roads were in disrepair and not suitable for wagons. Many were impassable during the rainy season. There were no rivers running through major population centers to provide low-cost transportation. (The Ohio-Mississippi-Missouri River system provided such transport alternatives for the United States.) The largest cities were located inland and thus unable to take advantage of inexpensive shipping by sea. (Many of South America's major cities, such as Buenos Aires, São Paulo, Rio

---

This chapter owes an incalculable debt to the meticulous, thought-provoking research and writing of Enrique Cárdenas, Margaret Chowning, John H. Coatsworth, Roberto Cortés Conde, Stephen Haber, Carlos Marichal, Jaime E. Rodríguez O., Richard Salvucci, and Barbara Tenenbaum.

de Janeiro, and Montevideo, are located on or near the coast.) In Mexico many coastal areas were virtually uninhabitable, because of climate and disease.

Third, there were human constraints to the development of domestic markets. The vast majority of Mexicans in 1821 were poor. Many lived almost entirely outside the money economy. The disparities between rich and poor were enormous, and per capita income did not increase during the period. Despite the abolition of slavery in the 1820s and the nation's potential wealth in precious metals, Mexico, unlike Argentina, Brazil, and the United States, was unable to attract European immigrants, which accounted for much of the population growth of these countries in the last half of the nineteenth century. Undoubtedly, political instability discouraged prospective migrants.

Fourth, Mexico lacked the institutional framework that would enable a modern capitalist economy to emerge. The legal structure, in part a heritage of Spanish colonial rule, allowed a wide gap between laws and their enforcement. This created widespread uncertainty about the rules of business. Corruption flourished as a means to maintain a semblance of stable economic relations. The nation lacked adequate legal infrastructure, as well; Mexico was late in establishing legislation to permit banks and joint stock companies. Undoubtedly, turbulent political conditions stymied the government's ability to pass and enforce laws. Governments at all levels lacked the necessary revenues to conduct daily tasks, such as providing security, or to make public investments, such as building and maintaining roads and schools. And, finally, Mexico lacked investment capital due to the plummeting fortunes of silver mining and capital flight caused by the departure of Spaniards during the Wars of Independence and the expulsion of those who remained during the 1820s.

The Wars of Independence

The Wars of Independence ruined the economy and pushed the nation into a prolonged crisis, placing Mexico at an insurmountable disadvantage in the highly competitive world economy that emerged in the nineteenth century. The loss of human life was enormous. An estimated 600,000 people died from war, famine, and disease in the 1810–16 period alone. Government revenues dropped from 39 million pesos in 1806 to 5.4 million in 1823. During the last two decades of colonial rule, revenues averaged 24 million pesos annually, but in the first decade of Independence the average fell to 12.2 million.

Mining was especially hard hit, as guerrillas forced mine owners to abandon their properties. Untended mines fell into disrepair. Mining output dropped from 25 million pesos a year on average before 1810 to 6.5 million in 1819, and rebounded to an average of 11 million a year for the next four decades. This precipitous decline represented a drop in production, not lower silver prices on the world market. From 1811 to 1821 silver extraction declined to about half the level of the previous decade.

Physical damage to agricultural properties was staggering. Rebels destroyed farms, stole crops, and killed livestock. Counterrevolutionary terror by the Spaniards in response to the rebels' guerrilla activities damaged the countryside even further. The wars inflicted the most damage to the large estates that had supplied food to the mining camps and nearby cities. Nonetheless, agricultural production continued to provide subsistence for the population, for there were no reports of widespread hunger or starvation.

Generally, non-mining sectors did not decline precipitously, but rather stagnated for a decade. Most probably severe disruptions in production and distribution occurred for a year or two, not the entire period. Some regions and industries, however, suffered substantially. Querétaro's textile production plummeted by seventy percent between 1810 and 1812. The wars disrupted trade routes, destroying local commerce.

The prolonged wars had other important consequences. Many Spaniards fled the fury of the Mexican masses and the uncertainties of guerrilla war, taking with them the lion's share of the investment capital used in commerce and mining. Mexico was unable to replace this capital until the last quarter of the century, when U.S. investors channeled capital into mining and transportation.

Silver in Decline

Some historians attribute the entire collapse of the Mexican economy in the three decades after Independence to the dramatic decline in silver production. Because the amount of silver exported continued at about the same level as prior to Independence, the quantity of silver retained for the domestic market plummeted. Consequently, the money supply contracted, prices fell, and commerce stagnated.

To make matters worse the flight of Spanish capital in the aftermath of Independence and the drastic curtailment of foreign trade cut back the amount of money available to finance mining. Large Spanish commercial houses had furnished financing for the mining industry during the colonial era. Mexico had neither foreign nor domestic investment capital to take advantage of new technologies (railroads were the most notable) and economies of scale that transformed the U.S. and Western European economies as the nineteenth century unfolded.

The mining crisis also shrunk public revenues. Mining taxes had been the colony's chief source of funds, but with the downturn in mining, taxes on international trade became the biggest source of revenue for the Mexican government. Tax revenues declined by half after Independence. The new nation rarely had enough funds to pay for its daily expenses, let alone to finance road maintenance or other public services that would encourage economic enterprise. Most government employees went for long periods without pay.

Geography

Mexico has limited natural resources. Climatic extremes, ranging from chilly mountains to tropical coasts to deserts, have made subsistence quite difficult for its inhabitants and commercial agriculture a risky business. Half of Mexico endures chronic water scarcity. Rain is adequate for dryland (non-irrigated) farming in only thirteen percent of the country's land area. With man-made improvements only fifteen percent of the land is arable. The entire nation of Mexico has only the same amount of arable land as the U.S. state of Kansas.

High transportation costs and poor communications were critical obstacles to economic development. Most Mexicans have always lived in the valleys and plateaus of the highlands running down the country's interior. They lived and traded far from the sea. Mexico's only navigable rivers were in the south, far away from major population centers. The only method of transport was over land, either by animal (burro, mule, or horse) or animal-drawn wagons, all of which were slow and expensive. This form of transport, in comparison to railroads and waterways, increased the cost of goods by an estimated forty percent. Moreover, reliance on animal transport severely limited the range of even local and regional markets. Historian John Coatsworth has concluded that the lack of inexpensive transport alone accounted for one-third the difference in productivity between Mexico and the United States at the end of the nineteenth century. Transportation was also an obstacle to recovery of the mining industry. A flurry of foreign investments during the 1820s failed, in part, because it was too difficult and costly to import the equipment necessary to restart the mines. It could take as long as a year just to move machinery, broken down into the smallest possible pieces, by wagon and mule train from Veracruz to the mining camps in central Mexico.

Domestic Market

The national market would have been small, even if transportation was safe and cheap. Although a much debated premise, it is possible that in the first half of the nineteenth century a large portion of the rural population lived and worked outside the money economy. The US$56 per capita gross domestic product (GDP) estimate for 1845 suggests that only a very small amount of discretionary income was available for purchasing manufactured goods. Given the greatly skewed income distribution, most Mexicans had little or no money to spend in the marketplace (except, perhaps, to purchase necessities, such as salt). The richest ten percent of the population controlled 35 percent of the nation's wealth in the 1790–1810 period and 43.8 percent in 1850–59. Struggling to survive the exigencies of daily life, average Mexicans were lucky to be able to buy sufficient food for their families.

A combination of low levels of immigration and high death rates limited Mexico's population growth. In 1800 the Mexican population was roughly the same size as that of the United States and one-third to one-half that of Great Britain. By 1910, however, the difference in population was huge. Mexico had grown to 15 million people, but the United States had 92 million and the United Kingdom 45 million. Brazil, perhaps a better comparison, had only 3 million people in 1800, but grew to 22 million during the same period. Thus, the domestic market was not large enough to sustain economic growth, whether in terms of sheer numbers or affluence.

Institutional Framework

The environment for conducting business in newly independent Mexico was problematic. This circumstance resulted from a combination of the colonial heritage of ineffectual administration (including endemic corruption), regionalism, the uncertainty of constant warfare, and relatively unstable governments after 1821.

The Spanish colonial administration had been a curious and damaging combination of limited supervision and overregulation. On the one hand, much of the colony escaped all but cursory administrative oversight, while on the other, regulatory minutiae existed for nearly every economic activity. The intent was to maximize the Crown's tax revenues, but the maze of laws and regulations made businesses expensive to start and operate. The inefficient and unpredictable colonial judicial system never established or enforced a "well-defined set of property rights," and also discouraged new enterprise. In addition, Spain set up numerous monopolies and closely guarded the privileges of important economic constituencies. These policies limited competitiveness. The whole system was uncertain and arbitrary. As a result, prospective entrepreneurs were either discouraged from investing or forced to circumvent legal limitations. Corruption was one method to ensure equal opportunity for at least certain periods of time. Smuggling, for example, was rampant, because the high cost of transport and the Crown's heavy taxes undermined the profits of honest operators.

Independence presented the new nation with an unprecedented opportunity for creating an environment more favorable for business, but the chance to start over without the encumbrance of policies, laws, and institutions that had stymied the economic development of the colony was quickly squandered. Instead, government policies, laws, and attitudes continued to inhibit economic entrepreneurship. The laws of newly independent Mexico poorly defined and unevenly defended property rights and restricted banking and commerce. Inheritance laws were antiquated. Government, with the notable exceptions of the experiment with a state-run development bank in the 1830s and a couple of unsuccessful attempts to promote railroad construction in the 1860s, rarely undertook positive actions to foster economic development until the regime of Porfirio Díaz after 1877.

Mexico failed to clear away institutional obstacles to economic growth, in part because the very same people who had benefited from the colonial system held the reins of government and tried, with some success, to replicate the arbitrary centralism of the colony. These large landowners and merchants, mostly based in Mexico City, sought, above all, to protect their own privileged status. They found close allies among the clergy of the Catholic Church and the officers of the national army, who also enjoyed special privileges left over from the colonial era. Theirs was a shortsighted vision for the nation, for they wanted to protect what they had from what they perceived to be the clamoring, threatening masses, rather than to facilitate national economic development.

The constant turnover in national governments meant that the rules of conducting business were continually changing. Three different constitutions and innumerable turnabouts in law and policy did not promote entrepreneurship. Laws were administered in an arbitrary and capricious manner. To make matters worse, the federal government had little jurisdiction in the states, each of which had its own laws and taxes. Internal sales taxes, known as *alcabalas,* levied on interstate business transactions impeded commerce and the creation of regional and national markets. It was virtually impossible to operate a business in more than one region.

Federalism, in the form of the Constitution of 1824, kept the nation together, but also left the national government in permanent fiscal crisis. The Congress transferred almost half of colonial-era revenue sources to the individual states. To make up for this shortfall, the national government adopted new higher tariffs (taxes on imports) and added an assessment on each state government proportionate to the revenues from taxes formerly collected by the colonial government. Several factors adversely affected central government income, including economic stagnation, declining tariff revenues from imports, difficulties in collecting taxes, and foreign interventions. For example, Spanish troops controlled the fort overlooking Veracruz harbor from 1821 to 1825, which prevented customs collections at the nation's largest port. Veracruz had contributed between 20 and 50 percent of Mexico City's revenues for much of the century. National government revenues slumped further when the volume of foreign trade leveled off through the 1830s and then experienced a slow downward trend in the 1840s, reaching bottom during the war with the United States. Imports fell approximately three percent a year from the mid-1820s through 1845. To make matters worse, state governments refused to pay their allotted contributions to the central government, mainly because they could not generate enough income to pay their own bills. Other colonial-era moneymakers, such as the tobacco monopoly, slipped greatly after Independence because of poor management. Some reforms meant to free the economy from colonial restraints sharply reduced government revenues. To lower mining costs, for example, the new government lowered the total tax on mining production from ten to three percent. At the same time the new government abolished formerly lucrative monopolies on gunpowder and mercury. The Indian tribute system (a head tax assessed on each Indian) gradually ended.

The resulting loss of revenues was disastrous. The national government ended 1821 with barely 6,000 pesos in the treasury! Emperor Augustín I (Iturbide), ignoring this unfortunate state of affairs, spent 255,000 pesos on pomp and circumstance in only nine months. By the end of 1822 the deficit stood at almost 3 million pesos. Matters only worsened. When ousted by Santa Anna in 1832, Anastasio Bustamante left a public debt of 11 million pesos. Constrained by politics from raising taxes, Bustamante simply spent the money he thought necessary.

Centralist regimes fared no better than federalist. The deficit was more than 5 million pesos every year from 1835 to 1844. On the eve of war with the United States, President Mariano Paredes y Arrillaga adopted a series of drastic measures. He suspended repayment of national government loans and cut the salaries of the military by twenty-five percent. His administration demanded all revenues from port taxes, coinage taxes, land sales, the tobacco monopoly, the lottery, salt deposits, the federal district, and Church property. He also imposed taxes on property and a fifty-percent surcharge on businesses. None of these measures solved the fiscal crisis.

There were times when the national government sustained itself on foreign loans and indemnities. Guadalupe Victoria financed his administration (1824–29) with loans raised in Great Britain. Since the proceeds from the loans were used to cover the deficit between revenues and the cost of day-to-day functions, it was inevitable that the government would be unable to repay the loans. Where was the money to come from? Mexico predictably defaulted on its British debt in 1827. As a result, foreigners were subsequently wary of lending money to the new nation. The US$15 million indemnity paid by the United States in 1848 for territories taken from Mexico as a result of the war underwrote the national government for a number of years. Another injection of US$10 million in 1852 from the Treaty of Mesilla/Gadsden Purchase was spent recklessly by Santa Anna. By mid-1855 he had no money left to pay public employees, including the army. No Mexican central government balanced its budget until the mid-1890s.

The national government had few alternatives. Foreign loans were not available after the default, there was only so much territory any administration could sell off, and direct taxes failed to produce substantial revenues, because rich Mexicans, especially landowners, refused to pay. As a result, the government made up the difference between expenditures and revenues by borrowing internally. The national government's lack of funds led to the rise of a class of moneylenders (agiotistas), whose sole client was the national government. They enriched themselves on high-risk, high-interest loans to desperate governments. Loans to the government soaked up all the available capital in the country. Rather than invest in industry, technology, or even agri-culture, the agiotistas chose the lucrative returns earned on the public debt. In 1848 the Mexican government owed 92 million pesos in internal debt and assigned two-thirds of tariff receipts to debt repayment. No government could long survive on this course.

Worst of all for daily life and commerce, neither state nor national gov-ernments could protect people or property. Endemic banditry disrupted the economy. Mexicans were afraid to travel because roads were unsafe. The sto-ries of robberies on the highway were legendary. In more than one instance, according to the lore of the time, robbers accosted the stagecoach traveling from Veracruz to Mexico City so many times that the passengers arrived in the capital with only newspapers to cover them — successive groups of bandits had taken the last stitches of clothing off their backs!

The Church as Banker

The lack of capital for investment was a crucial element in the stagnation of the Mexican economy. The private sector did not have the necessary insti-tutional framework for promoting economic development and growth nor the mechanisms for raising capital for entrepreneurship. Capital flight in the wake of the Wars of Independence certainly played a major role in this defi-ciency, but the most important disruption in the financial and credit system was the change in the status of the Catholic Church.

During the colonial and early Independence eras, the Church was the most important creditor in Mexico. It had accumulated enormous wealth through the tithe (donation of ten percent of one's income to the Church required by law) and bequests. Although much of the wealth was in the form of property (Church institutions were the largest urban landowners in Mexico), the Church's revenue stream was huge. It invested heavily in mortgages and com-mercial loans. The Church was widely known for its fair terms, especially rea-sonable interest and lenient repayment schedules. Independence, however, radically transformed the Church's financial status. The national government ended the tithe and the collapse of mining and estate agriculture badly cur-tailed bequests. To make matters worse, Liberal governments attacked the Church as an obstacle to economic development, because it had accumulated so much of the nation's capital. Governments of all political persuasions levied forced loans on the Church in order to pay for the defense of the nation. Often the Church had to liquidate outstanding loans to private individuals in order to satisfy government demands. The Church as banker was ruined in the half-century after 1821 and there was no Mexican institution that could replace it.

The Case of the "La Constancia Mejicana" Cotton Mill

Fanny Calderón de la Barca, the diplomat's wife whose memoir so vividly depicts nineteenth-century life in Mexico, tells the tale of a textile enterprise in Puebla. Her memoir illustrates the trials and tribulations of conducting business in Mexico during the first half of the century. In the early 1830s Don Esteban Antuñano bought the Santo Domingo mill for US$178,000. He spent large sums to construct a building, "employing foreign workmen at exorbitant prices." He borrowed an additional US$178,000 from the Banco de Avío (1830–42), the Mexican development bank, founded by Lucas Alamán, ordering nearly 4,000 spindles from a company in the United States. While Antuñano waited for his equipment, he and his family lived "with the strictest economy . . . almost suffering from want." He was frequently "unable to obtain credit for the provisions necessary for their daily use."

When the commercial house that had lent Antuñano money to buy machinery lost confidence in him and called in the loan, he had to sell off his clothes to purchase food and pay rent on his home. The machinery finally arrived a year after it embarked from Philadelphia, but, unfortunately, it proved unsatisfactory. Nearly four years later, Antuñano procured replacement equipment, only to have it lost on two different occasions in shipwrecks. One final obstacle, a brief French blockade, was overcome and 7,000 spindles were installed. It took an enormous investment and five years to establish the mill. Señora Calderón de la Barca does not tell us whether the venture was ultimately profitable. Antuñano experienced all the major hazards of doing business during this era: struggles to raise capital, high costs involved in purchasing foreign technology and expertise, and the prohibitive expense and difficulties of transportation. One might wonder what possessed him to take such a risk!

The Hacienda in Crisis

Historians have often characterized the hacienda as an obstacle to economic development. Large estates were very inefficient operations, whose owners saw them as symbols of prestige rather than profit-making enterprises.

While there were innumerable regional differences, this stereotype is generally incorrect. In both colonial and post-colonial Mexico haciendas were capitalist enterprises operating on a rational profit-seeking basis for the market. Haciendas arose in the sixteenth century in order to supply wheat and livestock to the Europeans. The catastrophic decline in the indigenous population brought about by the introduction of deadly European diseases, such as smallpox and plague, facilitated the acquisition of land by the Spaniards. Mexican agriculture in general functioned rationally: large estates had comparative advantages in the production of livestock, cereal grains, and export crops like sisal and sugar; and small farmers had the advantage in garden crops, fruit orchards, and poultry raising, all of which were labor-intensive activities.

In the aftermath of the Wars of Independence, many haciendas were heavily mortgaged, requiring periodic infusions of money to operate. But with the Church rapidly losing its ability to lend large sums and Spanish-owned commercial houses either closed or on the brink of collapse, there was little available credit. All of these conditions worsened in the turmoil and warfare of the next half-century. As a result, there was widespread, though not uniform, crisis in the countryside from the 1820s through the 1860s. There are two clear manifestations of this depression. First, many owners abandoned their haciendas because they were unable to repay their mortgages. In some cases, villages and small farmers took advantage of the hacendados' misfortune by expanding their holdings through the purchase of land from haciendas. One village in the Huasteca region of San Luis Potosí purchased a 40,000-acre hacienda for 3,120 pesos in 1826. Each of the 187 members of the community contributed twenty pesos to the acquisition of land they once rented. Two decades later, the municipal government of Tuxpan bought two haciendas. Again, public contributions paid for the land. In Michoacán the downturn in agriculture furnished opportunities for those willing to take risks in uncertain conditions. Historian Margaret Chowning found that numerous former administrators and tenants in Michoacán bought low-priced land. Second, as seen in chapter 1, a constant flow of people left rural areas in search of better lives in the cities.

The decline of the large estate was most likely not uniform, however. Chowning found that after an average forty-percent price decline in the 1810s, Michoacán haciendas recovered their value by the 1830s and 1840s. Rents for hacienda lands followed the same pattern, showing an increase in sharecropping and improved terms. Elimination of the tithe, decreased labor costs, and higher commodity prices helped raise profit margins. Chowning argues that estates were consolidated rather than broken up during the first fifty years after Independence. Estate expansion took place at the expense of Indian communities, especially after 1840. The new owners were not from the former colonial elite.

Recovery

The Mexican economy generally stagnated in the 1860s, but deterioration was not uniform. Some areas recovered faster than others. Michoacán, for example, rebounded briefly in the early 1830s and recovered colonial levels of production by mid-century in some sectors. The mainstay of the Mexican economy, silver mining, however, did not bounce back as quickly, growing in the 1830s and 1840s at an average rate of 2.3 percent, only to fall again to an average 0.8 percent per year in the 1850s. At the end of the French Intervention (1867) silver production rose rapidly, stimulated by new silver deposit discoveries. Nonetheless, total silver production between 1860 and 1870 was still ten percent lower than in 1810. Throughout the 1870s production grew at an annual growth rate of over two percent.

Mexican industrialization made surprising progress before 1880, especially in light of numerous impediments and the comparative record of other Latin American nations. High transportation costs sometimes acted as protection for domestic industry from foreign manufactures. With the cost of transportation added to their price, some imported goods were too expensive to compete against local products. In addition, for a short period the government maintained an activist role in fostering industry, with the establishment of the Banco de Avío, which financed a large number of textile enterprises. Compared to the rest of Latin America, the Mexican textile industry was quite large and modern.

Manufacturing began to use the new technology of mass production in the late 1830s, particularly in textiles. The Banco de Avío's seed money helped increase the number of spindles by fourteen times in eight years. An expansion of the money supply along with protective tariff policies during the 1840s also helped the manufacturing industry. The number of textile spindles increased from 113,000 in 1845 to 152,000 in 1865, and the number of mechanical looms rose from 2,600 in 1843 to 4,400 in 1854.

As silver production gradually returned to pre-Independence levels, the amount of currency in circulation rose, which in turn led to increased commercial activity. Trade with the United States rose four percent a year in the 1860s. (Much of this trade was probably contraband Confederate cotton sold through Mexican ports during the Civil War, when the Union Navy blockaded southern ports.) Tax revenues grew with the increase in foreign trade. During the 1867–68 to 1877–78 period, fiscal revenues reached an average 18 million pesos per year, double that of the 1840s.

During the first half of the nineteenth century the Mexican economy functioned on two levels. Economic activities with international connections declined precipitously, mainly because of the severe damage wrought by the Wars of Independence. So-called everyday economic activities operated at a roughly even level, perhaps declining slightly.

Constant warfare affected all levels of the economy and society. Armed conflict brought devastation to the battlegrounds, created widespread insecurity and uncertainty, and absorbed resources that would have been better used to develop the nation. While the North Atlantic countries and a few South American nations expanded rapidly, Mexico stood still. For fifty years economic progress was virtually nonexistent. As a result, Mexico fell irretrievably behind; it remains so today.

Chapter 4

THE DISASTROUS WAR

Mexico was a nation at war for much of the nineteenth century. The most damaging of the wars was fought against the United States from 1846 until 1848. As a result of this conflict, Mexico lost one-half of its national territory, including what are now the southwestern and western states of the United States: Arizona, California, New Mexico, Texas and parts of Colorado, Nevada, Oklahoma, Oregon, Utah, and Wyoming. These areas contained enormous agricultural and mineral resources, which greatly contributed to the subsequent economic development of the United States. The loss of Texas in 1836 and then the rest of the north in 1848 resulted from the convergence of two underlying currents: the Mexican government's inability to secure its territory, because of the nation's political and economic instability, and the United States' relentless push for territorial expansion.

After Independence, Mexico, like Spain during the colonial era, struggled to extend control over its northern frontier. Two thousand miles lay between Mexico City and the Californias, and more than a thousand miles between the capital and Texas. Barely passable roads made communications with these northern territories difficult, if not impossible. Insufficient rainfall for crops made much of the north unattractive for agriculture. Entrepots, such as San Francisco and Santa Fe, New Mexico, drew settlers, but these communities remained isolated from the major Mexican population centers.

The Indian peoples of the region fiercely resisted incursions into their lands. During the first half of the nineteenth century, Apaches and Comanches often took the offensive, rendering much of the north uninhabitable for set-

Many thanks to the excellent work of William DePalo, John Eisenhower, Richard Griswold del Castillo, James M. McCaffrey, Ramón Ruiz, Elizabeth Salas, Pedro Santoni, Otis Singletary, Captain Franklin Smith, and John Edward Weems.

tlers. The Yaquis and other Indian peoples in Sonora and Sinaloa also fought stubbornly to retain their lands and their political autonomy. The Spanish colonial government had tried various strategies to maintain peace, with modest success. It had granted subsidies paid in staples to some of the Indian peoples. The Catholic Church had dispatched missionaries to inculcate them with religion. Spain also established military settlements, known as presidios, across the northern provinces.

Independence destroyed the precarious peace established in the colonial era. The new regime was unable to pay for either food for the Indians or upkeep for the presidios. Understaffed Catholic missions were ineffective. To the Mexican government, the obvious solution, both to the problem of protection and the need for tighter political control, was to increase the population of the north through immigration from Europe and the United States. The unanticipated consequence of the Mexican government's policy of luring foreign settlers to the north was the loss of half its territory by 1848.

The Loss of Texas

The first settlers from east of the Mississippi River trickled into Texas during the 1820s. Over the next decade their numbers increased, escalating tensions with their Mexican hosts. There were fundamental differences in language, religion, and culture between the newcomers, who steadfastly refused to learn either the Spanish language or the customs of their new home, and the original colonizers. At the same time, these Anglo-Texans became embroiled in the crucial political issue of the era in Mexico: the extent of local and regional autonomy (federalism versus centralism). The "anglo" settlers, like their north Mexican neighbors, deeply mistrusted the government in Mexico City, which rarely, if ever, contributed to their security or welfare.

Mexicans well understood the danger from their northern neighbor. General Manuel de Mier y Terán, in a report on conditions in the north in 1827, warned that growing U.S. influence would lead to loss of the territory. On at least two occasions, the Mexican government refused offers by the United States to purchase the area north of the Rio Grande. Various Mexican governments tried to limit immigration, particularly in the early 1830s, by insisting colonists affirm the Roman Catholic faith and pledge not to practice slavery in Texas. Finally, Mexico prohibited further immigration to Texas from the United States (the Law of Colonization of April 6, 1830). But these measures were too little too late. By 1830, of the 28,700 residents of Texas, only 4,000 were native-born Mexicans; the majority of the foreign born were overwhelmingly *norteamericanos* (translated as North Americans, but used to refer to people from the United States). The "anglos" (another term for people from the United States) ignored the constraints on immigration. Instead, they asked the Mexican government to repeal the Law of Colonization and create a separate state of Texas, which the Mexican government rejected. When the centralist President Santa Anna eliminated all autonomy for the states in 1835, the Texans rebelled.

Santa Anna confidently marched north to quell the revolt in early 1836. His army was large at the outset, perhaps 6,000 soldiers, but it was soon in shambles. His soldiers were almost all unwilling draftees, who had received little or no training and had no combat experience. Their uniforms were unsuitable for the northern climate and their weapons were outdated. As a commander, Santa Anna was known to regard his troops as little more than cannon fodder. The Mexican officer corps was little better than the troops. (Poor military leadership was a definite problem on both sides.)

The campaign began badly. Santa Anna left much of his force in the environs of Monclova, Coahuila, where severe winter weather devastated the underdressed soldiers, most of whom were Maya Indians from the hot lands of Yucatán. To make matters worse, the general planned for his army to live off the land, but southeast Texas was not able to provide provisions for a large armed force. In March Santa Anna engaged the Texans at the Alamo. Victory was his, but, unfortunately for Mexico, casualties (killed and wounded) amounted to more than half his force. Worse still, he gained nothing strategically. A few weeks later, General José Urrea, Santa Anna's most competent subordinate, won a more important battle at Goliad. Santa Anna then ordered the execution of the captured Texans, an act that brought with it an enduring notoriety in the United States. With victory seemingly in his grasp, Santa Anna lost a crucial engagement in late April at San Jacinto. To his humiliation, Santa Anna was captured; legend has it he tried to escape from the field poorly disguised as an enlisted man. The prisoner Santa Anna ordered his commanders to withdraw from Texas. Remarkably, his second-in-command, General Vicente Filisola, obeyed the order. Texans declared their independence and set up the Lone Star Republic. Texas would remain an independent nation until annexed by the United States nine years later.

Prelude to a Larger War

For a decade the situation in Texas festered as an open wound in Mexican politics. Mexico's revolving governments and their persistent financial short-falls prevented any serious effort to reconquer the lost territory. On a number of occasions both the Texas and British governments offered proposals for a negotiated settlement, but no Mexican government could have recognized the loss of Texas and survived politically. Successive Mexican administrations, re-flecting public opinion, advocated reconquest. Behind the scenes, however, there was sentiment that Texas was forever lost, because not only was the na-tion bankrupt and the army in disrepair, but the population of Texas was mostly non-Mexican. Some believed it was time to move on and build a na-tion out of what remained.

Although there was sporadic fighting along the border, war did not loom on the horizon until the U.S. Congress voted the annexation of Texas and President John Tyler signed the resolution March 1, 1845. Mexico regarded this action as an act of war. All that was left was the appropriate provocation to provide justification.

The War with the United States

Political instability and the government's lack of funds badly hampered Mexico's war effort. During the prewar and war period from December 6, 1844 to June 20, 1848, twelve different governments presided in Mexico. None had the authority to negotiate a compromise. Because the nation was penniless, there simply was no money to fight effectively. The political turmoil began with the overthrow of Santa Anna in December 1844. José Joaquín de Herrera, the new president, a moderate Liberal and a former military officer with a rep-utation for honesty and integrity, tried to bring the various factions together and sought to negotiate a peaceful settlement with Texas. He failed on all counts. U.S. President James K. Polk sought to prevent war by sending an emissary, John Slidell, to Mexico in November 1845. Herrera refused to meet with Slidell, because he feared that the adverse public uproar against the meet-ing would lead to the fall of his regime. Despite the reluctance of Herrera and others to enter negotiations, it may have been possible to arrange a peaceful solution to the issue of Texas, but it was impossible for any Mexican officeholder to accept any further territorial losses. Polk's obsession with the acquisition of California made war inevitable.

The immediate provocation for war took place when Polk ordered General Zachary Taylor into a disputed sliver of land between the Nueces River and the Rio Grande. Mexico claimed the Nueces as its border with Texas, while Texas claimed the Rio Grande as its boundary. A small skirmish between the two sides followed. Polk used the incident as the pretext to recommend war, which the U.S. Congress declared on May 13, 1846.

José Joaquín de Herrera

General Mariano Paredes replaced Herrera as president in early 1846. He declared war against the United States in May 1846 and his administration suffered the war's first military defeats the same month. In June Paredes left office to take charge of the army. Meanwhile, in an ironic twist of fate, regional boss Juan Álvarez and Valentín Gómez Farías joined forces to bring back their once bitter enemy, Antonio López de Santa Anna (see chapter 2). Leaving exile in Havana, Santa Anna slipped through the U.S. blockade at Veracruz with the connivance of the U.S. commander, who may have hoped that Santa Anna would make peace under favorable terms for the North Americans. It may have been enough for the invaders for Santa Anna to have intensified the chaos. After months of political maneuvering, in December the Mexican Congress chose Santa Anna as president and Gómez Farías as vice president. Hailed as "a man with . . . [an] heroic halo . . ." and the only one who could save the day, Santa Anna had returned yet again to lead Mexico to ruin.

Three factors caused the Mexican defeat: chronic lack of funds—which left the military badly supplied and obsoletely equipped—inadequately trained soldiers, and poor leadership. Although Mexican forces often outnumbered the invaders, they suffered from severe disadvantages in equipment, especially artillery. Mexican troops, though quite brave and resourceful, were not well prepared for combat. They had outdated heavy weapons, insufficient provisions, and substandard rifles and uniforms. The officers, Santa Anna in particular, were irresolute, inconsistent, and often distracted by personal vindictiveness and political scheming, which at crucial times led to costly mistakes in battle.

The North Americans invaded the north with the hope of bringing a quick victory. They sought to force Mexico to sue for peace by capturing the northern tier of states: California, Chihuahua, Coahuila, New Mexico, Nuevo León, and Tamaulipas. To this end, one army was sent from San Antonio to capture Chihuahua; another smaller army was dispatched from Fort Leavenworth, Kansas, to take New Mexico and then move on to California; and the major force under General Zachary Taylor moved west from Matamoros to capture Monterrey. At the same time, the U.S. Navy blockaded the Gulf coast.

The war went badly for Mexico from the start. General Mariano Arista lost battles at Palo Alto, northeast of Matamoros and north of the Rio Grande, and at Resaca del Guerrero to the southwest, due largely to the North Americans' superior artillery. Taylor took Matamoros and Monterrey, the most important

city in northeast Mexico, in late September. North American troops then occupied both Saltillo and Tampico in November. Meanwhile, another U.S. army
took Chihuahua. The north was effectively in the hands of the United States.

By a stroke of fortune in January, Santa Anna's scouts intercepted a dispatch
that revealed North American plans to land at Veracruz. Discovering that Taylor's forces were reduced in strength and, therefore, perhaps vulnerable to attack, Santa Anna decided to fight in the north, rather than defend Veracruz.
Just as he had in marching northward to Texas, more than a decade earlier, the
Mexican dictator encountered severe winter weather. During the desert cross-
ing, his troops endured scarcities of food and water, and a fifth of his force deserted. The battle of Angostura (known in the United States as Buena Vista)
on February 23, 1847, located southwest of Saltillo, Coahuila, was the largest
engagement of the war. In the early part of the battle Santa Anna nearly carried the day, but the combat ended in stalemate. It was a battle characterized
by missed opportunities. During the night Santa Anna withdrew his battered
army southward. On other fronts Mexico suffered additional defeats. New
Mexico and California fell in rapid succession. But to the chagrin of the North
Americans, Mexico did not surrender. The northern strategy of the United
States did not succeed. Scott would have to conquer the remainder of the
country.

The major campaign of the war lay ahead. The United States determined
to land and take Veracruz, the main Gulf port, and then march inland to Mexico City. The main obstacle for the North Americans was the maintenance of
long supply lines. The danger of tropical diseases, especially yellow fever, also
loomed threateningly over the occupation forces. The United States landed an
army of 10,000 in early March and laid siege to Veracruz. The city fell shortly
thereafter. The terrible artillery bombardment heavily damaged the city and
caused a thousand civilian casualties. After the Battle of Angostura, Santa
Anna reorganized his army to meet the invaders on the road from Veracruz.
He had lost more than 10,000 soldiers at Angostura and subsequent retreat to
San Luis Potosí, but was able use the remnants of this force to form yet another army. The decisive engagement took place at Cerro Gordo, not far from
Jalapa, Veracruz (state), where Santa Anna waited with between 10,000 and
12,000 men, outnumbering U.S. commander General Winfield Scott, who had
8,500. The defeat for Mexico was bloody and devastating.

General Scott had exclaimed that after Cerro Gordo, "Mexico no longer has
an army." But the war was to continue. The invaders despaired about the Mex-

icans' stubborn willingness to fight on. There were, moreover, a number of difficulties confronting the victors. As a result, the Mexican situation was not as grim, perhaps, as the successive defeats might indicate. The North Americans still faced the problems of provisioning. Mexican guerrillas along the main highway from Jalapa to Veracruz were making life miserable for them, disrupting this crucial supply line. The imminent departure of 3,000 volunteer troops, whose enlistment had expired, further jeopardized the U.S. army. The war would not end unless the North Americans captured Mexico City. It would be a costly campaign.

One of the shabbier episodes of the war occurred at this juncture. Santa Anna, stalling to reorganize his army yet again, negotiated with Scott for a US$1 million bribe to end the conflict. Scott actually sent Santa Anna US$10,000. Santa Anna, of course, never had any intention of ceasing hostilities, but nonetheless kept the money. By the middle of the summer the general had reconstituted his forces with 20,000 to 25,000 troops, whom he positioned at the major entrances to the capital. Santa Anna's army was approximately twice as large as that of the North Americans.

Surrounded by lakes and marshes and with access over a limited number of causeways, Mexico City presented a difficult task for any invader. The U.S. army arrived at the outskirts of the capital in August. Santa Anna strongly fortified the entrances, but the norteamericanos successfully circumvented the Mexican troop concentrations. Amid heavy fighting, the initial battle for the city hinged on the poor relations between Santa Anna and one of his subordinates, General Gabriel Valencia. Valencia refused Santa Anna's orders to redeploy his soldiers. The vindictive Santa Anna then refused to aid him when the North American attack began. A series of brief, bloody battles followed with heavy casualties on both sides.

Despite their victories, the North Americans were in some distress, for they were exhausted and low on supplies and ammunition. Outnumbered, they now faced having to fight for the city in bitter, house-to-house combat. However, victory came suddenly, for Santa Anna surprisingly abandoned the capital. The U.S. flag flew in the Zocalo on September 14.

The residents of the capital were not ready to surrender, and resisted as U.S. troops entered the city. Snipers shot at the invaders. Some *capitalinos* even hurled stones and broken bottles from rooftops. It took two days to restore order. Outside the city, guerrillas disrupted communication and supply lines.

Soldiers

Although on paper Mexico had a large number of men under arms at the outbreak of war with the United States—almost 20,000 permanent troops, scattered in garrisons all over the country, and slightly more than 10,000 active militia reserves attached to regional commands—the dismal reality was quite different. There were far too many officers and far too few soldiers. When war came, the government had to raise a large number of troops quickly. Panicked officers could not pick and choose from the population. Conscription filled the ranks, but of necessity took unwilling men.

The soldier's life was not a comfortable or happy one. Most important, there was no time to train the new soldiers. Poorly trained troops were more likely to desert or to panic in battle. Conditions experienced by the common soldier were generally abominable. In 1835 a soldier's pay was approximately 20 pesos a month, with deductions for laundry, barber, shoes, and assorted other expenses, if the government paid him at all. Armies fight on their bellies, but for Mexican forces supplies were hard to come by. Mexican soldiers often had to live off the land. Most civilians were uncooperative when it came time to provision the army. Most country people had little to spare after providing for their own families and the government commonly paid them in worthless currency for their produce. Hungry troops deserted or mutinied. Arms and equipment were outdated; weapons were usually British army discards. Mexican artillery was no match for the North Americans'.

The lack of equipment was also a cause for dismay. For example, Mexico City's Matamoros battalion, a militia unit comprised of 500 men, in November 1846 had only 90 usable rifles and an estimated 300 others that were irreparable. By late December one commander complained that his troops still had not enough uniforms three months after they had organized. His men had "a frock coat and skintight pants, and they lacked a shirt, a short cape, and a blanket; in sum, the clothes were useless and infested with lice."

The soldiers were further disadvantaged by poor leadership. The general staff was not trained to undertake large-scale military operations. One report on the Mexican army criticized the "prodigality of ranks and decorations conferred on a multitude that does not know how to lead . . . [A]s a result of this disorder, well-trained and punctilious officers have retired. . . ." Officers commonly mistreated their subordinates.

An incident at the Battle of Churubusco in late August 1847 is telling. After a long bloody struggle, during which both sides suffered heavy losses (the United States experienced many more casualties than the Mexicans), a North American officer inquired of the Mexican commander: "General, where is your ammunition park?" The general replied, "If I had ammunition, you would not be here."

Discipline was lenient. Saluting individuals, for example, was not required until 1847. On the other hand, there were specific regulations for the spacing between soldiers and the pace of march during battles. Officers often ignored crucial regulations. In an especially egregious case, at San Jacinto in 1836 commanders failed to post the required sentries.

Despite all their disadvantages, Mexican soldiers fought well. There were notable examples of bravery and endurance. Though on average barely over five feet tall, the Mexican soldier had extraordinary stamina and resilience and was capable of exceptional bravery. Lieutenant William S. Henry described them:

> The infantry were miserably clad, brawny, thick-set fellows, chiefly shod with sandals; one regiment of Lancers were as fine looking men as I ever saw. Their horses were inferior animals. . . .

In September 1846, U.S. forces attempted to capture Monterrey, Nuevo León. In an engagement at a fortress known as the Citadel, Mexicans troops inflicted terrible casualties on the invaders, who lost ten percent of their force. Hand-to-hand street fighting in the city ensued, accompanied by vicious artillery barrages and heavy civilian casualties. Nonetheless, the Citadel held. Mexican troops were still attacking when their commander offered surrender. The armistice allowed evacuation of the fort on the most honorable terms. The Mexicans left with "their flags held high, giving the appearance of a victory parade." Before the battle of Angostura in February 1847, Mexicans marched forty-eight miles and plunged into battle without rest. They captured an important ridge the first day and kept it without camp fires through the night, protecting their powder from the pouring rain with their bodies. The next day they took additional hills and broke through North American positions all over the field. Despite their accomplishments, their commanders ordered them to withdraw ten miles, abandoning their wounded. The soldiers clamored to attack again, but their officers ordered retreat instead.

Armies on both sides marched with considerable numbers of women, who formed supply and medical auxiliaries. They also suffered casualties. More than 1,500 women and children went with Santa Anna on his Texas campaign. Only 300 survived. The rest died from starvation, thirst, and exposure. Generally, without the women soldiers would have either deserted or died of hunger. Women served foreign soldiers as well as Mexican. They traveled with the U.S. Army, and they often nursed both sides in battle. One U.S. soldier described these women as follows:

> The woman of sixty or more years—the mother with her infant wrapped in her rebozo—the wife . . . the youthful señorita frisking along with her lover's sombrero upon her head; even to the prattling girl who had followed padre and madre to the wars. . . . In addition to their bedding and wearing apparel, they pack upon their backs the food and utensils to cook it in, and worn out as they are by the toils of the day, while their husband or lover sleeps, they prepare his repast.

It was not just the enlisted men who had an entourage. Lieutenant Henry noted that

> The streets were filled with followers of the army, mounted on everything from a decent mustang to a humble, uncomplaining donkey. Some of the officers' wives, picturesquely wrapped in their gay-colored ponchos, were slowly riding after their chivalric husbands.

Although women's greatest impact was in providing medical care and supplies, there were some who fought as soldiers. Their heroism was widely admired.

For all soldiers, the horror of war was immense. A North American soldier described the aftermath of one battle:

> [It was] such a sight as I had never seen before, and which I would have been satisfied never to see again. The ground was covered with gore from the wounds of the dying and dead. . . . The sight was horrible. . . . Some had a leg, a foot, an arm or hand mangled to pieces and were lying upon the cold, muddy ground, shivering with cold, begging . . . [a] drink of water.

On both sides to be wounded meant death. The weapons used inflicted terrible wounds and there were no medicines to prevent or treat infection. Hospitals were unsanitary. Since there was no anesthesia, treatment brought brutal pain.

Context for
Today

The Peace

For Mexico, the crucial decision at this point was whether to continue the war by setting up a government in the countryside and fighting as guerrillas against the North Americans, or to surrender. After the battle of Cerro Gordo, Captain Kirby Smith of the invading army wrote of the Mexicans:

> They can do nothing and their continued defeats should convince them of it. They have lost six great battles; we have captured six hundred and eighty cannon, nearly one hundred thousand stand of arms, made twenty thousand prisoners, have the greatest portion of their country and are fast advancing on their capital which must soon be ours—yet they refuse to retreat! Those the gods wish to destroy, they first make mad.

How do we reconcile the above quote with the Mexican capitulation after the fall of Mexico City? There were some circumstances that actually favored a guerrilla movement. Public opinion in the United States, where there was from the beginning opposition to the war, would probably not have supported a prolonged occupation. The cost of the war both in terms of human life and funds was considerable and not very popular. An extended occupation marred by casualties in a guerrilla war would most likely have produced loud objections in the U.S. Congress and among voters. The occupation forces were inadequate to govern Mexico. Even with the arrival of reinforcements at the new year, General Scott had only 15,000 soldiers under his command, a force marginally sufficient to keep the peace in the huge city, let alone pacify the adjacent regions. To make matters worse, the idle North Americans soon began to engage in unseemly squabbles among themselves over who was to receive credit for the victory. Scott found it impossible to maintain his line of communication with Veracruz. The supply line from the United States was incredibly long and uncertain. The invaders had to rely on sending ammunition over thousands of miles by sea and then by wagon or mule.

The precedent for guerrilla warfare was ample. More than a decade of guerrilla warfare had won Independence. Though aging, most Mexican political and military leaders were veterans of the Independence wars. Men like Juan Álvarez, the boss of southern Mexico, had used guerrilla tactics as the basis for their power. The guerrillas active in Puebla and environs had in recent times proved successful against the North Americans. Resistance was much discussed as the army crumbled.

Why then did Mexico end the fighting? One answer perhaps lies in the lack of credible leadership. No one with charisma and persistence rose up out of the muck of Mexico's fragmented politics to rally resistance. The lack of consensus among Liberal factions, Santanistas (supporters of Santa Anna), Conservatives, and monarchists surely undermined continued widespread, organized opposition to the North Americans. Another possible answer is the lack of funds. The North Americans occupied all the major cities and ports, leaving the government without resources.

More important, the hombres de bien who ruled Mexico feared that continued war would unleash the masses. The riots in Mexico City that greeted the occupation served to remind them of the destructive forces that had erupted before in the Wars of Independence. The outbreak of racial wars in Yucatán and the Sierra Gorda in 1847 exacerbated their anxieties. These men had spent the past two decades establishing a political system they could dominate for their own goals. They were not about to abandon their rule to the rabble. Peace—even a peace that would cost Mexico half its territory—was a better alternative to them than allowing the lower classes to enter the political system. Some believed that Mexico should keep what territory it could. They surmised that public opinion in the United States would limit territorial gains to the land north of the Rio Grande, but that further resistance might lead the United States to wrench away more of the north or annex the entire nation. Finally, there is some evidence that the agiotistas (moneylenders), who had financed the largest part of the government's debt, exerted pressure for peace, so that the proposed indemnity to be paid by the United States to Mexico for its lost territories would be used to repay their loans.

The main proponents of continuing the war were the radical Liberals (puros), who may have sought the total destruction of the army as a way to ensure democracy in Mexico. A few puros may have advocated a U.S. protectorate or even annexation. One group reportedly offered General Scott the opportunity to become dictator of Mexico. He turned down the proposal. The puros were, however, a distinct minority among the ruling classes.

Peace talks proved slow and difficult. After a number of unsuccessful secret attempts at negotiation, the first formal discussion began in late August 1847, when Santa Anna and Scott agreed to an armistice. The first tentative agreement gave the United States Alta California and New Mexico, but the boundary between the two countries would start with the Nueces River and run along the Gila and Colorado Rivers to the Pacific. But both Santa Anna and

Polk rejected it. In the meantime, the armistice ended, the North Americans occupied Mexico City, and two new Mexican administrations took office. To further complicate matters, Polk, frustrated by the lack of progress on a treaty, recalled his chief peace negotiator Nicolas Trist in mid-November. In early December Trist decided to disregard his recall in order to hammer out the treaty. Despite a third Mexican change of administration, the two parties reached agreement. Negotiators signed the Treaty of Guadalupe Hidalgo on February 2, 1848. In May the Mexican Congress ratified it.

The terms of the treaty ceded the territory north of the Rio Grande and Gila Rivers and San Diego Bay to the United States. Mexico received an indemnity of US$15 million. Because its Constitution forbade the transfer of national territory, Mexico regarded its losses as conquest, not as a sale or negotiated settlement. A later agreement, the Treaty of Mesilla (known in the United States as the Gadsden Purchase) in 1853 transferred land in Arizona and New Mexico from Mexico to the United States in exchange for US$10 million.

The Cost of War

The cost of the war was enormous. The United States lost more than 12,000 dead, eighty-seven percent of whom died from disease and exposure, the highest cumulative mortality rate of any war fought by the United States. Thousands more were badly wounded. The cost to the nation was US$100 million. Mexico's casualties, though difficult to calculate accurately, were probably heavier in combat, but lower from disease. Perhaps 10,000 Mexicans died in the war, with 4,000 to 5,000 of the total killed in battle. Countless more civilians perished. The economic damage to Mexico was immense.

Civilians in many regions paid a high price for the war in several different ways. There were, of course, direct damages and disruptions, which extracted the heaviest toll. There were also forced loans and taxes levied by both the Mexican and U.S. armies. The worst damage occurred during the siege and bombardment of Veracruz in March 1847. Many buildings fell on their occupants and others were burned out. The bombardment was horrible. Shells flew in day and night. Only because the town was mostly masonry prevented it from being burned down in its entirety. One U.S. officer recounted: "I shall never forget the horrible fire of our mortars. . . ." There was no safe place for the wounded. Errant shells crashed into churches, where hospitals were es-

Map 2. Mexican Territorial Losses from 1836 to 1853

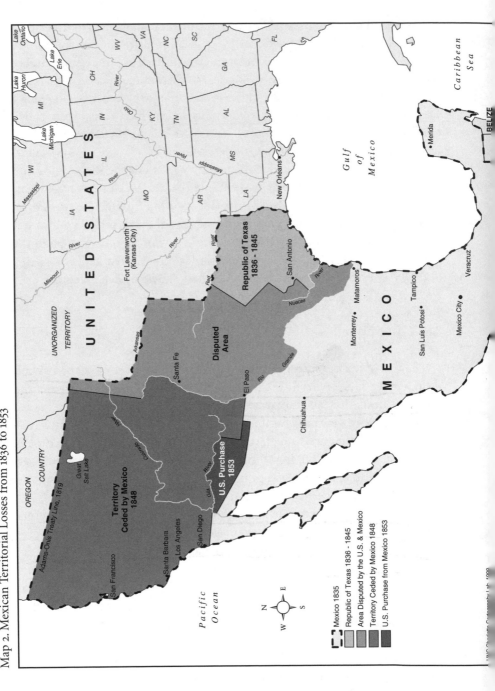

tablished. The yells and screams of the victims were heard above the din by the attackers.

Needless to say, Veracruzanos were not the only victims. Mariano Riva Palacio related in his memoirs that in Chalco "all the villages and haciendas have suffered great destruction at the hands of the malicious" norteamericanos. He claimed that in Chalco the norteamericanos had gone so far as to rob the little chapels of their sacred vessels and images. The invaders had left "fixed signs of the barbarity by burning the doors." Near Saltillo, Coahuila, the main house of the Hacienda Aguanueva, owned by the wealthy Sánchez Navarro family, was burned by retreating North American troops just before the battle of Buena Vista and required extensive repairs.

As in all wars, civilians were tragically caught in the middle. The invading North Americans inflicted considerable damage during their occupation of Mexican territories. In the early days of the war the U.S. army reported that its "wild volunteers . . . committed . . . all sorts of atrocities on the persons and property of Mexicans." The situation grew serious enough that in February 1847, General Winfield Scott had to establish military courts for crimes committed by North Americans against Mexican civilians. It took the examples of public whipping and a hanging to restore good behavior.

In the combat areas civilians were constantly in danger. Mexican guerrillas in the northeast, for example, burned down the haciendas of owners who refused to aid them. The North Americans, in turn, burned haciendas whose owners cooperated with the guerrillas. Many landowners, consequently, had to abandon their properties. As one traveler in the northeast observed, "[A]ll the haciendas are blackened shells, . . . abandoned by their residents."

Sometimes the war required the government to take drastic steps. In October 1846, the governor of San Luis Potosí ordered all Church properties, schools, and government buildings turned into hospitals and barracks for Santa Anna's army. Wealthy families had to furnish livestock, provisions, and shelter in addition to subscribing to forced loans. Everyone suffered as the city grew very crowded with refugees from other regions fleeing the North Americans.

On at least one occasion, civilians refused to endure unnecessary hardship. After the Mexican army retreated from its defeat at the siege of Monterrey, the inhabitants of Saltillo would not allow General Pedro de Ampudia to take a stand there, reasoning that if he had lost Monterrey, he had no hope of defending Saltillo. He concurred and retreated further.

The U.S. occupation also had its costs for the Mexican people. After the capture of Mexico City, North American commanders demanded war taxes of 3 million pesos from the states, of which 400,000 pesos were to come specifically from the capital and the Valley of Mexico. At the same time, in Mexico City Yankee troops occupied barracks, convents, hospitals, and schools; officers were accommodated in hotels, inns, and private homes. In some instances, they were guests and paid rent, in others they shared dwellings with Mexicans, and in some cases they lived in houses abandoned by owners who had fled the city.

Because spontaneous riots and stone throwing erupted and there were continuous rumors of uprisings in the barrios, the worried, undermanned North Americans staged public punishments, such as lashings, in the Zocalo. Far from curtailing popular civil disobedience, these measures aroused protests; the main plaza, where these spectacles occurred, was full of hundreds of lower-class Mexicans, who resisted when ordered to disperse and threw stones at the soldiers.

As in all wars, some civilians profited substantially. Business relations, however, did not mean Mexicans and North Americans lived harmoniously. The invaders, out of necessity, contracted locally for food and supplies. In 1846, for example, they purchased 1,000 mules at a cost of US$15,000. The camps themselves were often open to peddlers and food vendors. Mexicans sold the U.S. troops alcohol and took their money in gambling. More than a few of the norteamericanos sought the company of Mexican women. Business dealings often gave rise to mistrust. The racism of North American soldiers also affected relations.

The price of Mexico's defeat was, perhaps, as great politically and psychologically as the impact of the wars of Independence. The traumatic loss of the northern half of the nation caused a wide reevaluation of Mexican politics. That reevaluation would in turn lead to a devastating decade-long civil war. It is to this second tragedy that we turn next in chapter 5.

THE AGE OF CIVIL WARS

Benito Juárez

Benito Juárez

Above all the caudillos of the nineteenth century, Benito Juárez stands as Mexico's greatest hero and his legacy continues at the center of Mexican political mythology. Juárez was extraordinary in that, despite his enormous disadvantages as a full-blooded Indian, a country bumpkin from Oaxaca, and a civilian, he dominated mid-century Mexican politics. Juárez was also, perhaps, the most qualified president of the era, because he had extensive legislative, judicial, and administrative experience at every level of government. Juárez was the first Indian to become president of Mexico. He served in the office from 1858 to 1872, fifteen brutal years that included the vicious War of the Reform (1858–60), the French Intervention (1861–67), and innumerable revolts. Although he endured discouraging defeats, he persisted in fighting on. More than any of the other major leaders of the nineteenth century, Juárez helped form Mexican national identity. After the nation's humiliating defeat by the North Americans, Juárez restored his nation's dignity and self-esteem.

Juárez was not physically imposing. According to the Princess Salm-Salm, the wife of one of Maximilian's officers, "Juárez is a man a little under middle size, with a very dark complexioned Indian face, which is not disfigured, but on the contrary, made more interesting by a very large scar across it. He has very dark piercing eyes, and gives one the impression of being a man who reflects much, and deliberates long and carefully before acting. He wore old English collars and a black neck-tie, and was dressed in black broadcloth."

Juárez was actually a little over five feet tall, strong, and stocky. His black coat and tie, cane, and white shirt were trademarks. His wife made the shirts. He was neat, despite his hectic life on the run. He carried a pistol on occasion when warranted.

Despite his unexceptional appearance, throughout his career he displayed, in the words of biographer Wendell Blancke, an "iron will and inexhaustible self-confidence." His unprepossessing manner was legendary. In June 1855, he arrived in Acapulco to offer his services to Juan Álvarez, who was leading the Liberal rebellion (Plan de Ayutla) against Santa Anna. Dressed almost in rags, Juárez, who had once been well-known as governor of his home state of Oaxaca, found Diego Álvarez, the son of Juan, and volunteered for the cause. Young Diego did not recognize the name, but brought the shabbily dressed man along to his father's camp, where they outfitted him with some new clothes. Juárez started work as a secretary to the general. It was only after several days, when letters arrived for him addressed to "attorney" Juárez that the Álvarezes finally realized the former governor was among them. When asked why he had not introduced himself more elaborately, Juárez replied: "Why should I? What importance does it have?"

Later on, while president during the War of the Reform, a similar incident occurred. Six weeks of traveling had finally led to Veracruz, where he was greeted with a band and speeches. Nonetheless, when he arrived at his lodgings, his welcome was somewhat less enthusiastic. The mistress of the house, thinking him a servant, scolded him loudly when he requested water, bidding him to serve himself. He did so with no remark. He had endured much worse in exile. It was not until the midday meal, when he sat at the head of the table, that the landlady realized her mistake. She fled from the room to the great mirth of Juárez's entourage. Nondescript as he may have been, Juárez had a steel backbone.

Benito Juárez was born in 1806 into a poor Zapotec Indian family in the town of Gueletao in the state of Oaxaca. He was orphaned as a child and worked as a shepherd for his uncle. When he was eleven, he journeyed to Oaxaca City, where he apprenticed as a printer. He spoke no Spanish, only his Zapotec dialect, until he moved to the city. Later, Juárez attended the local seminary. In those days, the priesthood was, perhaps, the best path toward upward mobility for an Indian lad with talent and ambition. When the Institute for Arts and Sciences opened in 1828, however, he transferred there to study law. He taught at the Institute to pay for finishing his degree.

In 1832 Juárez won election to the Oaxaca city council with the support of the governor. While beginning his political career, he earned his living serving as secretary of the Institute. He won election as a Liberal to the state legislature in 1833 and to the state court a year later. In 1834 Juárez became the first person to receive official qualification as a lawyer in the state of Oaxaca. After Santa Anna overthrew Liberal president Valentín Gómez Farías in 1834, Juárez left government and returned to the practice of law. Although he mainly represented wealthy clients, Juárez in one controversial case was jailed for nine days because of his persistent defense of a village against its local priest. He continued his steady rise in politics. He became secretary of the Superior Tribunal of Justice in 1839 and one of its substitute magistrates in 1839 and 1840, and then civil justice of the first instance. The latter office paid him the comfortable annual salary of 1,200 pesos, a sum which qualified him as an hombre de bien. This enabled him at age thirty-seven to marry Margarita Maza, twenty years his junior, the illegitimate daughter of Italian immigrants. The Juárezes were to have nine children.

After serving in the state legislature, Juárez became governor of Oaxaca from 1847 to 1852, first as an interim appointment by the state legislature and, then, in August 1848, by election. Juárez was the first Indian elected a state governor in independent Mexico. He served his full term, in part because he built up his own armed forces.

His political career brought him considerable pain and suffering. In May 1853, Santa Anna, just reinstalled as president, had him arrested without explanation and held him for seventy-five days, followed by another twelve days in solitary confinement at the horrible prison of San Juan de Ulua in Veracruz harbor. His wife Margarita had to flee from the harassment of government agents. Eventually Juárez was tossed onto a steamer on its way to Europe. He left the steamer in Havana and made his way to New Orleans, where he resided from October 1853 to June 1855. During his time there, he earned a living rolling cigars and cigarettes, and then peddling them at suburban cafes and bars. Residing in a flophouse in the poorest section of the city, he survived on a diet of cafe au lait and black bread.

Juárez found his political salvation when Juan Álvarez and a Liberal coalition overthrew Santa Anna in 1855. The interim president Álvarez appointed him to his cabinet as Minister of Justice and Ecclesiastical Affairs. It was in this post that he promulgated the Ley Juárez (Juárez Law) on November 23, 1855. An executive decree on the administration of justice, it abolished ecclesiastical and military privileges (fueros) that had provided special courts for clergy and soldiers. The law also gave the federal government the right to nominate the members of the Supreme Court, previously nominated by state legislatures. (Both before and after the War of the Reform, members of the Supreme Court were elected by the federal Congress.) After Álvarez stepped down, his successor Ignacio Comonfort in 1856 sent Juárez back to Oaxaca as governor. Juárez returned to Mexico City the next year as minister of the interior in Comonfort's cabinet. The same year he was elected president of the Supreme Court, a position from which he succeeded to the presidency when Ignacio Comonfort resigned in 1858.

In the meantime, the War of the Reform between Conservatives and Liberals had erupted. Juárez, as president, had to abandon Mexico City in the face of military defeats. His government eventually settled in Veracruz, while the Conservatives held the capital. His party, the Liberals, was bitterly divided. Liberal regional bosses were reluctant to accept the leadership of the national government under Juárez. Santiago Vidaurri, who ruled in the northeast, went so far as to proclaim his region's secession from Mexico. These regional leaders wanted Juárez to lead their cause during the War of the Reform, but they also strove to keep him subordinate to their interests. They wanted a figurehead president and nothing more. Governors appropriated federal tax revenues and took advantage of any diminution of central authority. Juárez worked against these tendencies throughout his presidency with few resources other than his consummate political skill. One by one Juárez disarmed or broke the regional bosses, including Vidaurri, whom he ran off to the United States.

In 1860 the Liberals defeated the Conservatives on the battlefield and Juárez returned triumphant to Mexico City. In March 1861 he won election as president. Soon thereafter, Juárez, whose administration was unable to find revenues to pay for daily operating expenses, suspended repayment of Mexico's international debt. This action precipitated armed intervention on the part of Great Britain, France, and Spain. The French stayed on to attempt to conquer the country.

The French Intervention was the most severe test for a man who already had endured imprisonment, impoverishment, civil war, and exile. The invading French army, after suffering a humiliating defeat on May 5, 1862, at Puebla, overwhelmed the Mexicans. From late 1864 to mid-1866, Juárez and his government holed up in the state of Chihuahua, at times in Paso del Norte (today Ciudad Juárez), while the French installed the Austrian nobleman Maximilian as emperor. When his term expired in November 1865,

Juárez faced a constitutional crisis. There was no possibility of holding an election, for there was no Congress and the French occupied almost the entire nation. Jesús González Ortega, the president of the Supreme Court, claimed rightful succession, but Juárez sustained himself in office by declaring a national emergency. The president was unbending in his unwillingness to negotiate with either the French or Maximilian. It was for him a war to the death; and by the decree of January 25, 1862, anyone who collaborated with the French was subject to the death penalty. Again Juárez lived through personal agony. He had sent his family to the United States, where they barely survived. When his son became deathly ill, the president suffered greatly as the result of unreliable communications and uncertainty.

Eventually, he outlasted the French, who pulled out their troops in 1867, and defeated Maximilian. On June 19, 1867, Juárez ordered the execution of Maximilian, and his two best generals Miguel Miramón (1831–67) and Tomás Mejía (1820–67), despite an international outcry to save them. Juárez was a hard man, indeed.

Having persevered, the weary president sought a second election (third term) in 1867, which he won against two other Liberals, General Porfirio Díaz, the hero of Cinco de Mayo, and Sebastián Lerdo, a long-time loyal aide to Juárez. With considerable difficulty, he kept the nation together during the so-called Restored Republic, ruling by decree for much of the time. He moved to limit the army, to enforce the Reform Laws, to strengthen the executive branch, and to assist the transition to economic development. As ever, he suffered more defeats than victories. Juárez was reelected in 1872, despite growing evidence that he had lost the support of his fellow Liberals. Done in finally by his struggles, Don Benito died in 1872.

Juárez presided over and encouraged the emergence of modern Mexico. He was an unifying force in a nation torn by regionalism and ideology. He forged Mexican identity by standing up to foreign invasion, despite the long odds against him. At the same time, Juárez's political legacy, still predominant today in the ruling political party, the PRI (Party of the Institutionalized Revolution), was authoritarian. Out of necessity, most of the time he ruled by decree, not through representative government.

Juárez, too, implemented the Liberal vision of economic development, based on individual initiative, which ignored the majority of the population who lived in rural areas. Nonetheless, Benito Juárez towered over mid-nineteenth-century Mexico, courageous and undaunted.

TIMELINE

The Age of Civil Wars

1853–55 Santa Anna's last presidency

1854 Liberal revolt against Santa Anna

1855–61 Reform Era

1857 Constitution (Liberal)

1857–60 War of the Reform

1858–72 Presidency of Benito Juárez

1861 Tripartite Intervention (France, Great Britain, Spain)

1862 Cinco de Mayo (defeat of French at Puebla)

1861–67 French Intervention

1864–67 Maximilian

1867 Election of Benito Juárez as president

1871 Reelection of Juárez

1872 Death of Juárez

1872–76 Presidency of Sebastián Lerdo de Tejada

Chapter 5

POLITICS AND ECONOMY IN CIVIL WAR, 1848–61

The disastrous war with the United States caused a reevaluation of Mexican politics and political ideology. Two of the major groups, who had ruled in both centralist and federalist regimes, the army and the hombres de bien, were badly shaken. Humiliating defeat discredited the army. Emerging from the national debacle, Mexico's political debates reconfigured around Conservatism and Liberalism (see introduction). Members of each faction were convinced that their way was the best for the nation. Their conflict was irresolvable other than by bloodshed. It would take a vicious civil war (the War of the Reform) and a destructive foreign intervention before a new generation of Liberals emerged victorious. The War of the Reform from 1857 to 1860 marked, perhaps, a second watershed (Independence was the first) in the history of modern Mexico, because it not only ushered in a new age dominated by Liberalism, but also ended the transitional period of change from the colonial era's semi-feudal economy to a capitalist market economy.

The Liberals

There are two conflicting views held by historians of the Liberals at mid-century. One holds that they were an isolated minority, who, as a modernizing elite, were set on imposing new institutions and values on an either uncomprehending or recalcitrant population. The second maintains that because local issues, such as political autonomy, taxes, the draft, and access to

Thanks to the excellent work of Barbara Corbett, Brian Hamnett, Richard Johnson, Florencia Mallon, Simon Miller, Nelson Reed, Leticia Reina, Terry Ruggeley, Elizabeth Salas, Walter V. Scholes, and Guy Thomson.

land were so important, Liberals, who advocated federalism, attracted widespread popular support at the grassroots. Villagers guarding their prerogatives were moved to join Liberal ranks, because the Liberals defended state and local rights. Liberals organized locally based militia units, which formed the core of their popular base. There is no question, however, that in some areas Liberal policies elicited violent opposition from country people, who objected to the Liberal Reform Laws and Constitution of 1857, because they called for the destruction of the institution of communal landholding. In the end, however, the Liberals won over the majority of the lower classes, because with local autonomy the people in the countryside could best determine the rules of their everyday lives.

At mid-century Mexican Liberals were most closely associated with federalism and anti-clericalism, but they also adhered to the formalities of republican, representative, constitutional democracy. They advocated freedom of the press and freedom of speech, and expanded secular educational facilities. The Liberals favored capitalist development, especially "middle-class" land ownership, and recognized a need to imbue Mexicans with the virtues of hard work and frugality. The Liberals also aimed to eliminate what they saw as impediments to capitalism, most importantly, the extensive economic holdings of the Catholic Church. Central to their program was the expropriation of Church lands and their distribution among small landholders. The Liberals were by no means in agreement among themselves on policy or method. Through the 1840s, the civil wars, and the French Intervention, Liberals were increasingly divided by a bitter internal split between the radicals (puros) and the moderates (moderados) (see the introduction).

Post War

Mexico reached its low point politically in 1847, when, while enduring defeat by the United States, two major rebellions broke out in the countryside in the Sierra Gorda region north of the capital and in the Yucatán peninsula. Both were locally based movements of the lower classes, which threatened the Mexican *gente decente*. To make matters worse, regional bosses like Santiago Vidaurri (Nuevo León) and Manuel Lozada (Nayarit) declared themselves autonomous from the federal government. The old colonial order had passed and the new republic had shown little facility to reestablish either peace or order. Leaders from all over the ideological spectrum believed by 1853 that the nation was coming apart.

In crisis, Mexico looked again to Antonio López de Santa Anna. Even the leader of the rabble, Juan Álvarez, with his extensive base among mixed-blood small farmers in the tropical districts of Guerrero, agreed. He summed up the feeling of many Mexicans when he called the mercurial Santa Anna "the only man who could lead the country from its painful situation." Santa Anna returned from exile in 1853. The old war-horse reentered Mexico City in April, a little over five and a half years after he had fled in shame into bitter exile. Perhaps the hombres de bien believed, fooling themselves once again, that they could control the general. But there was no restraint to Santa Anna's excesses. He established a lavish court around himself, insisting that he be called "His Serene Highness." He also set out to centralize governance once and for all. So many scores to settle, so little time!

The Sierra Gorda

Between 1844 and 1857, a series of rebellions broke out in an isolated region that cut across the states of Guanajuato, Querétaro, and San Luis Potosí, known as the Sierra Gorda. The first and most serious outbreak took place from 1847 to 1849. Increased taxation, resulting from the state government's need to help finance the war against the United States, triggered Indians to revolt. As the uprisings spread, the rebels took on a heterogeneous mix of small-holders, tenants, sharecroppers, and villagers. Country people allied with regional elites who promised to remedy their complaints against oppressive taxation and to defend their communal lands. Eventually, these elites abandoned the "rabble" to preserve their own class interests and the rebellion faded. Although never a real threat to either the region or the nation, the Sierra Gorda underlined in the minds of the hombres de bien their worst fears of mass participation in politics.

The Caste War of Yucatán

If Mexico's elites were upset by the events in the Sierra Gorda, the eruption of rebellion in Yucatán in 1847 frightened them much more. The Yucatán peninsula had seceded from Mexico and returned to the fold various times during the 1840s. With the outbreak of war with the United States, Yucatán rejoined the union, but the state government grew weaker and weaker from a combination of growing unrest in the countryside and political conflict between competing elite factions. In 1847 the peninsula split along geographic lines—the city of Campeche against the state capital, Mérida—over issues of regional autonomy. Campeche residents wanted a separate state. This dispute further weakened elite defenses against revolt from below.

In order to furnish soldiers for their own forces, elite groups mobilized and armed the Maya Indians who comprised most of the population of Yucatán. Once the long-exploited Maya realized their collective strength, they were to come within a hair's breadth of destroying Mexican rule in Yucatán. The Maya had many old grievances, but their primary objection was to taxes. At one point in 1848 the Maya had won nearly complete control over the countryside, forcing the Mexicans to seek refuge in the larger cities. Eventually the tide turned and the Mexicans retook most of the region. Many Maya fled into the forests. By 1850 perhaps thirty percent, nearly 150,000 of the Maya population, had perished in battle or as a consequence of the rebellion. Despite defeats, the Maya did not surrender, maintaining their own independent area for several decades. As in the case of the Sierra Gorda upheavals, the Caste War and its aftermath added to the sense that Mexico was disintegrating and magnified the belief of the hombres de bien that only they could save Mexico from chaos.

The Liberal Rebellion (Plan de Ayutla)

In the regions and municipalities people resisted the incursion of central government power and merged the struggles for local autonomy and access to land with national issues of centralism and federalism. Santa Anna used the funds from the Treaty of Mesilla (Gadsden Purchase) to undertake a final assault on federalism. At the peak of his power, the dictator set out to oust his long-time enemy and the leader of the federalists, Juan Álvarez. In defense of his bailiwick in the state of Guerrero Álvarez rebelled in early 1854 (the Plan de Ayutla). After sporadic but bloody fighting (reports indicated 4,000 dead) that lasted for more than a year, Santa Anna again fled into exile in August 1855.

The rebellion of Ayutla marked the temporary victory of the periphery (the northernmost and southernmost states) over the center (the area dominated by Mexico City), the militia over the regular army, and the countryside over the city. These triumphs were transient, however, because the core of centralism, the regular army and the urban elite, survived this defeat. But most important, the coalition that routed Santa Anna was divided and soon fell apart. The revolt arose and persisted as an uncoordinated, heterogeneous movement, made up of regional political bosses like Álvarez and Santiago Vidaurri, the boss of Nuevo León and Coahuila, who balked at the dictator's encroachment on their own political fiefdoms. The major division within the Liberal coalition was between radicals (puros) and moderates (moderados). The crucial issue that separated these factions was the extent of the participation of the lower classes, particularly country people, in politics. The puros wanted to include the rural poor as active citizens of the new state, especially as participants in local politics. Moderates, much like the Conservatives, however, feared the masses and tried to limit the right of citizenship to men of property.

The Reform

The head of the coalition, Álvarez, was the logical choice to become interim president, but he had no stomach to remain very long in Mexico City. His protege, the moderate Ignacio Comonfort, took over as president in December 1855. Almost immediately he had to turn his attention to a Conservative rebellion, which broke out in January 1856, financed by high-level Church officials. Comonfort personally led the army in the siege that defeated the rebel stronghold of the city of Puebla. In the meantime Liberal regional bosses continued to assert their autonomy. Santiago Vidaurri unilaterally annexed Coahuila in defiance of the national government. Despite these difficulties, Comonfort was elected president in September 1857.

When they took control of the national government in 1855, Liberals were determined to eliminate the vestiges of colonial privilege, which they believed stood in the way of modern economic development. The cornerstones of their program were the three so-called Laws of the Reform, named for prominent politicians, and the Constitution of 1857. The first of the Reform Laws, decreed on November 23, 1855, was the Ley Juárez (Juárez Law), which reorganized the judicial system so as to eliminate the special courts for military, clergy, and other special interest groups. The Ley Lerdo (Lerdo Law), passed on June 26, 1856, which affected both Church property and communal properties held by Indian and mixed-blood villages, forbade corporate landholding. Under the new law, Church lands were to be sold and the proceeds turned over to the Church. Purchasers would pay a five-percent sales tax to the government. Church officials, of course, balked and, as a result, the Mexican government sold off the property without their compliance. As a result, the Church eagerly sought to back opposition to the Liberals.

In the countryside, villagers resisted government efforts to break up their communal holdings. The Liberals tried to mitigate the effects of the law on the lower classes in the cities by giving tenants on expropriated properties first rights to buy them. In rural areas Liberals reduced the costs involved in the transfer from communal to individual property in order to allow those who tilled the privatized land the first opportunity to purchase it. The Lerdo Law was intended to help Indians better their lot by transforming them into small landholders, but the law served instead to rob them of their ancestral lands. In January 1857, the third of the reform laws, the Iglesias Law (Ley Iglesias), forbidding clergy from charging exorbitant fees for the sacraments (e.g., baptisms, marriages, funerals), was adopted.

The Constitution of 1857 culminated these reforms and was to provide the basis of Liberal rule for the next sixty years. The new Constitution established a federal system of government with executive, legislative, and judicial branches. Because Liberals feared the recurrence of dictatorships like Santa Anna's, a unicameral Congress (a single legislative body) was to be the strongest branch with presidential authority relatively weak in comparison. The Constitution also provided for true democracy with universal male suffrage. For the first time, the president was to be elected by direct popular vote. Twenty-nine additional articles declared such rights as the abolition of slavery and debt peonage; freedom to choose one's occupation, work for just compensation; freedom of speech and association, petition and assembly; freedom of the press; the right to carry arms; freedom of access and exit from Mexico; prohibition of retroactive laws; elimination of the death penalty for political crimes; and the sanctity of private property except in instances of eminent domain. There was also a provision that allowed the suspension of these rights during time of crisis. Further, the Constitution granted the states considerable autonomy, a longstanding Liberal commitment. There were two important omissions from the U.S. model: trial by jury and religious toleration. The Liberal constitution makers believed the Mexican population was not prepared for either trial by their peers or freedom of religious belief.

The Liberal program manifested in the new Constitution was filled with contradictions. While Liberals formally adhered to democratic principles, at least one faction, the moderates, had serious misgivings about mass participation in politics and government. Once in power, the Liberals exhibited a clear predilection for authoritarianism. Firmly believing that only their program could save Mexico, they felt justified in manipulating elections in order to construct a one-party political system. At the same time, Liberals found that they could not win either peaceful elections or armed conflict without some form of alliance with the lower classes.

Moderates, for example, feared Juan Álvarez and his mulatto farmers from the hot country of Guerrero, known as *pintos,* whom one moderate called "wretched and indecent rabble . . . a horde of savages," but they could not have taken power without their support. The Liberal elite had to find a way to reach a working relationship with the masses. This dilemma was deepened when the Liberals, in earlier times advocates of federalism, increasingly centralized government in following their program for economic development and, as a consequence, encountered the persistent demand of the masses for local self-governance. Finally, although the Liberals publicly proclaimed their belief that all Mexicans were equal under the law, they aimed, in fact, to eliminate the basis for the Indian way of life, communal property holding. To Mexican Liberals communal landholding and the culture it sustained constituted an impediment to the development of individual initiative and enterprise. Liberals believed Indian culture was a major obstacle to modernization and Indian communities were the core of resistance to the Liberal program.

The first clear demonstration of these contradictions took place on December 17, 1857, when the Conservative General Felix Zuloaga issued the Plan of Tacubaya, which rejected the Constitution of 1857, but recognized Comonfort as president and offered him wide powers. Within two days Comonfort, who was convinced that the Constitution of 1857 was impractical, turned his back on the Liberals and joined Zuloaga, carrying out an executive coup d'etat that closed the Congress and revoked the Constitution, which was barely nine months old.

Born in 1812 in Puebla, Comonfort was a career military officer, who after the war with the United States had served as customs administrator in Acapulco. A protege of Juan Álvarez, Comonfort was one of the leaders of the Plan of Ayutla revolt that overthrew Santa Anna and then served in Álvarez's cabinet before succeeding him as president. He saw himself as a conciliator, who would bring together moderate Liberals and army officers in order to carry out the Liberal program. However, he soon found himself beset by both the radical Liberals and the Conservatives with little room for maneuver. Zuloaga eventually grew impatient with Comonfort's endless maneuvering and pro-

claimed himself president in mid-January 1858. Deprived of Conservative support Comonfort tried to return to the Liberals, but it was too late and he fled
into exile. The bizarre events of these three weeks in 1858 underlined the deep
divisions within the Liberal movement, unable to unite in the face of impending civil war.

The War of the Reform

According to the provisions of the Constitution of 1857, as the president
of the supreme court, Benito Juárez succeeded the deposed Comonfort. Since
the Conservative army held Mexico City, Juárez established his government
on the run. And, as we will see, for much of the next decade Juárez was to lead
Mexico from outside the capital city, ruling whatever share of the nation his
forces controlled from makeshift temporary headquarters.

For the better part of a year the Conservatives gained one military victory
after another. They had the best soldiers and the best leadership. Young generals such as Miguel Miramón and Leonardo Márquez were excellent soldiers.
Despite some squabbling over who was to be president, the Conservatives continued their military victories. Early defeats led Juárez's nomad government
from Guanajuato to Guadalajara to Veracruz (via the United States). Juárez's
itinerant government experienced several narrow escapes. In one incident in
mid-March 1858 a contingent of supposedly loyal soldiers mutinied and then
captured Juárez and his cabinet. These rebels determined to execute the president and the other prisoners. Just as the commander of the execution squad
ordered its members to fire, one of the cabinet, Guillermo Prieto, leaped in
front of the president and persuaded the soldiers to release the condemned
men.

Desperate for funds to purchase arms and supplies, both Conservatives and
Liberals resorted to foolhardy measures. In late 1859, Miramón contracted a
US$600,000 loan from a French banking house, Jecker and Company, which
obligated Mexico to repay US$15 million. For their part, Liberals agreed to the
McLane-Ocampo Treaty with the United States, which ceded the right to transit across northern Mexico and the Isthmus of Tehuantepec as well as the right
to send U.S. troops to protect U.S. citizens in Mexico in return for US$4 mil-
lion, US$2 million to be paid immediately and the remainder due on ratifi-
cation of the treaty by both sides. Luckily for Juárez, the U.S. Senate rejected
the treaty. Juárez received no money, but earned the unfortunate reputation
for selling out Mexican sovereignty.

The tide in the bitter bloody war slowly turned toward the Liberals and by the end of 1860 they had recaptured Mexico City. The Liberals won, because they ultimately attracted more popular support than the Conservatives. Although the Reform land program, which attacked communal village land-holding, alienated much of the countryside, the Liberal advocacy of federalism and local autonomy won over rural people in the end.

The War of the Reform exacted a devastating toll. Mexican politics were poisoned for a generation. Despite their military victory and the majority of popular support, the Liberals continued to be badly divided along personal and geographic, as well as ideological lines. The Liberals were a quarrelsome conglomeration of small guerrilla bands, private armies, and militias, with no one group having any inclination to cooperate with the others. On the local level, the war was marred by political assassinations and atrocities. Each side retaliated in kind. The war exacerbated inter-village rivalries, leaving people deeply embittered. It also widened racial antagonisms. The next stage in the struggle between Conservatives and Liberals, the French Intervention, would be a war to the death. The nation was armed to the teeth. Banditry, largely perpetrated by unemployed ex-soldiers, would torment the nation for the next two decades. The victorious Liberals faced the prospect at some point of having to confront an armed countryside if they were to carry out their program of individualizing communal land ownership. To the dismay of increasingly authoritarian Liberal leaders like Juárez, the civil war had strengthened regional political bosses, who would be difficult to control in the future.

Worst of all, the Liberal victory did not bring peace. Conservative armies stayed in the field with the stronghold of Puebla remaining in Conservative hands until January 1861. General Tomás Mejía, a Conservative leader, continued to operate in the mountains of Querétaro, north of Mexico City. General Márquez also refused to surrender. Although Juárez issued an amnesty to ameliorate the bitterness, many on both sides still had revenge on their minds.

Perhaps the biggest loser during the War of the Reform was the Catholic Church. Liberal wartime decrees separated church and state, declared religious toleration (both going beyond the Constitution of 1857), banned monastic orders, secularized cemeteries, made marriage a civil contract, recognized legal separation (though divorce was still illegal), and reduced the number of religious holidays. Liberal policies ended the Church's preeminent role in the nation's economy, most importantly by confiscating and selling off all Church property. In great part the Church had only itself to blame, for during the years after Independence the Catholic clergy had abused rural parishioners.

Many clergymen neglected their religious duties in favor of attending to private business, meddling in politics, and, in some cases, engaging in scandalous behavior. The Church steadfastly ignored even the most vile transgressions by priests. Many Indians, weary of exorbitant fees for the sacraments and masses and of condescending attitudes, came to regard the priests with "disdainful hostility."

Between Wars

After their victory Liberal vengeance came quickly. In January 1861, they fired all government employees who had served the Conservative regime. The Liberals also made the clergy financially responsible for damages from the war, because the clergy had allegedly instigated and supported the rebellion. Juárez expelled foreign diplomats who had cooperated with the Conservatives or had been hostile to the Liberal cause. He also exiled the Catholic archbishop and several bishops. Juárez was not a forgiving man.

The new Liberal government confronted difficult financial problems. Customs revenues (taxes collected on imports and exports) comprised almost all of Mexican government income during the nineteenth century, but were, for the most part, assigned to the repayment of international debt. Eighty-five percent of Veracruz customs receipts were so earmarked, as well as similar proportions of customs revenues from Tampico, Matamoros, and the Pacific ports. Under the new Constitution, the states were supposed to pay the central government a portion of their revenues, but rarely fulfilled their obligations. The government had no other income. Floating additional loans abroad was impossible, for Mexico was judged too great a risk. The proceeds from the sales of Church lands (the national government was supposed to receive five percent of each sale) proved insufficient to cover the government deficit. There was simply no money with which to operate the government. This fiscal crisis would propel the nation toward foreign war again.

The presidential elections in 1861 began as a three-way contest between Miguel Lerdo, the author of the law banning corporate landholding, Juárez, and Liberal general Jesús González Ortega. But Lerdo died in the middle of the bitter campaign, and Juárez won. His opponents contended that he had failed to gain a majority of the popular vote and that the Congress should therefore have resolved the election. Because Juárez's faction held a slim majority in Congress, his election was secure. Juárez surrendered the extraordinary powers he had taken during the civil war and Congress met for the first time in nearly four years. Democracy, however, would be short-lived.

Juárez faced more than his share of problems as he embarked on his first elected term as president. The national government confronted bankruptcy, for it had to struggle just to pay government employees on an irregular basis. The Liberal army that had supported Juárez during the civil war was reluctant to disband. Country people, armed and distrustful, bristled at the idea of white or mestizo city lawyers ruling their fate. Regional political bosses had agreed Juárez should lead the Liberal cause during the civil war, but, at the same time, they also strove to keep him subordinate to their interests. Now with peace, they wanted a figurehead and nothing more. State governors appropriated for their own needs federal revenues and took fullest advantage of shrinking central authority. Juárez, as a result, was forced to negotiate endlessly with uncooperative state governors and congressional factions, for which, thanks to the Constitution, he had few resources other than his considerable political skill.

In the countryside the face of politics had changed radically at mid-century. The civil wars provided an opportunity for country people to bargain for their interests through alliances with various elite political factions. Some historians believe that the intersection of the Liberal project to create a new national state and the patriotic stirring created by the foreign invasion in 1861 made possible the construction of a new, more inclusive, more participatory concept of citizen, challenging rural communities to become involved in politics. The overriding question was whether the Liberals would be able to carry out their vision of democratic capitalism (with its stern measure of authoritarianism) without the cooperation of the masses in the countryside. Would the Liberals consolidate national power in conflict or cooperation with regional struggles for ethnic and social justice? These issues would not be resolved until the later years of the Díaz era.

Economy

The economy during the years between the war with the United States, which ended in 1848, and the French Intervention, which began in 1862, was affected by the Reform Laws and the war they provoked. In the decade immediately following the war with the United States, the economy in some regions recovered quickly. This may have resulted in part from the end of uncertainty. War with the United States had loomed for so many years that it had cast a shadow over investment and commerce. Most importantly, there was stirring in the crucial mining sector. The once great silver producing center of Guanajuato, for example, showed signs of resuming mining. The region between Veracruz and Mexico City grew in population and economic activity.

The northern tier of states, however, was in ruins at mid-century, torn apart by separatism and war. National governments were unable to protect the region. The loss of the vast territories north of the Rio Grande to the United States had set loose a wave of raids by Apaches and Comanches that devastated the land. One raid in Sonora in January 1849, for example, resulted in the deaths of eighty-six settlers. Vast stretches of land were uninhabitable. For a time in the north the major economic enterprise was hunting Apache scalps for which state governments paid a bounty. Panic-stricken state governments like Chihuahua's, with meager funds to combat the Apaches and no help on the horizon from the federal government, resorted to this vicious enterprise, which brought no honor to its perpetrators and had little positive effect on public security. War also badly damaged the once-flourishing trade between northern Mexico, New Mexico, and Texas along such routes as the Camino Real (Chihuahua City to Santa Fe). The California gold rush virtually depopulated other areas in the north. Ten thousand people may have left Sonora for California from 1848 to 1850 alone.

Of the events in the years from 1848 to 1861, the Reform Laws had the biggest impact on the economy. The Ley Lerdo, which ended corporate ownership of land, was the most important piece of legislation. Liberals had intended that the nation's great estates be broken up and a new class of small farmer arise to form the basis for capitalist development, as it had (supposedly) in the United States and Western Europe. The most important target of the law was the Church, which owned vast tracts of land and was the largest urban property owner. Liberals sought to end collective ownership on the part of Indian villages as well.

The expropriation of lands held by the Church did not accomplish Liberal goals. The original intent of the law was for those who rented rural or urban property from the church to have the first right of purchase. Few such renters had the financial resources to acquire property. Moreover, there was no limitation under the law in the number of parcels or properties that one person could buy. In the long run the Reform served to concentrate landholding even more than previously. It also formed the legal basis for massive expropriations of village lands in the last quarter of the century that engendered widespread unrest in the countryside. In the state of Morelos, for example, the village of Annencuilco lost much of its land to the neighboring sugar estate. Eventually, after years of peaceful protests in the courts, the village, under the leadership of Emiliano Zapata, rose in rebellion in 1910. In urban areas, particularly Mexico City, the effect was somewhat more positive. In the capital the Lerdo Law created 9,000 new property owners. Though many of these people were later to lose their holdings, in the short term urban landowning was not as concentrated as it was before 1857.

The Reform Laws concerning land had other effects as well. Because the Conservatives had controlled many regions from 1858 to 1860, the status of many of the original property transfers from the Church to private individuals was complicated. The Conservatives had (temporarily as it turned out) nullified the transfers of ownership. The amount of litigation that ensued when the Liberals finally won and reinstated the Reform Laws was huge. Property holders would live with uncertainty for years.

As seen in chapter 2, the Mexican economy continued to function and in some places even prospered during this disruptive era, though as a whole it stagnated or declined slightly. An example was the Hacienda San Marcos in Jalisco. From 1850 to 1863 this sugar producing and stock breeding estate continued to operate. Unlike many haciendas it possessed fertile land and good growing conditions. But, typical of most Mexican haciendas, its access to markets was severely limited because there were no roads. The hacienda also endured two Indian uprisings in 1852 and 1857 and repeated bandit raids. Hacienda managers solved some of their marketing problems by selling low-grade sugar (*panocha*) and the cheap alcoholic beverage made from sugar, *aguardiente,* directly to customers, and by acquiring and maintaining its own mule teams. The hacienda owner lived on the hacienda and carefully supervised all activities. On the Hacienda de San Juanico in Querétaro another resident owner survived the foraging armies that repeatedly crisscrossed the region. The estate grew wheat that the proprietor hauled via his own means of transportation to Mexico City.

Mexican politics and economy staggered on in the wake of the civil war. The Liberals had the upper hand, but more dangerous obstacles lay ahead. The Conservatives with new allies from abroad would wage a renewed war to the death for the soul of the nation.

Chapter 6

FOREIGN INTERVENTION AND RECONSTRUCTION, 1861–67

From the time Mexico proclaimed its independence from Spain, some Mexicans advocated monarchy as the most appropriate form of government for the new nation. The ill-fated reign of Emperor Agustín I, who ruled less than a year, did not deter them. There was, for example, a brief, poorly conceived, unsuccessful monarchist plot, just before the outbreak of war with the United States in 1846. Later, Santa Anna obtained all but formal title of royalty during his last dictatorship in 1854. Despite these failures, monarchists obtained their most important opportunity in the early 1860s, when the circumstances of Mexican domestic politics and conditions in Europe came together to make the Second Empire possible. In Mexico, Conservatives, who had been defeated in civil war, looked for any means to overcome the Liberals. At the same time, the opportunistic emperor of France Napoleon III sought to enhance his international prestige by extending his sphere of influence over Mexico. He conspired with Mexican monarchists and Conservatives to install a European prince as ruler of Mexico, committing a large military force to this objective. His plan met fierce opposition from Benito Juárez, president of Mexico and the victor in the War of the Reform, who steadfastly refused to accept foreign conquest. Thus began the dramatic sagas of Maximilian and Carlota, the doomed royalty, on the one hand, and Benito Juárez, the persistent hero of Mexican sovereignty, on the other.

Underlying the personal dramas of the tragic couple and the indomitable Juárez were the crucial dilemmas, still unresolved, which had tormented Mex-

Thanks to Alicia Hernández Chávez, Egon Caesar Corti, Jack Dabbs, Will Fowler, Brian Hamnett, Alberto Hans, Florencia Mallon, T. G. Powell, Laurens Perry, James Ryan, Jasper Ridley, Ralph Roeder, Elizabeth Salas, Walter V. Scholes, Guy Thomson, and Charles Weeks.

ican politics since Independence. The French Intervention was essentially a continuation of the War of the Reform. The Conservatives, defeated in the civil war, found a foreign ally and restarted the conflict. Mexicans again fought over who should rule and how, the role of the Catholic Church, and the place of the military in society. Much of this struggle originated and played out regionally and locally. The issue, as ever, was elementary: who was to control government, most especially at the local level, and thus control the level of taxes and the access to land?

Ultimately, the Liberals won out, defeating both their domestic rivals and foreign invaders in a long, bitter war that lasted for more than six years. But, even in the face of these serious threats, the Liberals remained divided. The so-called Republican Restoration from 1867 to 1876 would be rancorous and conflict ridden. Juárez and his successor, Sebastián Lerdo de Tejada (a one-time ally of Juárez), presided over a transition period during which they reestablished basic order and governmental functions, but could not bring an end to internecine strife. Liberals were torn by a generation gap between the Juaristas (supporters of Juárez) and Lerdistas (supporters of Lerdo) on one side and the younger generation, led by Porfirio Díaz, one of the foremost resistance heroes of the French Intervention, on the other. Those who rallied behind Díaz, Porfiristas they were later called, believed that it was time for the old Liberals to step aside and let the newcomers modernize Mexico. Neither side of the generation gap believed in the ability of the people to choose the nation's path. Only they could lead.

Juárez and his Liberals discovered, perhaps to their chagrin, that their aims were contradictory. Liberal methods, too, were often inimical to their proclaimed goals. The Liberals sought to reestablish order after two decades of destructive war. They had long advocated federalism with strong state governments and a relatively weak president. But Juárez's Liberals, through hard experience, concluded that no government could bring order without a strong central authority and a powerful executive. Liberals extolled democracy, as spelled out in the Constitution of 1857 that they had drafted, but, to maintain themselves in power for what they believed to be the good of the nation, they stole elections and curtailed freedoms. More important, although they proclaimed the equality of all Mexicans, many Liberals disdained the common people, especially Indians. Finally, the Liberals dreamed of economic development, but development, they discovered, was possible only if they restored order and centralized authority.

Juárez himself was the embodiment of these inherent contradictions, and the difficulty in applying ideology to actual conditions. During the French Intervention, he prolonged his term as president in a way that was of dubious constitutionality. The presidential elections of 1867 and 1871 were tainted with impositions and dishonesty. After the defeat of the French Juárez unsuccessfully attempted to change the Constitution to strengthen the central government. As president, Juárez constantly interfered with state politics to ensure his allies' victories. His peacetime administration was, in fact, more a benevolent dictatorship than a democracy.

The French Intervention and the Empire of Maximilian

The history of the French Intervention and Empire actually involved five intertwined stories. The first was the dismal tale of Napoleon III's imprudence. He listened to Mexican monarchists, who had attached themselves to his idle court, fell victim to his own ignorant dreams of overseas glory, and ultimately betrayed an even bigger dreamer, Maximilian.

The second was the tawdry story of the Mexican monarchists and Conservatives who took the opportunity presented by Napoleon's pride to grab temporary victory after their defeat in the War of the Reform. Men like José Manuel Hidalgo and José Miguel Gutiérrez Estrada occupied center stage but briefly and with great cost to their homeland. Maximilian's is, of course, the best known of these tales. He and his wife Charlotte, known as Carlota in Mexico, were doomed to execution by firing squad and to madness, respectively. The Emperor, though probably well intentioned, consistently made faulty decisions. The fourth story was the most noble and heroic. At enormous sacrifice Benito Juárez and the Liberal patriots stubbornly stood against the invaders. For six terrible years, pushed to the ends of Mexico, Juárez persisted. This time Mexico did not surrender to a foreign power as it had in 1848. Humiliation by the United States had brought about a deeply felt reassessment on the part of the Mexican people, especially the nation's intellectuals. It was the victory over the French that was to forge Mexico's disparate regions into a nation. Finally, there was the story of the war at the local level, where people used the intervention and war to help formulate their construction of Mexicanness, while furthering their own political and economic interests.

Napoleon III

The fiscal disarray of the Mexican government was the initial cause of the Intervention. When Juárez returned to Mexico City after defeating the Conservatives in 1861, Mexico was near bankruptcy. In July 1861, the president suspended payment on foreign debts for two years. This sensible measure allowed the national government to apply all its revenues to finance its day-to-day operations and allowed it to pay its long-suffering employees and soldiers. The European holders of the Mexican debt, not surprisingly, objected to this plan. The government of France demanded that Mexico repay 12 million pesos owed to French citizens. The Conservative government had incurred this debt buying arms to fight Juárez during the War of the Reform. Napoleon's brother-in-law, it just so happened, owned thirty percent of the bonds in question. Spain and Great Britain demanded repayment of debts owed their citizens as well.

The three powers agreed to join together to use a show of force to persuade the Mexicans to reconsider. They would occupy Veracruz, if the Mexicans did not agree to resume regular payments. In December 1861, Spanish, French, and British troops landed. Juárez permitted them to move inland to avoid the outbreak of tropical disease. The European allies, however, soon quarreled. The Spanish and English realized that Napoleon had ambitions in Mexico beyond collecting debt and withdrew their soldiers after the Mexican government promised to resume payments as soon as it could. The French stayed.

Napoleon III simply misinterpreted the situation in Mexico. His head was filled with dreams of international glory. With the United States preoccupied in its civil war and Mexico barely recovering from the War of the Reform, circumstances appeared favorable to conquer the badly wounded nation. Napoleon did not anticipate the ensuing resistance, the end of the U.S. civil war, or a radical change in the balance of power in Europe that would threaten France itself.

After the Spanish and English pulled out of Veracruz the French embarked on a full-scale invasion. On the road to Mexico City, however, they were stopped at Puebla on May 5, 1862, by a ragtag Mexican army led by thirty-three-year-old General Ignacio Zaragoza. After a series of futile assaults on Puebla, the French withdrew defeated to Orizaba. Cinco de Mayo (the fifth of

May) became the second greatest modern national holiday ranking only below September 16, Independence Day.

Humiliated by the shocking defeat of his army, Napoleon III sent 25,000 more soldiers to Mexico led by two new commanders, Marshals Elie Frederic Forey and Achille Bazaine. Forey took Puebla in March 1863. The Mexicans were handicapped by a change in military leadership, for Zaragoza had died of typhoid in the interim. Nonetheless, they resisted the siege for two months before they surrendered. Juárez then chose to abandon Mexico City, establishing his government in San Luis Potosí. The French entered Mexico City in June and quickly selected a provisional government, which then invited Maximilian to be emperor. The French army completed this process with a rigged plebiscite (held on Maximilian's insistence) confirming this decision.

The Monarchists

Several important Mexican monarchists had found a respite after the War of the Reform in the court of Napoleon III and his Empress Eugenie. José Miguel Gutiérrez Estrada was born of a wealthy Mexican family and spent much of his life in the Mexican diplomatic service. His long-time commitment to monarchy began with his participation as a member of the delegation sent to Europe in 1821 to find a king for Mexico. Through his wife he had connections to the Austrian royal court and to Maximilian. Gutiérrez was fanatically pro-clerical and reactionary in his politics. After publishing a pamphlet expounding his extreme views in 1840, he had to flee the country in fear for his life. Gutiérrez never returned. Nonetheless, for more than two decades, he haunted the courts of Europe in search of support for a Mexican monarchy. In the mid-1850s he found an ally in José Manuel Hidalgo, the son of a prominent Conservative, who was a member of the Mexican diplomatic corps. The handsome, charming Hidalgo easily made connections in royal courts throughout Europe. It was the young Hidalgo who found the ear of the Empress Eugenie. Both Gutiérrez and Hidalgo remained in Europe during the Intervention and suffered expropriation of their estates in Mexico by the Juárez regime. Each had to rely on Napoleon III to restore their properties and provide funds for their sustenance. Hidalgo continued to accept large sums from Napoleon, even while he served as Maximilian's minister to France!

Maximilian and Carlota

The monarchists needed to find a European prince willing to take the throne of Mexico. The most eligible royal was the younger brother of the Hapsburg Emperor of Austria-Hungary, the same Franz Joseph whose diplomatic failures would help set off a world war in 1914. The young Archduke Ferdinand Maximilian was a bored sailor (an admiral to be sure), not trustworthy enough to have any real responsibilities in his brother's empire. He resided in a monumental castle, Miramar, with a beautiful princess as his wife. Perhaps only vanity and foolishness could have caused him to give up his creature comforts and his rights as potential successor to the Hapsburg throne to go to Mexico.

Born in 1832 amid rumors of his illegitimacy, Maximilian, called Ferdinand Max by his family, grew up "dreamy and artistic" in the shadow of his older brother. As a young man he was very religious and held himself to a strict code of conduct. At eighteen he commanded the Empire's Adriatic fleet. According to Count Corti, his biographer, he certainly looked the part of a king:

> Ferdinand Max was slender and slightly built, with fair hair, blue wide-open eyes, and a rather retreating chin, which was later concealed by a well-cared-for fair beard, parted in the middle, which he was often in the habit of stroking. His complexion was in general pale, and on the whole, he was a charming figure. . . .

He was not strong or energetic, though he had "spasmodic" bursts of activity when he thought himself underestimated. He had "romantic and exalted tendencies." In 1856 he met and courted Charlotte, the youngest child of King Leopold of Belgium; they married the next year. Charlotte was a fun-loving beauty, who at sixteen fell head over heels in love with the handsome Austrian archduke. She determined to have him and her father obtained what she wanted. After some haggling over Charlotte's dowry, the arrangement was completed. In the late 1850s Maximilian served as viceroy in the Austrian Empire's northern provinces of Italy. He then traveled without Charlotte to Brazil. Evidently separation did not make their hearts grow fonder, since after he returned they no longer slept together.

Napoleon III proposed that Maximilian take the throne of Mexico after France began its intervention in 1861. It was not an easy decision and Maximilian took many months to agree. He pouted and fumed when his brother Franz Joseph informed him that he would have to cede his rights to the Aus-

Maximilian

Carlota

trian throne. Maximilian then insisted that he would not journey across the Atlantic unless the Mexican people voted by plebiscite to accept him as their ruler. Finally, he and his wife arrived in Mexico in April 1864. The French army had by then obtained control over much of the country.

The imperial court was a dreamland. The dashing Maximilian presided over a horde of sycophants, eating rich food, drinking expensive imported wine, and chain smoking cigarettes. Between the cost of the high life and the upkeep of the military, the emperor borrowed enormous sums. Rumors swirled about his relationship with Carlota and their inability to have children. One of the rumors claimed the emperor had syphilis and had been rendered impotent; another that he had a child by another woman.

Maximilian tried, in his way, to meet the Mexicans halfway. He learned Spanish; Carlota already spoke it. In an effort to enhance his popularity among the masses, he abolished debt peonage, allowed freedom of religion, and promoted education, but these measures only succeeded in alienating the Conservatives, who composed the base of his support. Nothing could win over the people, however. He was a foreigner imposed on their nation by force. Thirty thousand French soldiers secured his throne.

The Tide Turns

By early 1865 the French army controlled nearly all of Mexico. Imperial forces had forced Juárez to Paso del Norte, on Mexico's northern border with the United States. Stalwarts like Porfirio Díaz were defeated. But in these darkest hours, the tide turned. A combination of drastically changing international conditions, a series of serious (and perhaps inevitable) blunders by the emperor and his government, the inherent contradictions that undermined the empire from the outset, and the persistence of Juárez defeated Maximilian.

The transformation of France's international situation was most crucial, for it resulted in the withdrawal of the French Army. The defeat of the Confederacy ended the U.S. civil war in 1865 and the defeat of Austria in war with Prussia in 1866 together drastically altered the international situation for France and shook Napoleon's support. The U.S. government pushed for the withdrawal of French troops from Mexico. Prussia threatened France. In response, in January 1866, Napoleon informed Maximilian that the French army would leave within the year. Although Maximilian refused to abdicate, he could not maintain his throne without French troops.

Maximilian was not at any point able to put his military house in order. The original convention signed between Maximilian and Napoleon III provided for 25,000 French troops and 8,000 Foreign Legionnaires to stay eight years. The agreement did not mention a commander-in-chief. The imperial army and government were divided in the best of times. The army consisted of small contingents of Austrian and Belgian troops, as well as French soldiers, and several thousand Mexicans, who operated without a unified command structure. Because of deep, personal dislike, Maximilian did not communicate at all with the French commander Marshall Bazaine. The Austrians never recognized French leadership. There was not enough money to properly fund the military. Mexico was supposed to pay for the expenses of the French expeditionary force after July 1, 1864, but could never fulfill this agreement. Napoleon III promised that "however events in Europe might turn out, the assistance of France should never fail the new empire." But Napoleon III, rather than maintain a minimum 20,000 troops in 1867, withdrew entirely.

The former archduke trusted Napoleon III, who wrote him in 1864: "I beg that you will always count upon my friendship . . . You may be sure that my support will not fail you in the fulfillment of the task you are so courageously undertaking." They would prove hollow words indeed.

Another important error was the emperor's difficult relations with the Catholic Church. Maximilian refused to rescind the Liberals' Reform Laws. A decree in early 1865 reaffirmed the sale of church property, revised Church procedures, and provided for liberty of worship. As a result, the Mexican Church hierarchy never committed its full resources to the empire.

The new ruler went to Mexico without adequate financial arrangements. There were never enough funds to operate the government, fight the war, and carry out new programs. If Maximilian had the monies to institute a more far-reaching public works program, for example, he might have won over more of the population.

Frustrated at every turn, Maximilian vented his displeasure:

> There are three classes which are the worst thing I have found in the country so far, the judicial functionaries, the army officers, and the greater part of the clergy. None of them know their duties and they live for money alone. The judges are corrupt, the officers have no sense of honor, and the clergy are lacking in Christian charity and morality.

And this was in October 1864! He was at the time still quite optimistic about his prospects.

Maximilian made other mistakes as well. Frustrated by continued guerrilla warfare in the face of his almost certain victory, in October 1865 he proclaimed that any Mexicans who continued to fight the empire would be shot summarily. Unfortunately for the emperor, Juárez would use this decree later to justify his order to execute Maximilian. The former archduke also erred when he dispatched his wife to Europe to drum up support for his faltering enterprise. For all her later reputation as unbalanced, Charlotte had acted as his most trusted counsel. Her sympathetic presence might have saved him from the firing squad. Her failed attempt to obtain support in Europe drove her to despair and pushed her over the edge to madness. Charlotte herself had misjudged badly, for it was she who had dissuaded her husband from abdicating in mid-1866. It had been Charlotte who had demanded that he "be a man and hold out."

As Maximilian and Charlotte tried mightily to win over their new Mexican subjects, Benito Juárez fought on. The defeats of 1864 led to even darker days,

The Battle of San Lorenzo, April 10, 1867

as his government wandered north through San Luis Potosí, then Saltillo and Monterrey, and eventually to Chihuahua in 1865 and 1866. The French pushed Juárez to the border at Paso del Norte, but the stubborn president refused adamantly to cross the border to the United States and safety. By early 1866, however, Juárez had turned the tide. In June 1866, the Conservatives' best general, Tomás Mejía, lost a crucial battle at Matamoros. The Liberals let him and his army go after they surrendered, opening the door for many desertions from the imperial army. Miramón, another Conservative general, suffered defeat at Zacatecas in February 1867, forcing Maximilian to leave Mexico City on February 13. A new group of young Liberal generals pushed the French south, taking back Chihuahua, then the northwest, Jalisco, and Oaxaca. In March 1867, Bazaine took the last of the French army home. Maximilian again decided to stay. With his generals Miramón, Mejía, and Márquez, the emperor set up his headquarters in Querétaro. In May 1867 after a long siege Querétaro fell. On June 19 the Mexicans shot Maximilian, Miramón, and Mejía. (Márquez avoided capture.) The nation had regained its self-respect.

The War for Soldiers and Civilians

The six-year war of the French intervention had cost dearly, with approximately 300,000 dead and inestimable damage to infrastructure and commerce. Marauding armies demanded provisions and there was much pillaging of villages by both sides. Sometimes the suspicion was that the roving bands were more interested in plunder than politics. The Liberal strategy was to fight guerrilla war, favoring ambushes and avoiding major battles, unless they had an overwhelming superiority of numbers. The objective was to avoid decisive defeats and demoralization. After each small setback in the mid-1860s, republican forces would disperse, resupply, and reorganize.

The republican soldiers were, despite their allegedly "slovenly and unkempt appearance," quite capable. One study by the French Foreign Legion determined that the Mexican soldier "whether regular, guerrilla, or bandit—was a formidable and resilient opponent who gloried in the charge while displaying the courage of a lion." The observer continued that he believed the Mexican soldier "seldom evinced fear of death," though he sensed a hesitation "to engage in hand-to-hand combat." Another Legionnaire described the Juarista Cotaxtla Squadron, led by Captain Tomás Algonzas.

The latest generation of a lengthy line of crafty, saddle-hardened warriors, the men of the Cotaxtla Squadron disdained wearing regulation military uniforms in the style of the brigade's blue-jacketed dragoons, clinging instead to their traditional *ranchero* outfits:

> [L]avishly ornamented leather waistcoats, tight leather breeches with flaring bottoms, broad-brimmed felt hats over colorful bandannas, and huge metal-coated spurs attached to high-heeled leather boots. . . . The Mexican horsemen heightened their macho image by arming themselves with the U.S. pistol carbine, U.S. 1855 model rifle carbine, and one of a dozen different types of revolvers slung in heavy leather holsters fastened low on the hip. The lance was favored over the sabre. . . .

Although to the Legionnaires, at least, the Mexicans were a formidable enemy, as in the War of the Reform, most Mexican soldiers on both sides were conscripts coerced into service and, consequently, desertion was a chronic problem. The Europeans had further difficulties in recruiting and leading, because they did not speak Indian languages and often the Indians did not speak Spanish.

Bravery came at a price, of course. Alberto Hans, one of the empire's European soldiers, writes of one of his admired foes, a Spaniard named Regules, who fought on the side of Juárez in Michoacán, and of his troops:

> One cannot but admire his obstinacy in continuing to fight without mercy a struggle which cost the lives of his two predecessors as commander in Michoacán. After many defeats his soldiers have attained a state of nakedness and misery which is impossible to describe and for which there is no remedy, for unlike the northern republican generals, he cannot gain ready access to arms and supplies in the United States. In spite of it all, Regules, always sick, continued to fight, suffering defeat, but revitalizing himself with small victories.

Hans went on to say that these were not the undisciplined masses who had fought under the banner of Father Hidalgo in 1810 or Juan Álvarez in 1854.

There was among the Mexicans a marked improvement in leadership compared to the war with the United States, especially once the younger generation, such as Porfirio Díaz and Ignacio Zaragoza, assumed larger roles. Nonetheless, old habits died hard. The Mexican armies remained corrupt, exacerbating the already unfortunate circumstances of the soldiers. In just one example, senior officers among the Conservative ranks commonly bought horses and fodder at low prices (or stole them) and resold to the French at very high prices.

As was the case in the war with the United States, the Mexican army relied on women to function as the supply and medical branches. *Soldaderas,* as women auxiliaries came to be known, were with the Mexican army on Cinco de Mayo and afterwards. Camp followers provided food, medical attention, and solace for the soldiers of all armies. The French called the Mexican camp followers "zopilotes en jupons" (vultures in petticoats), probably because they collected still useful items from the battlefields. They formed a transport unit carrying soldiers' equipment, thereby enabling them to move faster. Women's participation in the French army must have reached a significant number, for the Mexican army tried to elicit patriotism among women in order to keep them from aiding the French. One propaganda tool was the song "Yo soy un chinaquita" ("I am half Indian and half African") aimed at Afro-Mexican women, who might find themselves attracted to the French army's African troops.

Although there was considerable indifference toward the programs and ideologies of the contestants, civilians were deeply affected by the demands of war. In one region in Puebla studied by Florencia Mallon, local guerrilla forces required a supply of tortillas each day from each of five villages. A soldier's daily ration was twelve tortillas. By her calculations the women in these towns had to produce between 1,800 and 2,400 tortillas a day to feed these men; and this was in addition to their other daily tasks. Tortilla making was arduous and time consuming and the demand was enormous. There were no rewards for women when the war ended—no land, no promotions, no medals.

The French ultimately lost, because they failed "to appreciate the magnitude of the physical task before them and the nature of the war they would have to fight." They thought that they could impose their will on the Mexicans as they had on native populations in North Africa. They had, however, less than 40,000 troops to rule a nation with difficult terrain half the size of Europe. The French and Austrians expected set-piece battles; instead they confronted a very different type of engagement. The enemy would not stand and fight. It raided and ambushed where the Europeans were weak. The Mexicans were mostly cavalry with great mobility; losses were light. The Europeans suffered fewer losses in numbers, but because reinforcements were not forthcoming these losses were proportionately much more damaging. Eventually, the guerrillas controlled the countryside, leaving only the cities to the French. Language and cultural barriers prevented optimal cooperation between the

French and their Mexican allies. The Mexican republicans led by the stubborn
Juárez simply outlasted the French, who could not afford a prolonged war of
attrition.

At the Grassroots

The republicans led by Juárez ultimately won over the majority of the Mexican people. They were successful because politics were essentially regional
and local. National issues like monarchy versus republic were deeply mixed
with local interests. Political alliances often depended on local ties and issues.
If one's enemy was a Liberal, then one became a Conservative in order to acquire the outside support needed to carry on the rivalry. Communities often
followed their leaders into one camp or the other. In many places, the conflict
took the form of resistance to forced loans, taxes, the draft, and imposed outside leadership. Juárez drew support at the local and regional level, because he
was a Liberal and, as such, stood for a weak central government, strong state
governments, and local autonomy.

However, at the same time, Liberals most assuredly threatened the community life of villages by advocating a strong secular state and private property. They opposed patriarchal government by elders; the system of
compulsory and community services; religious celebrations and confraternities; and communal ownership of land. In the end the republican Liberals
overcame the stigma of the Reform Laws, because they adopted policies that
addressed other concerns of villages, such as taxes. For example, the Liberals
replaced the *capitación* or head tax on Indians with a mustering-out tax that
fell on those not serving in the National Guard. Since Indians regarded the
capitación as an instrument of repression, its abolition and replacement was
a symbol of equality before the law. No longer were they singled out as Indians for taxation; under the new laws everyone was taxed. The Liberals also
abolished unpaid forced labor. The Liberals provided an environment in
which upward mobility was possible. For example, Indians became leaders
of the republican National Guard.

Privatization of land remained the most explosive issue, for villagers deeply
resented and opposed the transfer of collective holdings to individuals. But
counterbalanced against the issue of communal landholding were those of
local and regional autonomy, local politics, and patriotism. Local political autonomy, which meant local control over taxes, courts, and conscription, probably overwhelmed the land issue in most areas. It is likely that encroachments

by hacendados and politicians had not reached a critical extent by the late 1860s in most parts of the country. If the locals envisioned the impending crisis, they also knew local control could delay or frustrate such redistribution. The only hope for stalling or overcoming privatization of landholding was to control local courts and municipalities. The Liberals made seemingly minor, but to local communities quite important, changes. Some barrios received municipal status and therefore were entitled to common lands at the expense of local hacendados.

There was also an issue of trust. The Conservatives were known for their pro-clerical leanings. The villagers had learned the hard way in many regions that the clergy were the least trustworthy officials of all. The long pattern of neglect, not to mention broken vows (like scandalous sexual activity), eroded the legitimacy of the clergy, which should have had enormous influence at the local level. The clergy had been more likely to exploit people in the countryside than provide any solace or guidance in hard times. Catholic priests were more agents of central authority than protectors or advocates of their parishioners.

Crucial to country people were the institutions and traditions that affected everyday life. The Liberal program allowed the people of the countryside the most leeway in running their daily affairs. But the Liberals would seek also to control and change Indian communities to fit their idea of progress. Eventually, this aim would clash with centuries of tradition, leading to renewed violent conflict. The Liberals tried to disguise this inevitable conflict until they were stronger. Indian communities fought on both sides. The republicans in some regions got support from Indians, who traded military service in exchange for keeping their communal lands and municipal autonomy. In other places, Indians fought to retain communal holdings against the Liberal Reform Laws by joining the French.

The empire certainly understood the importance of local issues. In March 1864, for example, the imperial army offered Juan Francisco Lucas, the political boss of the Puebla Sierra, the mountain region of northern Puebla state, a settlement of the land problem in his municipality in return for laying down his arms. Lucas refused and remained loyal to the republic. Nonetheless, Conservatives controlled the Puebla Sierra by 1866. Given the Reform Laws regarding communal landholding, it is surprising that the Liberals obtained any support in the heavily Indian regions.

Initially, Maximilian concurred with the Reform Laws, which ended communal landholding and rejected village petitions to regain their lands from

encroaching haciendas. In 1865 and 1866, however, as it became clear that
French support would diminish, Maximilian had to rethink his agrarian policies. He openly sought the support of country people. "The best of them . . .
are, and always will be, the Indians," Maximilian wrote to his father-in-law
King Leopold. "I have just promulgated a new law for them, forming a council that shall go thoroughly and helpfully into their desires, complaints, and
requirements." This initiative was stymied because the empire's local officials
were invariably in cahoots with the hacendados. Maximilian's government had
no means to enforce its laws.

Given the overwhelming importance of local issues in Mexican politics at
mid-century, it is most difficult to analyze patriotism's role in the republican
Liberal victory. As part of their project to build a modern nation, the Liberals realized that an idea of citizenship among the people was needed. They
therefore attempted to construct citizenship through secular education, the
National Guard, and patriotic institutions and rituals, such as *juntas patrióticas* (patriotic committees) and even brass bands. The most important of these
was, perhaps, the National Guard. Guy Thomson's studies of the Sierra Puebla
indicate that the National Guard, comprised of mestizos and Indians—the
bottom of the social hierarchy—shifted the balance of power in the region
away from the clergy and Conservatives. In Sierra Puebla, Juan Lucas recruited
for the National Guard using incentives rather than the *leva* (draft) or other
types of coercion. Recruits got tax exemptions, pay, promises of land, and protection against conscription or military service outside the region. Those who
did not serve could contribute supplies or taxes. For these soldiers, the Guard
embodied the nation (at war) at the same time that it inculcated localism and
local concerns.

The juntas patrióticas were organized to celebrate the anniversaries of important national events, such as the Grito de Dolores and the Cinco de Mayo.
These fiesta days had an educational component, because they invariably included the participation of school children. While music and fireworks hardly
indicated a sense of citizenship, they certainly were beginnings for tying local
with national concerns.

The Restoration

Juárez returned triumphantly to Mexico City in May 1867. The Conservatives were finally defeated and consigned to oblivion. In the next few years,

Juárez would rule over the beginnings of what some have called the second Mexican revolution (the first was Independence). The Restoration marked the transition from the mainly creole hombres de bien who had ruled Mexico since the 1820s to a new generation of mestizo and Indian leaders. In nine-teenth-century Mexico, however, no victory was ever complete. The split be-tween radical (*puro*) and moderate Liberals, always lurking beneath the contrived unity of the War of the Reform and the French Intervention, burst out in the late 1860s in the Restored Republic. The moderates advocated a strong executive and central state, primarily to bring about order and to en-courage economic development. The main battles during the Liberal Restora-tion were fought over the nature of the relationship between the national government and the states and between the state and national governments and the municipalities. Some historians believe that villages and municipali-ties quite clearly modified Liberalism, at least on the level of the localities, by making it more democratic. Nonetheless, in the long term the authoritarian version of liberalism won out.

From the outset the Restoration was not a triumph for democracy. Juárez asked for and Congress consented to the suspension of constitutional rights nine times in nine years, for a total of 49 of the 112 months of the Restored Re-public. The president also held extraordinary powers throughout all but 57 days of this period. The Mexican Congress, which with considerable courage had consistently defended the nation against executive excesses for four decades, nearly disappeared from the political horizon.

There was no peace either. During this period, a large number of insur-rections erupted and banditry was endemic. Uncertainty was everywhere. There were endless rumors that parts of Mexico were to be torn off and an-nexed by the United States or established as independent entities. Juárez needed to reestablish order and tranquility, but he confronted two immedi-ate problems: the enormous military created to defeat the Conservatives and the French, and the fate of those who had collaborated with the French. His first important measure was to reduce the size of the military by seventy-five percent from its peak of 80,000 in July 1867. Juárez, despite the harshness of his execution of Maximilian, exhibited a pragmatic generosity toward many collaborators. He ended the confiscation of their property and eventually a general amnesty was legislated.

The Presidential Election of 1871

Juárez won a three-way presidential election in 1871 among Sebastián Lerdo, Porfirio Díaz, and himself, using incumbency to utmost advantage. Although Juárez constructed an efficient political machine that controlled the electoral system, he did not receive a majority. The Juarista Congress reelected him president. Porfirio Díaz represented the new impatient generation, which felt its time had come and, as such, remained a long-term threat to Juárez. Luckily for Juárez, however, the Porfiristas were divided over whether to acquire power peacefully or by rebellion.

The opposition to Juárez protested voting fraud—with undoubted justification. Díaz determined that he could not attain the presidency by election and his followers proclaimed the Plan de la Noria rebellion. Many factions sided with Díaz in their disgruntlement with Juárez. Rebels raised the issues of local autonomy and privatization of land. This odd revolt—concentrated in Oaxaca, the northeastern states, the Pacific coast, and Puebla—featured only one major battle, which took place at La Bufa near Zacatecas in March 1872, where the rebels were defeated. Díaz exhibited a degree of ambivalence about the movement, which was disorganized and poorly led. Amazingly, Díaz did not participate in a single battle fought on his behalf! The rebellion ended with the death of Juárez (by natural causes) in July 1872. Lerdo as president of the Supreme Court then ascended to the presidency and quickly issued amnesties to the rebels.

Sebastián Lerdo de Tejada won new elections called after the death of Juárez, but the next four years were filled with local upheavals, assassinations, and disruptions. Before entering politics, Lerdo had begun studies for the priesthood and then switched to an academic career. Changing careers again, he served in the governments of Santa Anna and Comonfort. He was a cabinet member of Juárez's government during the Intervention. He emerged as one of the heroes of the courageous internal exile, standing with Juárez in the most difficult times. As a result, Lerdo entered office with much good will. The fifteen-year rule of Juárez was over; people expected a different outlook. Lerdo, however, kept the same political apparatus intact in order to maintain himself in power.

The new president sought to enforce the Reform Laws, especially those concerning religion, such as limitations on clerical garb in public and bell ringing, the institution of civil registry for births and marriages, abolition of religious vows, suppression of religious orders, and banning religious processions and festivals, which no previous Liberal governments had implemented. When combined with his efforts to rein in local and state governance, these measures resulted in widespread tension and conflict. Lerdo, like Juárez, was firmly convinced of the need for a strong executive. Toward this end he succeeded in reinstituting a bicameral Congress with the addition of the Senate, reestablished in 1874. The Senate had wide-ranging authority to intervene in state politics. Lerdo used this power to further exert his influence.

Like his predecessor, Lerdo sought reelection. The up-and-comers, however, had not learned patience in defeat and rebelled again. The Plan de Tuxtepec rebellion erupted in January 1876. Its motto was "no reelection." Díaz, again the leader of the outsiders, drew support from many ex-army officers left with no patronage after the wars ended in 1867. It is also likely that he drew behind-the-scenes support from Conservatives and clergy, who saw him as a moderating force. He also apparently received support from a number of Texas cattle barons. On the other hand, the regular army and most state governors remained loyal to Lerdo. Ironically, the rebellion established the script for Díaz's downfall thirty-five years later. The Porfiristas fought guerrilla warfare with the goal of starting brushfires in as many places as possible, which would eventually overwhelm the government. Lerdo's problems were compounded in October 1876, when José María Iglesias, the president of the Supreme Court, also pronounced revolt against him. This betrayal left him with no hope of maintaining his power. Díaz took the capital in December 1876. A new era began.

Ramifications

The decade of civil strife that included the War of the Reform and the French Intervention had torn the nation asunder. Endless violence magnified everything from alliances to rivalries. In some regions the violence had been unprecedented.

Clearly, the Liberals had won, settling a number of the political disputes once and for all. Mexico would never again have a monarch, at least named as such. The Liberals pushed aside the Catholic Church, which would never again have an official public place in politics and society. Capitalist economic development with strong orientation toward an export base was the wave of the future.

Other issues were not resolved. Although the Liberals were proponents of federalism, they had deep misgivings about its compatibility with their plans for economic development. The contradictions that resulted from their promotion of order and progress, while adhering to the concept of a weak central state were out in the open for all to see. The dying gasps of federalism were to have wide-ranging effects on life at the local level.

Politics were still very much local phenomena. Each level had its hierarchy. Pre-colonial and colonial tradition and years of war had evolved a system of paternalistic patron-client relations, which heavily relied on village, municipal, and district leaders who acted as brokers or intermediaries between the local entity and the next higher authorities.

Each village had a cacique, usually a village official or a school teacher, who might have a store or lend money, to whom villagers looked to for advice on legal matters. The modernizing Liberals added more local officials, such as captains in the National Guard and justices of the peace. The new liberal cacique (local boss), usually the president of the ayuntamiento, was not appointed from above like before, but elected from the community. He was supposed to represent the community in the outside world. Another kind of cacique was the *jefe político* or district boss. These men were almost always whites (*gente de razón*). The crucial aspect of the caciques' authority was their control over taxation and access to land.

The lives of the lower classes, especially in the countryside, began to change. For the first time upward mobility existed for Indians, for war opened the doors. Indians became municipal officials after successful careers in the National Guard. There was an Indian in the presidential palace. A mestizo general became dictator in 1877. To be sure, most Indians possessed little more than local identity, despite migration and increased contact with other communities. Nonetheless, years of warfare had thrown people together. The population became more mobile. Language barriers had eroded.

Civil war and Intervention left hard memories. Indian villages had experienced their women raped, their property stolen, and their children taken for the draft against their will. There was much physical destruction. Moreover, country people confronted a new era that offered them endless challenges to their traditions. The presidency of Benito Juárez presented only the beginning of the transformations to come. Porfirio Díaz and his lieutenants would threaten the very essence of their culture.

Chapter 7

EVERYDAY LIFE, 1849–76: THE IMPACT OF WAR

The wars and Reform Laws of mid-century disrupted all aspects of Mexican society from landholding patterns to gender relations. The brutal civil strife, which raged from 1854 to 1867, killed hundreds of thousands of people and inflicted enormous hardship on soldiers and civilians alike. The fighting also caused incalculable damage to commerce and industry.

Repercussions from the wars continued for several years thereafter. Thousands of unemployed soldiers, unwilling to return to their former status as poor country people, roamed as bandits. Lawlessness and disorder ruled. Since casualties of war hit disproportionately among males, the resulting demographic imbalance affected marriage and migration patterns for a generation. The Reform Laws, most especially the Ley Lerdo and the expropriation law of 1859, profoundly altered relations among rural people. They created unprecedented opportunity to redistribute property wealth by privatizing large amounts of land formerly owned by the Catholic Church or held collectively by rural communities. Mexican rural dwellers would continue to experience the reverberations of these laws for the next fifty years.

The effects of the Reform Laws were equally important in the cities. In the immediate aftermath of the Reform, some urban areas, like Mexico City, had a turnover rate of fifty percent in the ownership of buildings and lots. Renters in the cities had their lives turned upside down. Concurrent with the wars,

Profound thanks the following scholars and other observers upon whose research and writings I have relied for this chapter: Ana Alonso, Jan Bazant, Charles Berry, Margaret Chowning, Moises González Navarro, Michael Johns, Jonathan Kandell, Robert Knowlton, Frederick Ober, María de la Luz Parcero, Brantz Mayer, Ricardo Rendón, Heather Fowler Salamini, Carl Sartorius, Frederick Shaw, Guy Thomson, John Tutino, and Stuart Voss.

Mexico had begun to feel the full force of the technological advances developed during the nineteenth century. These would deeply affect the way Mexicans viewed and experienced rural and urban workplaces. The 1848–77 period marked both the nadir of the dismal conditions of everyday life in Mexico and the initial stage of their modernization (but not necessarily improvement).

As Mexico turned from war to peace and reconstruction, its people confronted new challenges to adapt to these changes. Through it all, of course, Mexicans survived and lived their lives, having good times as well as bad. A small minority prospered. Though many aspects of life remained as they had for centuries, few Mexicans would ever be the same. The era of the civil wars and reform at mid-century ushered in a new Mexico, which its people resisted, at times fiercely, but whose emergence proved impossible to halt.

The transformations of everyday life and politics intertwined. Local government presided over much of the redistribution of wealth brought on by the Reform Laws. It determined the extent and pace of implementation. In many areas, sympathetic local authorities could and did delay the implementation of laws for decades. Thus, as the national Liberal government pushed for the end of communal landholding, control over village, municipal, and district authorities became more critical than ever to the everyday existence of average men and women. A way of life was at stake.

The Impact of the Civil Wars

Without a massive investigation of local records throughout Mexico, we will probably never compile even a reasonably accurate estimate of the physical destruction of property and the loss of life caused by the civil wars and the French Intervention. They most certainly took an enormous toll. The contending armies left a wake of devastation. The U.S. consul in Veracruz reported in 1859 that haciendas were abandoned, ranchos deserted, and villages pillaged and sacked. And this was an assessment made when another eight years of hard fighting lay ahead. Carlton Beals (writing long afterwards) described conditions similarly:

> Already the countryside was desolate. Robbers swarmed on all sides; bandits . . . swept into towns, first one band, then the other, looting, burning, murdering, raping. Scarcely a village had a girl under twenty-five left, even the ugliest ones had been forcibly carried off. . . . On the roads were few travelers; the inns had been burned down, mills abandoned, fields laid waste,

cane fields trampled down by cavalry of either faction. Walls had great holes like toothless mouths. . . . An army of children, of adults, of ragged old folk with hungry faces, begged . . . with shrill, weeping voices.

The consequences of these conflicts, however, went far beyond the brutality of battle. War thoroughly disrupted commerce. Merchants faced intermittent forced loans, erratic taxation, and currency scarcities. Agricultural production suffered because the military draft created labor shortages. Rural routines were in shambles. Hacendados had to adapt to labor losses resulting from the draft. Haciendas and villages had to survive the ravages of foraging armies, which constantly demanded provisions from their already depleted supplies. A substantial part of the population became transient. Soldiers, unwilling to return to their status as landless country people, shunned returning home and turned instead to banditry. Gangs of bandits became commonplace, contributing to a widespread sense of insecurity. Urban areas suffered equally. One observer described Mexico City as "great stretches of abandoned terrain, vast mud holes, and swelling trash heaps," with rampant misery and marauding gangs.

The combination of casualties and reduced numbers of men of marriageable age had extensive demographic and social repercussions. As part of a natural readjustment to the large number of male military deaths during the war with the United States, men married younger. There were fifty percent fewer bachelors in 1848 than earlier. The same male casualties caused the number of widows to rise dramatically from 33 to 35 percent of all women in 1811 to 41 percent in 1848. There were also many single-parent households led by women, who raised their children alone. As the civil wars intensified during the next two decades, it is likely that these numbers grew larger.

War brought about a substantial flow of people, mostly women without prospects of employment or marriage, who moved from the countryside into the cities. Many women between the ages of fifteen and thirty-nine sought employment as domestics. Given the low regard society paid to domestic service, we can imagine how difficult life was in the war-torn countryside for women to push them to migrate. In cities such as Zacatecas, where migrants made up a substantial portion of the residents, the proportion of women in the population far exceeded fifty percent.

There were more women working in 1848 than previously. The loss of young men and migration allowed women to enter the workforce in greater numbers and also, in some instances, to upgrade their occupations. A few gained access to formerly all-male occupations and, as a result, the proportion of women who labored as domestic servants declined. If we exclude laundresses, cooks, and porters, the number of maids as a percentage of female employees decreased from 54 to 30 percent. If we include these three categories, the decline was somewhat less dramatic, from 57 to 43 percent. Food services and commerce took up the slack. Seamstresses increased from 3 to 14 percent of working women.

In the countryside the wars affected relations between hacendados and their peons. Successive governments demanded that peons serve in the civic militia (leva or draft). The republican government meted out harsh punishment, such as fines and prison terms, for those who tried to evade conscription. It regarded evading the leva as treason. But many hacienda administrators, desperate for workers, did their utmost to keep their peons from the clutches of the leva. Caught between government demands on one side and a combination of the need to preserve their labor force and a moral obligation to protect their employees on the other, hacendados commonly handed over a few of their peons to authorities in order to save the majority. Labor scarcity forced hacendados to provide additional incentives, such as wage advances, to make sure their employees stayed. Temporarily, the balance tipped in favor of the workers. For example, in order to compensate for the acute shortage of currency during wartime, haciendas had to provide workers with their sustenance in advance. But given the competition for workers, employees were unlikely ever to repay this debt.

The effects of war and reconstruction were not always beneficial to the lower classes. In Michoacán, for example, they may have increased the disparities between rich and poor. There the top ten percent of the elite controlled 44 percent of the total wealth during the 1850s compared with only 32 percent in the two previous decades.

War polarized the politics of everyday life. In Morelos, for instance, confrontations between villages and haciendas over land and water not only increased, but grew more embittered. Traditional rivalries between villages deepened, the result of assassinations, plunder, and atrocities committed in wartime. In areas such as the Puebla Sierra hard feelings left over from the civil wars lasted for years. Insurrections marred the region for a decade after the departure of the French. The civil conflicts had not only set village against village, but fragmented villages internally as well. With their shifting local alliances, the civil wars upset the balance of social and ethnic power. The land redistribution mandated by the Reform Laws only intensified these tensions.

The Reform Laws

To the victorious Liberals, traditional landholding villages obstructed progress; they were symbols of the colonial past, which held back the nation. The Liberals believed it was crucial to transform land into a commodity and to change country people into wage laborers or capitalist agricultural entrepreneurs. At the same time the Liberals sought to break down local loyalties and replace them with a sense of national citizenship. Conversely, country people wanted to maintain their communal landholding and local autonomy. For the most part they successfully resisted the Liberal program until the mid-1880s, when Porfirio Díaz strengthened the central government.

The Liberals' Reform Laws were intended to create a middle class of modest urban property owners and small farmers. With this in mind, the laws gave tenants the first opportunity to purchase Church property. Although in the short term, the result was a massive shift in land ownership both in urban and rural areas, often to small proprietors, in the long term the Reform Laws led to the increased concentration of land ownership. The worst excesses, however, would not come until after the construction of an extensive railroad network. Few tenants had the necessary funds to sustain the payments required to purchase urban or rural properties made available by the Reform Laws, despite provisions in legislation for extended payment schedules. Given the precarious employment possibilities in major cities, the average tenant had a difficult enough time putting food on the table, let alone servicing a mortgage. Individuals with ready cash, not the poor, took advantage of the opportunities furnished by the Reform Laws. In the cities, for example, merchants obtained two-thirds of the properties sold off by or expropriated from the Church for sale to the public. Professionals and government officials bought the remaining third. Mexicans purchased two-thirds and foreigners one-third of the properties.

The expropriation of Church lands and the legislation that ended the legality of corporate, collective community holdings profoundly affected the countryside. The symbiotic but conflictual relationship between Indian villages and large estates began to change at mid-century, because land prices rose as the economy righted itself after decades of civil war and foreign intervention. Since there were no limitations on individual acquisitions, the law created a new class of large landowners. This process was at work in Oaxaca where many original buyers of Church properties could not maintain payments and soon resold their newly acquired properties.

Serious challenges to corporate village landholding began in some areas as early as the 1860s. Namiquipa, a village in the foothills (sierra) in the western part of the state of Chihuahua, suffered huge land losses to a hacendado, a foreigner named Enrique Müller. In Namiquipa, although the village held lands communally, access was traditionally individual. Men had earned the use of their own plot as a reward for (often) gallant military service in the Indian wars. The commodification of land under the Liberals, then, not only inserted a new set of economic relationships into village life, but altered traditional values and status as well.

To the Chihuahuans who resided in pueblos like Namiquipa their well-being and honor were tied up in the land they cultivated. As seen in chapter 1, the essence of manhood in rural communities was inextricably entwined with control of the land, which enabled the head of household to provide for his family. Without access to land either through individual or collective ownership, lease, sharecropping, or residency on a hacienda, men could not feed their families. They could not be men without the land. In Namiquipa and other villages in the north, when the Indian wars ended in the mid-1880s, peace shut off the main road to honor and status. Coupled with the widespread assault on small, individual, and collective landholding that began at the same time, elimination of access to land via reward for military service shook their society to its very core. Until the mid-1880s regional elites, needing the support of the villages in their internecine squabbles, had left the communal lands alone. The advent of the railroads increased property values, however, and the villages suffered a heavy onslaught against their land by the very same elites who once had sought them as allies.

The land redistribution laws disrupted everyday life on several other levels as well. Most tenants could not afford to buy the property they rented and had to adjust to new ownership. The Church had generally been an excellent landlord, because it charged reasonable rents. Although tenants were protected by the Reform Laws, in that they could stay for three years without any alteration of their lease contract, conflicts arose immediately. Because of loyalty to the Church, many tenants renounced their rights to buy the land they rented. In places like Guadalajara, out of loyalty to the Church tenants refused to pay rents to the new owners.

The Reform Laws intruded on other aspects of everyday life, often to the dismay of country people. To some village residents, the Liberals' establishment of state-run public schools usurped responsibilities better left to fam-

ily and church. Families, most especially mothers, were expected to teach the
tenets of honor and propriety. It was the father's exclusive right to discipline
his children. As a result, country people viewed state education as an in-
fringement on patriarchal authority. The residents of the Chihuahuan sierra,
for example, believed that the government's appropriation of church functions concerning marriage dishonored women. Civil marriages challenged
male control over female sexuality and reproduction. Country people saw this
as a threat to the purity of their women.

The Liberal program threatened the core of everyday life and political in-
teractions among people. From the mid-1850s, Liberals sought to establish law
and rationality as the principles of government. They sought to substitute
(at least in theory) electoral democracy for patron-client relations and authoritarian rule. In terms of daily life this meant that Liberals worked to
change the foundation of crucial institutions and relations. The Reform also
altered the dealings between hacendado and country people, among villagers,
between landlord and tenant, and between husband and wife. For the Liberals marriage was grounded on a profound contract, not coercion. While the
Liberals did not challenge the fundamental authority of a husband over his
wife and children, aspects of this authority were changed by law. Until this
time the state (and the Church) accepted the right of husbands to beat their
wives as a form of discipline. The criminal code of 1871, however, included wife
beating in the category of common crime. In the extreme case, a man could
no longer murder his adulterous wife without punishment; he would spend
four years in prison.

Another 1859 law regulated marriage and divorce, declaring marriage both
a civil contract and sacred union. Liberal reforms did not grant women suffrage or citizenship, nor did they alter women's submission to men. The civil
code of 1870 obligated men to feed and protect their wives, and women were
to obey their husbands, who continued to control their wives' property. The
law maintained the double standard for adultery. If a woman committed adultery, then it was grounds for divorce, but for men adultery was grounds for divorce only if abuse accompanied philandering. The Liberals created enormous
pressure on traditional, patriarchal values, because they enacted these new
laws at a time when the basis of manhood, the ability to feed and shelter one's
family, was under threat.

The New Workplace

Mid-century began the transition from artisan to factory production of manufactured goods. The introduction of modern machinery, first in the textile industry, reduced the need for skilled artisans and started a process of deskilling the workforce. Entrepreneurs established large factories with thousands of employees, some of whom worked in one area and others who labored at home. By the 1850s, local officials were already bemoaning the decline of tailoring, shoemaking, and other traditional crafts. The governor of the state of Querétaro, for example, went so far as to attribute the rise of banditry in his region to the establishment of the modern textile factory, Hercules, which caused extensive unemployment among artisans displaced by machines. These changes would accelerate after the end of the civil wars and the construction of the railroad network in the 1880s.

Secondary Cities

Despite the disruptions, dislocations, and terror of war, life went on. Some of Mexico's large and medium-size cities flourished, perhaps due to the business of war and the energies of migrants from the countryside. Some of these secondary cities remained sleepy with steady routines; everyday life revolved around family, church, work, and market. We have this picture of a Sinaloan municipality at mid-century, painted by Stuart Voss:

> . . . [T]he central, and usually single, plaza was a meeting place for those who brought in their wares and produce from the surrounding countryside. A few shops surrounded the plaza. . . . The plaza was also a gathering place for peddlers, tradespeople, and muleteers to sell livestock and other items stolen from haciendas by bandits or their own peons, small contraband, and other merchandise they had come by legally. . . . A few artisans labored at their trade in shops along the streets near the plaza—baking bread, making shoes, molding pottery. Near the plaza, standing out among the one-story adobe flats of the poor and modest of means, were the well-built homes of the few prominent families of the community, who often owned the haciendas outside of town. Located on one side of the plaza, a focal point of the town, was the parish church, whose priest was usually only slightly better educated than his parishioners. If the town were fortunate, there was a municipal building on the other side of the square, most of the time looking worn and badly in need of repair. . . . [T]he slow pace of life matched the largely static economic activity.

Charles Berry described life in Oaxaca City, a southern state capital, with about 20,000 inhabitants at mid-century, in much the same terms. People rose early, some as early as 3:00 A.M., to recite the Rosary (prayers), followed by a procession (a parade of worshipers and clergy) that marched around the town for half an hour ending with a snack of chocolate. Most residents heard mass at 5:00 A.M. Marketing and house chores filled up the hours before breakfast at 9:00 A.M. Children went to school. The male head of household went to work. The female continued to labor at home. At noon there was a light meal of fruit, and more prayers. The whole family came together at 2:00 P.M. for dinner and an hour's siesta. The men returned to work, while the women gathered in the veranda to sew until evening prayers, which they recited at dusk. The family ate a light dinner at 7:00 P.M. An hour later there were more prayers. Conversation took up the remainder of the evening until 9:00. Life revolved around family, church, and meals.

While Oaxaca City was undoubtedly more pleasant than noisy, smelly Mexico City, it suffered many of the same problems. Most important was the terrible incidence of disease. Intestinal parasites and respiratory ailments struck many of the residents. Oaxaca endured deadly cholera epidemics in 1833 and 1854 and smallpox in 1851–52.

By the 1830s Zacatecas, a city of 25,000 in the center of an important mining district, had recovered from devastating losses during the Independence era, only to slide back during the succeeding tumultuous decades. Puebla, too, had undergone a resurgence, becoming by the 1850s an industrial city, mainly producing textiles. Its factories, equipped with modern machinery, turned out half of the nation's textiles. The city also had a large porcelain factory. Veracruz, in 1856 a city with a population of 10,000, underwent a boom. Although it had suffered badly in the war with the United States, the city revived with the establishment in 1850 of daily stagecoach and telegraph service between Veracruz and Mexico City. Veracruz remained an unhealthy place, however, for yellow fever struck every year.

Mexico City

Mid-century brought the beginning of the physical relocation of the middle and upper classes to the western sections of the city. The massive sell-off of Church property—half of the city's buildings—during the late 1850s created new landlords who carved up older buildings into apartments and shops. In the 1860s the wealthy moved from the central zone around the Zocalo. The refurbishment of the Alameda Park and the construction of the massive boulevard, which later came to be known as the Paseo de la Reforma during the Maximilian era, pushed the rich into the new residential districts in the western part of the city.

Ironically, the initial force behind the beautification of the capital came in the 1860s from the French invaders and Maximilian. As soon as the French arrived, they poured funds into the city. Typical of the Intervention, the new regime paved the streets with cobblestones, but because they had not adequately accounted for the city's poor drainage, the cobblestones were soon lost underneath the mud produced by recurrent flooding that had tormented the city since the colonial era. The empire also installed gas lighting. Maximilian and Carlota remodeled Chapultepec Castle in grand style to suit their royal tastes. The emperor then built the grand boulevard to connect the park and castle to the Alameda. Whatever the invaders' efforts to make the capital the rival of Paris and London, in the end they did little to enhance its livability. As the city grew, conditions for the multitudes became more crowded. Then as now the management of Mexico City was beyond the capabilities of Mexican governments.

Food, Clothing, and Shelter

For most Mexicans the fabric of everyday life, the food they ate, the housing that sheltered them, and the clothing that covered them, remained much the same throughout these tumultuous decades. Nowhere were disparities between social classes as clear as in these three basic aspects of daily existence.

The average Mexican's diet, as it had in earlier eras, generally consisted of maize, beans, squash, and chiles with small amounts of eggs, pork, meat, and cheese. The essential dietary element was the corn tortilla. Women shucked the corn and soaked the kernels in water with small bits of limestone, which loosened the sheath of the corn, imbued it with calcium, and increased the content of amino acids. The latter created proteins from the mix of corn and beans, crucial in a diet that lacked meat. Next the women beat the corn in the metate (grinding bowl) for hours. Finally, small pieces of the resulting dough were worked between the hands, tossed and patted and flattened out, until no thicker than a knife blade, after which they were thrown on the steaming hot *comal* (griddle). The combination of maize tortillas and beans (tucked inside the folded tortilla) was not only delicious, but also provided almost all of the required daily protein. Squash, which is made up of ninety percent water, supplied badly needed liquid in an arid land, and filler to make meals more satisfying. Chiles added to the beans were the source of crucial vitamins A, B, and C and also killed bacteria that caused intestinal disorders.

For the wealthy food was plentiful, varied, and rich. Meals were leisurely. In the morning at 8:00 they partook of a small cup of chocolate with sweets. Two hours later, they ate a hearty breakfast of roasted or stewed meat, eggs, and beans (boiled soft and then fried with fat and onions). Dinner was at three in the afternoon. It began with a cup of clear broth, followed by highly seasoned rice or some other starch, beef or mutton, pork, fowl, and sausages, various vegetables and fruits, and dessert. After such repast a siesta (nap) was in order. At six there was a warm drink of chocolate or in summer a cold, sweet beverage. Cigars and conversation or a walk followed. Wealthy families ate supper at 10:00 P.M. Roasted meat, salad, beans, and sweets comprised this "light" meal. Domestics served all meals on elegant china and silverware with tablecloths and napkins.

Tortilla seller

A middle-class diet in Mexico City consisted of the following. Breakfast started with a hot drink, chocolate for the adults or *atole* (a corn gruel) for the children. Toast, biscuits, or pastries with coffee and milk came next. At 11 A.M. chocolate or atole was drunk with anisette. The large meal served in mid-afternoon consisted of bread, soup, a roast, eggs in chile, vegetables, beans flavored with pickled onion, cheese, and sauce. Dessert was honey with grated orange on a toasted tortilla. A light dinner in the evening was comprised of *mole* (a spicy sauce), stewed meat, and a lettuce salad. The serving staff was more modest in these homes than in the mansions of the rich.

The diet of the urban poor was far less nutritious and satisfying and hardly plentiful, but sufficient for survival. Pastry or brioche rolls with atole and clear tea or aguardiente made up breakfast. During the day, corn tortillas, beans, and chile with bits of unappetizing meat or fat, all purchased from street vendors and restaurants, sustained them. The poor took few, if any, meals at home for there was no place in their crowded rooms for cooking appliances. Bread was far too expensive for the poor. The tortilla was used as fork and spoon.

The sale of contaminated, spoiled, and adulterated food was woefully common. Unscrupulous bakers were known to substitute rust and lead for more expensive ingredients. Because wealthy capitalinos feared the masses with their long history of riots in times of shortages, Mexico City's municipal government made sporadic efforts to sustain low staple prices. The water was, as discussed previously, unhealthy.

In the countryside meals for the poor were more plentiful, perhaps, than for the urban working class, but were nonetheless simple. The center of the meal was the corn tortilla, usually filled with beans, sometimes supplemented with an egg and broth of peppers. Vegetables, most commonly squash, and fruit were also central to the rural diet. Water or pulque was drunk with the meal. The more prosperous small farmers, known as *rancheros,* ate more meat, mostly pork. Many farmers raised chickens to be eaten during fiestas. Their eggs, if not sold, comprised the farm families' breakfasts. Lump sugar provided the sweet part of meals.

Differences in dress were also stark. Affluent urban women conformed to the latest fashions from France, often adding traditional Spanish garb, such as the mantilla. Brantz Mayer described one rich woman in Church in the 1840s: "She wore a purple velvet robe embroidered with white silk, white satin shoes, and silk stockings; a mantilla of the richest white blond lace fell over her head and shoulders, and her ears, neck, and fingers were blazing with diamonds." The dandies who frequented the fashionable spots in Mexico City might wear a "French cutaway suit, American patent leather shoes and an English stovepipe hat." The more sedate wore broadcloth suits and silk hats.

Few Mexicans, of course, could afford rich silk and woolen apparel. Frederick Ober described mestizo dress in the early 1880s: "In the warmer regions he wears (on Sundays) a carefully plaited white shirt, wide trousers of white or colored drilling, fastened round the hips by a gay girdle, brown leather gaiters, and broad felt hat, with silver cord or fur band about it." Rancheros wore "open trousers of leather ornamented with silver, with white drawers

A mestiza and a mestizo

showing through, a colored silk handkerchief about the neck, and a *serape*—
the blanket shawl with a slit in the centre. . . ." The women "seldom wear stockings, though. . . . [F]eet are often encased in satin slippers; they have loose,
embroidered chemises, a woolen or calico skirt, while the *rebozo*—a narrow
but long shawl—is drawn over the head, and covers the otherwise exposed
arms and breast."

Most Mexicans dressed in simple, practical clothes. They wore sandals or
went barefoot. Their *huaraches* or footwear were simply and easily made from
rawhide or plaited fibers. Despite the laws that demanded they wear pants and
hats in public, Indian men usually wore a breechcloth. Other rural Mexicans
wore collarless, buttonless cotton shirts and pants with long legs that covered
their feet. Belts were strips of rawhide or cloth. The serape, a brightly covered woolen blanket, was an all-purpose garment that protected its wearer
from the elements. The one common luxury was a hat, usually of straw. Rural
women wore no fancier apparel than the men. Indian women often wore only
a few yards of cloth wrapped around their bodies. Rebozos were used similarly to serapes, protecting women from the elements and, in addition, providing modesty. The rebozo when folded just the right way could be used to
carry small children. Other women wore a scarf bound at the hips with a girdle extended to the feet. A broad mantle with openings at the head and arms
covered the upper part of the body. This wool garment was often ornamented
with colorful embroidery. Wealthier Indian women wore a white petticoat
with embroidery and ribbons. Some girls wore simple white cotton dresses
with the head, neck, shoulders, and legs below the knees left bare. Women also
wore heavy earrings and necklaces of cut glass. On their feet were the same
sandals as on the men or they wore no shoes at all. Mostly they went without head coverings. Often men and women carried rosary beads in religious
devotion.

The vaqueros (cowboys) of the north were, perhaps, more "dashing," according to one traveler:

> . . . [An] Indian, dressed in a pair of leather unmentionables, without sus-
> penders, buttoning from the knee downwards, which are usually left open
> in warm weather for comfort, and to exhibit the white drawers underneath;
> a common cotton shirt . . . ; a red sash tied tightly around the waist; a pair of
> sandals on his feet, and enormous iron spurs on heel; with a heavy conical
> felt hat . . . on head, and a long iron-pointed goad in hand.

As in the case of diet and clothing, housing, too, sharply differentiated the classes. The wealthy lived in opulence. As the century moved on, their conspicuous consumption grew. Carl Sartorius described a mansion in one of Mexico's smaller cities. The house was one story. One entered through a great gate beneath the archway over which was the porter's room or a part of the merchant owner's office. There was a square yard surrounded by a piazza. A fountain adorned the middle with vases of flowers everywhere. Each room opened onto this courtyard. The living room was in front next to the street. It contained fine furniture, religious artwork, and carpets. There were many chairs and sofas, presumably for entertaining family guests. The bedrooms had real beds with imported bed clothing. Opposite the entrance a smaller gate led to a second yard off of which were the stable, coach house, and apartments for the servants. In larger cities houses of the affluent often had two stories. The ground floor in these buildings was for shops or other businesses, while the second floor was for the family.

The house of Vicente Riva Palacio, well-known soldier-statesman and literary figure, located on the Alameda, had fifty rooms. One entered through a vestibule from which branched a spacious stairway leading to the living quarters. The stairs and the floors of the corridors were made of the finest Italian marble. Tropical plants decorated the halls and an aviary was filled with singing birds. Of the numerous rooms, there were three parlors, a grand salon, and two smaller ones. There was also an impressive private chapel adorned with luxurious drapes and beautiful religious ornaments. The dining room, measuring one hundred by fifty feet, contained furniture of mahogany and rosewood. The wooden floor consisted of other rare woods. Mirrors and massive sideboards filled the walls. On these shelves were thousands of pieces of china, crystal, and silver. There was a magnificent silver service sent to the owner's father Mariano Riva Palacio by the Emperor Franz Joseph of Austria for the former's efforts on behalf of the monarch's brother, Maximilian. The more than thirty bedrooms each had a bedspread of velvet, silk, lace, or crochet, each one more elegant than the last. The linen was hand stitched. The bedrooms also had brass bedsteads and canopies. The large living room had furniture with golden trim, fabulous mirrors and chandeliers, and rich carpets. The ceilings were thirty feet high. Finally, the family had its own theater, seating two hundred. Maintenance of this remarkable establishment required thirty-five servants.

In the north hacendados lived more modestly, perhaps, because transportation reduced the access to imported luxuries. Fanny Gooch described one such plain adobe house not far from Saltillo in the 1880s. It was low and flat with pounded dirt floors. The parlor had homemade chairs all around the sides of the room. At one end was a built-in sofa that extended the entire length of the room. Seven hard, stiff pillows decorated with lace adorned it. A "gay chintz" covered the sofa. Since the sofa was high, two feet off the ground, one had to almost leap on to it. There were also some homemade rocking chairs, which were more comfortable.

The typical middle-class home in Mexico City looked something like this, according to social critic Guillermo Prieto:

> A steep stairway led to a corridor paved with red varnished millstones. [The middle class usually lived on the second floor—a location of considerable importance, because of the flooding that periodically afflicted the city—and the servants occupied rooms on the first floor.] The corridor was embellished with cages filled with stuffed birds, squirrels, wind chimes, and earthen crocks packed with stored foods and vegetables. Landscapes . . . adorned the walls. Comfortable chairs and couches . . . furnished the principal chamber. Cuspidors occupied its corners, and a large brazier for cigarettes and heat stood on the floor. In the bedroom were a large bed of fine wood, easy chairs, and wardrobes. The small children of the family slept in the halls. Those of a small family slept with their parents in curtained compartments of the main bedroom. The dining room contained a washstand holding towels, soap, straw, and a scouring stone for scrubbing. Colored vegetables, pots and pans, and jars lined the kitchen walls . . . with strips of garlic and pepper for a festive air. A huge barrel of water stood at its center.

Housing for farmers in the countryside was little more than a hut. Because wood for construction or fuel was very expensive in these deforested or arid areas, neither lumber nor bricks were practical. (Wood was too costly for use in ovens that baked bricks.) The relative availability of wood dictated the range of building materials used in a particular region. Consequently, in temperate climates country people constructed their huts with adobe made from sun-baked straw and mud blocks. In the highlands houses consisted of unburnt brick (or stones plastered with mud) with a flat roof constructed of beams laid close together with a covering of carefully stamped, finely washed clay. Stone walls were built without mortar. In the tropics huts were comprised of saplings and leaves held together with mud. Occupants drove unhewn logs into the ground to support the beams and roof and used bamboo sticks for

Railroad bridge overlooking rural home

the walls. The normal hut measured twenty by fifteen feet with one room, no windows, and no flooring other than packed earth mixed with ashes. Door-ways (without doors) provided ventilation and light. Most commonly roofs were made either with thatch or by laying rows of poles across the tops of walls, and then covering these with one or two feet of dirt and over the dirt a layer of pine boards. Where it was colder, roofs were covered with shingles. Native vegetation, like palm leaves or straw, served in the tropics.

The kitchen area, where a fire burned continuously, was outside or in a sep-arate, smaller building. The ever-present metate for tortillas was beside the fire. Huts had no furniture. Mats known as *petates* served as sleeping pallets. Better-off rural dwellers might have a fancier bed consisting of four mounds of clay crossed with rough boards. No one could afford bedding or mattresses. Men and women slept in their clothes, wrapped in serapes and rebozos in cold weather. Since most people had only the clothes they wore, there was no need for chests or closets. Pottery and baskets stored their possessions and food. The only decoration in the hut was a picture of the Virgin of Guadalupe or a saint. Most regions required no heating and no one could afford it anyway. The more prosperous rancheros lived in slightly less simple abodes. They might have a bench, table, and board beds with mats with skins for pillows. There were low stools around the table for mealtimes.

The Countryside

For most Mexicans the routines of life remained constant. Rural women arose at four to grind maize. They drew the water, brought the wood for the fire, cared for the children, prepared three meals, did the wash, and spun and weaved. They made pottery and then hauled it to the Sunday market. It was very common that, if the men hired on at the hacienda, the women's work was included either as a field hand or as a domestic in the hacienda house. Women received no pay. In the Veracruz coffee region, for example, the ranchero's wife concerned herself mostly with household and children, except in the three or four months of coffee harvesting and processing. As one traveler observed, "Picking the ripe berries, cleaning, and drying them is the work of women and children, and is all the easier, as they continue to ripen from November till March and the harvests can therefore be got in most leisurely." Market day each week in the village, when Indians from surrounding towns sold their pro-duce and bought what they needed, provided a respite from the dull and routine. All was not work, for at the market women vendors had the opportunity to gossip and laugh with friends.

Perhaps the most important difference compared to the past was the number of people who were transients. Often there was not enough work in any one place for subsistence. In Guanajuato, for example, in the 1860s peons labored for miserable wages on haciendas for three months, then wandered from region to region during the rest of the year. "They lived for the day, without house, without family, without fate, on the margins of any notions of morality."

On the haciendas life continued as it had since Independence with adjustments for such factors as labor shortages due to war. As discussed in chapter 1, there were four types of workers: permanent resident peons, known as *peónes acasillados* or gañanes, who comprised a minority of the workforce; temporary laborers employed at planting or harvest, who carried out most of the work, and who came from the ranks of inhabitants of neighboring villages, or small landowners who sought to supplement their incomes; tenants; and sharecroppers. Debt peonage was prevalent in a few areas, most notably Yucatán, where peons had to work without pay on Mondays. There were some efforts to mitigate this onerous institution. Maximilian, for example, outlawed the company store in 1865. As we will see, conditions on the haciendas in agricultural export regions worsened considerably after 1880.

Wash day

Even with the general outline presented above, it is not easy to reconstruct what it was like on an actual working estate. Fortunately, the fates have preserved a number of illuminating documents. We have detailed employment records for the early 1850s for the Hacienda de Bocas, located thirty-five miles north of San Luis Potosí. Bocas had between 350 and 400 permanent workers. The better-off minority of these had free title to land they used for a house, corral, and cultivation. These workers lived either on or around the hacienda casco (the hacendado's house). They were "subject to work discipline as a price for their rights." The best-treated permanent workers also received a corn ration.

One of the permanent workers, Pioquinto Liñán, was illustrative of the practices of the hacienda regarding this relatively privileged group of fifty-five. He earned six pesos a month, slightly less than 1.50 pesos a week with a weekly corn ration of fifteen liters. Since this was not enough to feed his family—one liter a day per adult was necessary for sustenance—Pioquinto purchased another seven or eight liters a week on account for 0.125 pesos each, leaving him with roughly fifty centavos a week to cover all the family's other expenses. The worker received a plot of 3,000 square meters for which he paid no rent. He bought seed for planting from the hacienda. Other purchases during the year included food, huaraches (sandals), leather pants, and a burial. His expenditures totaled just over 72 pesos for the year, approximately the same amount as his annual salary. Another group of 265 permanent workers earned a daily wage that totaled 1.30 pesos a week without a corn ration. It is likely that the more trusted permanent workers, like Pioquinto, supervised these men to see that they actually performed their assigned tasks. Pioquinto's kin, Jacinto Liñán, as one of this category of workers, spent much of his salary on corn. Although he had to expend 4 pesos on a funeral, he managed to end the year only a half peso in debt. The last group of permanent workers were known as muchachos (boys). They earned 3.75 pesos a month. They were probably young married men without children.

Temporary workers' circumstances on Bocas were not nearly as favorable. Depending on the season, they ranged in numbers from 100 to 500 and earned the equivalent of 10 pesos a month if they labored thirty days, which most did not. Nor did temporary workers have the guarantee of subsistence rations provided the permanent workforce. Many of Bocas's tenants also worked as temporary labor on the hacienda. It was necessary for temporary laborers to have had additional sources of income or sustenance, for otherwise they would have lived "on the edge of misery and hunger."

The 794 tenants on Bocas in 1852 fell into three categories, according to whether they rented pasture and cropland, only pasture, or only their home site. Approximately 200 sharecroppers were also on the hacienda's books. It appears that on Bocas, the hacendados selected hardworking peons already employed on the estate to become sharecroppers. Sharecroppers handed over half their harvest to the landlord. Although there were varying results for individuals, it is clear that neither tenants nor sharecroppers made ends meet without supplementing their incomes with temporary work for the hacienda.

Commercialization of agriculture altered the landscape. On the one hand it led to concentration of landholding and worsening working conditions. On the other, it provided considerable new opportunities. In the mid-1850s, for example, the landowners of Córdoba, Veracruz, renovated their plantations to grow sugar, coffee, and tobacco. The demand for workers to farm the new crops brought about a considerable influx of migrants. In the Chalco region north of Mexico City in the decade after the war with the United States, large landowners modernized through the introduction of new seeds, manure fertilizer, and modern implements to increase the yield of staple crops. At the same time, they began dairy operations. These innovations, like those in Veracruz, worsened an already existing labor shortage and exacerbated conflicts with neighboring villages, because of increased demands for water resources. Villagers challenged the estate owners in court and, when that failed, resorted to taking matters into their own hands. As a result, in the late 1840s and 1850s the central highland basins around the capital quite commonly broke out in violence.

In both regions commercialization created a niche for small farmers. A new group of producers known as rancheros arose in Veracruz on lands leased to them in perpetuity by town councils. These rancheros cultivated subsistence crops with small surpluses sold in local markets. Coffee proved the perfect commodity for family farms. One person could tend 5,000 trees. Rancheros grew subsistence crops in between the coffee trees or on small plots and, during the rainy months, planted beans, tomatoes, chiles, and bananas. One of the adaptations large landowners made in Chalco was to institute sharecropping arrangements, until then quite rare. Dismayed by low profits, and the fact that they could not attract workers with traditionally low wages, they turned to sharecropping because it did not require them to use scarce cash for wages. If the crop failed, the estate lost little. If the harvest was good, the estate obtained half the value for little investment. The tradeoff was to accept minimal profits in return for low risk.

Country people needed to supplement their incomes on the estates one way or another. Sharecropping was the only possibility and so they took the opportunity, and gained control over production. The problem was that when droughts or other climatic catastrophes ruined crops, sharecroppers suffered badly. In earlier times, country people earned their wages regardless of the outcome of the harvest. Now there were no such guarantees. Commercialization of agriculture, then, increased the insecurity of small producers, while increasing the profits and economic power of the estate owners.

Entertainment

As miserable as statistics and anecdotal evidence depict everyday life in Mexico, all was not grim. People found ways to enjoy their lives. The Church, family, drinking, and gambling were the most common sources of everyday entertainment for people of all classes. The solemn Church masses were spectacles in and of themselves. The rites and rituals, resplendent priests, and majestic music surely were the best entertainment of the time. While no parish in the capital nor anywhere else duplicated the magnificence of the great cathedral in Mexico City, there were many inspiring churches elsewhere to stir the people. Even in villages with their modest chapels, a visiting clergyman might put on a good show without the trappings of opulence.

Religious fiestas took up a large number of days; in Aguascalientes in the 1860s there were forty per year. They were both occasions of solemn consideration and joyous fun. The cities, towns, and villages prepared carefully for these celebrations. Streets were repaired and cleaned. Processions marked the special days. On Palm Sunday the march represented Jesus's entrance into Jerusalem. On Good Friday the crucifixion procession took place. Repentant sinners paraded half naked with crowns of thorns. Mexico City celebrated Corpus Christi in "uncommon splendor." The archbishop conducted high mass in the great cathedral in the Zocalo after which he led a grand parade from the church through adjacent streets, walking under a canopy of white linen decorated with a red border. Everyone who was anyone—presidents, generals, cabinet ministers—appeared in full regalia. The procession was a time to show off. The wealthy displayed their fine clothes, perhaps imported from Paris. The surrounding homes were decked out with carpets, flowers, flags, and streamers. A vast crowd made up of people of different races, colors, and costumes watched the pageantry. What a sight!

Going to Mass

Corpus Christi in a large Indian village was more modest than celebrated on the main square in Mexico City, but impressive nonetheless. In the square in front of the church the people constructed a green avenue of trees, branches, and flowers at the top and sides. Flower altars stood at each corner of the plaza. Flowers were everywhere. Wonderful scents burned. Animals were sacrificed.

All Saints and All Souls or the Day of the Dead, celebrated in late October and early November, required an enormous effort. The celebrants burned massive numbers of candles and consumed large quantities of food. Poor Indians expended years of earnings in remembrance of loved ones who had passed on. The night of the last day of October families decorated their homes with flowers and candles and set out a colorful mat on which they lay a feast to lure the dead children back: chocolate, sweet maize porridge, stewed chicken, tortillas, and maize bread shaped into animals made for this day only. The next day the family repeated the ritual, adding other dishes too hot for children, like turkey mole, and tamales. On this day they offered liquor. The Day of the Dead celebrations indicated that many Mexicans knew death well and they did not fear it.

After the Reform religious processions were banned from the streets (though it is not clear when the laws were first enforced nor is it evident that enforcement was widespread). This did not put much of a damper on celebrations, however, for there were enough feast days and festivals to keep people quite busy.

Drinking was an important aspect of religious celebrations and, perhaps, for many a crucial outlet for alleviating the pain of daily life. As seen in chapter 9, it became a serious problem among the poor as the alienation of urban life and industrialized working conditions became widespread at century's end. Made from the maguey (agave) plant, pulque had been the alcoholic drink of the region since Toltec times (1000 CE). This cactus has leaves of up to ten feet in length, a foot wide, and eight inches thick. After some years it sends up a giant flower stalk twenty to thirty feet high, on which grow greenish yellow flowers. The plant dies after it blooms. Just before the plant is about to emit its stalk the Indians cut into the plant in order to extract the central portion of the stem. The incision leaves only the thick outside rind, forming a natural basin two feet deep and a foot and a half in diameter. The sap that would feed the stem, called *aguamiel* (honey-water), oozes into the core and is extracted. A small amount is taken to ferment for ten to fifteen days. This becomes the *madre pulque,* which acts as a leaven inducing fermentation in the aguamiel. Within twenty-four hours it is pulque. As one draws off the pulque, one adds aguamiel to the mix. A good maguey yields eight to sixteen liters of aguamiel a day for as long as three months. Although the pulque has a lumpy consistency and tastes something like stale buttermilk and smells like rotted meat, it is quite nutritious and many believe it helps digestion. The alcoholic content is six percent. Frederick Ober quoted the following verse:

> Know ye not pulque,
> That liquor divine?
> Angels in heaven
> Prefer it to wine.

Many observers of the time believed gambling was a Mexican obsession. Cockfighting was a passion (see Santa Anna). Certainly, it was a nineteenth-century entertainment industry. These fights necessitated considerable preparation. Handlers bred and selected the cocks carefully, fed them strictly, and trained them assiduously. The event required an arena, consisting of a six-foot diameter area fenced in by three-foot boards with benches around it. From the gallery spectators urged on their favorites. Wagers abounded. The spectacle of the birds was bloody and brutal. The brave cocks exhausted themselves, but would not quit until one of the two contestants lay dead. Money then changed hands.

And, of course, bullfighting was the most famous entertainment of Mexico. Thousands frequented the Sunday afternoon spectacle in Mexico City. Although it was a sport shared by all classes, status was clear by virtue of seating. The wealthy sat in the shade, while the masses suffered the sun. The spectacle proceeded in traditional stages. The bull entered to have *picadores* and matadores goad and tease him with lances and red cloaks. They had to be agile to avoid death on his horns. Then, amid trumpet sounds, the bull's tormentors stuck small lances into his neck. The bull, snorting and thundering to no avail, attacked anyone and anything. Finally, the chief matador emerged, with more trumpets, to do battle armed with his red cloak and long blade. After some flourishing, the matador plunged his weapon between the bull's shoulder blades to the heart. On to the next and more blood.

On his arrival in the 1840s, diplomat Brantz Mayer was told that Mexico had three great "'amusements': a Revolution—an Earthquake—and a Bull Fight." Unfortunately, they all had rather high costs. It is to the Revolution that we turn in the next chapters.

THE AGE OF ORDER
AND PROGRESS

Porfirio Díaz

Porfirio Díaz

On **midnight** September 15, 1910, Porfirio Díaz, "bent a little forward by the weight of his medals. . . . an old man, rather ill now, growing deaf, forgetful, irritable, overbearing . . . ," stood on the balcony of the government palace overlooking the Zocalo in Mexico City, and prepared to strike the Independence bell to celebrate the *Grito* (Cry) *de Dolores,* Mexico's proclamation of freedom, on the occasion of its centenary. Cheering crowds acclaimed his three decades of remarkable rule. Perhaps in his heart the dictator knew it was to be his last hurrah. Within eight months the most powerful man in the Americas would flee into exile. That night and perhaps later after his ouster on board the Ypiranga, the ship that took him into European exile as it crossed the Atlantic in May 1911, the old man undoubtedly reflected on what he had achieved. It was (and is) an extraordinary story. Porfirio Díaz had, building on the foundation laid by Benito Juárez, forged a nation and brought it (kicking and screaming) into the modern world economy. But as with almost all dictators, he had overstayed his time, unwilling to release the reins of power.

Mexican history has reviled Porfirio Díaz, because the triumphant revolutionaries of 1910 (the political heirs of whom retained power in Mexico through the 1990s) who rose against and defeated him, needed a villain to justify their actions. Ironically, as it turned out, the new revolutionary leaders modeled their regime after his at the same time as they condemned him.

On September 15, 1830, in the state of Oaxaca, Petrona Mori, a pure-blood Mixtec Indian, gave birth to Porfirio Díaz, eighty years to the day before the centenary celebration. His father, José Faustino Díaz, died of cholera in 1833, leaving Petrona with five children. Porfirio had to grow up quickly. While his mother worked variously as a hostess at a local inn, a cochineal (a plant used for dye) farmer, and a supervisor at a local school,

161

the young man learned to build furniture and repair firearms. He studied at a local seminary and the State Institute for Arts and Sciences, where Juárez had earlier studied. Given the conditions of the era, it is not surprising he turned to a military career during the Liberal uprising against Antonio López de Santa Anna in the mid-1850s. As a captain during the War of the Reform (1858–60), young Porfirio fought and was wounded. President Benito Juárez rewarded his efforts with an appointment as military com-

Carmen Romero Rubio de Díaz

mander of the Isthmus of Tehuantepec, where as the sole representative of the government, he had wide-ranging authority. While in Tehuantepec the backbone of his command was a coterie of fifty Indian men from the Mixes nation and a force of a couple of hundred Zapotecs from Juchitán, a village known then and now for its fierce independence. From these men he learned about the motivations of country people.

Díaz fought thirty-seven engagements over a dozen years as one of the Liberals' best military leaders. In the War of the Reform he fought in twelve battles and was badly wounded and then later gravely ill from the resulting peritonitis. Porfirio excelled in guerrilla warfare. He showed early on that he could get men to do what he wanted. This precocious officer gained legendary status during the French Intervention, when as commander of the Army of the east, he experienced a number of narrow escapes from death and capture. In 1862 Díaz was one of the Mexican commanders at the Cinco de Mayo victory over the French. Although he subsequently endured a number of discouraging defeats, he continued to fight, winning a major victory at Puebla in April 1867. It was Díaz who liberated Mexico City from the forces of Maximilian on July 15, 1867. Throughout the long ordeal of the Intervention, he was always loyal to Juárez. That allegiance, however, would not outlast his ambition.

When he finally became president in 1877, he was nothing if not ruthless and crude. His ruthlessness appeared early on in two instances related by biographer Carlton Beals. During the war of the French Intervention, he reportedly ordered the execution of every tenth man of a rebellious National Guard battalion in Toluca, not far from the capital. On another occasion, when a small town in the state of Guerrero would not surrender unconditionally, he not only seized and impressed a contingent sent to negotiate an agreement with him, but forcefully took 400 other residents off to conscript into his army. Beals described the new ruler of Mexico in stark terms:

> . . . [He] looked about him with hardness, almost ferocity. Very dark of skin . . . bronzed as an Indian . . . thick, black, close cropped hair . . . mustache not very large. The gilt buttons on the vest of his three-piece gray suit were half unfastened revealing his shirt front, mussed and wrinkled. Stretched out on his seat, his left arm thrown over the back, he stuck out his legs, his short trousers high on the accordion-shaped uppers of his boots. He picked his teeth with a gleaming quill.

To this portrait novelist Federico Gamboa added:

> ... [Díaz had] broad shoulders, strong neck ... dominant, profound, and determined gaze ... thick eyebrows; abundant loose hair; ... his lower jaw prominent; his ears large and red. ...

In 1867 Porfirio married Delfina Ortega Díaz, his niece, the daughter of his sister Manuela. She bore him two sons, Porfirio and Luz. Delfina died in childbirth in 1880. (Some said she had died heartbroken over Porfirio's illicit affair with a servant.) He then married a young woman thirty-five years his junior in 1882, socialite Carmen Romero Rubio, whose father became Díaz's finance minister. She was widely recognized for helping bring about Díaz's reconciliation with the Catholic Church and its hierarchy. Carmen soon made him over.

> ... [H]e seemed another man. ... [H]e had been "rude, heavy, a provincial. ..." [N]ow his dignified gray hair, formerly so unruly and coarse but at last obedient to brush and comb made even his skin seem much lighter; his mustaches, "which formerly drooped on either side of his mouth Indian style, had taken on a civilized and martial appearance." Now his shoes were always shined; collar, cuffs, and shirt bosom were white and starched; his clothes well pressed.

The new Díaz was comfortable in tie, gloves, and tuxedo! He had become courtly. No matter how hard she worked, however, Carmen could never erase the Oaxacan accent, nor teach him to write grammatically or spell correctly.

The changes in the dictator's appearance can be seen as a metaphor for what Mexico had become, and not become, under his rule. Mexico was no longer an Indian country. Its elite, despite the fact its members were often *mestizos,* had labored mightily to disguise the nation's Indian heritage. *Mestizos* like Porfirio were upwardly mobile, for the most part, because of the opportunities presented them by the nearly constant warfare from the 1820s through the 1870s. Theirs were the politics of pragmatism, forged by the experience of struggle. Like Díaz they too were hard-eyed men. The new rulers of Mexico could acquire new citified clothes and trim their hair elegantly, but their country accents and manners were unmistakable. Thus it was with Mexico. The rhetoric of progress and the trappings of technology continuously banged up against the resistance of country people who sought to maintain the way of life of their fathers and mothers.

Díaz in the late 1860s represented the new generation of *mestizo* Liberals who had defeated the French and believed that their time had come to rule Mexico; old-timers like Benito Juárez and Sebastián Lerdo de Tejada should step aside. Juárez and Lerdo, however, had different ideas. Díaz ran against Juárez for the presidency in 1867, but a grateful nation in admiration and recognition of Juárez's long fight against the French, reelected him. In 1871 Díaz faced Juárez and Lerdo. Again Juárez won. The up-and-comers then rebelled (Plan de la Noria), though Díaz did not actively participate in the short-lived fighting begun in his name. The revolt ended when Juárez died in 1872. Porfirio tried to win the presidency through election yet one more time in 1876, only to lose to Lerdo, who had succeeded Juárez from his post as president of the Supreme Court. Frustrated by his electoral defeats, Díaz led a coalition of army officers in rebellion against Lerdo (Plan de Tuxtepec), emerging victorious at last. His victory in the presidential election in January 1877 legitimized his triumph.

With the exception of a brief interregnum from 1880 to 1884, when his ally General Manuel González served as president, Porfirio Díaz ruled over Mexico as head of state for the next three and a half decades. His long years in the army had forged extraordinary skills of leadership: pragmatism, ruthlessness, and charisma. Born and raised in one of the nation's least developed, most isolated regions, and having led rural troops in virtually every part of the country, Díaz knew the Mexican people very well. Most of all, after surviving the exhausting civil wars and the French Intervention, three losing presidential campaigns, and two failed rebellions, Díaz had a clear, definitive vision of what had to be done and how to accomplish it.

Reflecting the revolutionary party line, historians have claimed Porfirio Díaz kept hold of his power through brute force. But the reality was far more complicated. As discussed in chapter 10, the general was a brilliant politician, who constructed a carefully crafted network of political alliances, which held together by virtue of a combination of personal respect or fear of the president, shrewd maneuvering that played off various factions against each other, and an expanding economy that provided the wherewithal to pay off his opponents and allies alike.

Benito Juárez had through his persistence brought forth the idea of Mexican nationality. It was, however, Porfirio Díaz who actually forged the nation, suppressing the long-dominant centrifugal forces that had pulled it apart region by region for half a century. Díaz built the railroads that tied the nation together and provided the vision and the reality of modern economic development.

Like so many other Latin American strongmen who preceded and succeeded him, Díaz failed in the end because his genius was only his own; he failed to build an enduring system that could have outlived him. Economic depression undermined his political deals and a multi-class alliance of outraged country people who were robbed of their land; desperate unemployed workers; ambitious middle-class people who were impatient (as Díaz once had been) for their turn to rule; and traitorous elites, whose interests and greed he had thwarted, rebelled and overthrew him in 1910 and 1911.

TIMELINE

The Age of Order and Progress

1876	Porfirio Díaz rebellion, Plan de Tuxtepec
1877–80	First Presidency of Porfirio Díaz
1880–84	Presidency of Manuel González
1884	Completion of Mexican Central and Mexican National Railways
1884	Commercial Code
1884–1911	Presidency of Porfirio Díaz
1888	Mining code
1890–94	Economic depression
1892	Tomochic Rebellion
1893	José Yves Limantour becomes finance minister
1905	Mexico adopts gold standard
1906–07	Strikes in textile and mining industries
1907–09	Depression
1908	James Creelman interview with Porfirio Díaz
1910	Outbreak of Revolution
1911	Resignation and exile of Porfirio Díaz

Chapter 8

THE ECONOMY OF PROGRESS

Under Porfirio Díaz, Mexico's economy grew spectacularly. The combination of internal peace, the end of foreign invasions, burgeoning markets for Mexican food commodities and mineral ores in Western Europe and the United States, and the large sums of international capital in search of lucrative investments caused unprecedented expansion in Mexico. Exports led the way with a ninefold increase from 1877 to 1911.

While peace and prosperity reigned on the surface, there was a dark underside to the Porfirian economy, which would lead after 1900 to the erosion of the regime's political support. Foreign investment-financed, export-led development had several shortcomings. Although it produced impressive rates of growth—an average increase in the gross national product of eight percent a year—it could not sustain such growth on a steady basis. Export demand was subject to cyclical booms and busts. There were severe downturns during the mid-1880s, early 1890s, and from 1907 to 1909. Mineral prices, for example, fluctuated radically. While booms brought prosperity, the busts caused widespread dislocations, especially among the urban and rural working classes. Prolonged upturns would have probably benefited a broad spectrum of the population eventually, but short bursts of growth tended to concentrate wealth even more than the highly inequitable distribution that existed previously. Busts worsened inequalities. Just as important for the long term, export-led development did not expand the domestic market for either consumer goods or capital goods (industrial equipment, for example). Export revenues financed new industries, but the small size of the domestic market limited their competitiveness.

Great thanks to the work of Thomas Benjamin, Marvin Bernstein, John Coatsworth, Roberto Cortés Conde, Stephen Haber, Ian Jacobs, William Meyers, Fernando Rosenzweig, Alex Saragoza, and Allen Wells.

Two aspects of Mexico's economic development led directly to revolution in 1910. First, periodic depressions tore at the political and social fabric of the nation. Second, Porfirian politics depended on a web of arrangements, which the expanding economy underwrote. From 1907 to 1909 a severe economic depression unbalanced this system, leading to the rise of a substantial faction of dissident notables. The depression also erased a decade of upward mobility, which had created an entrepreneurial middle class. This middle class organized and vocally protested its plight. In addition, the commercialization of agriculture under Díaz created unrest in some rural regions, because hacendados expropriated the lands of villages in order to expand production of export crops and, in some instances, to ensure a cheap labor supply. The subsequent resentment, unemployment, and decline in the production of staple crops deeply disturbed the countryside.

To implement their development strategy, Díaz and his allies had to eliminate economic bottlenecks that had prevented earlier expansion. Political stability was, of course, the initial step. Díaz believed that a peaceful, well-run Mexico with laws amenable to private investment would result in economic growth. Although it took several years, Díaz pacified the country so that it was safe for foreign investors. (This considerable accomplishment is discussed in chapter 10.) At the same time, he and his ally Manuel González, who served as president from 1880 to 1884, set about to create the legal and administrative basis for private enterprise. Díaz and González reformed the nation's commercial and mining codes in order to open the nation to foreign investment, particularly in the mining sector. The reforms also laid the groundwork for a new banking system. The last and most crucial obstacle to overcome was transportation. Díaz encouraged the construction of a large railroad network, which greatly decreased the cost of hauling both commodities and people.

Administrative and Legal Reforms

The Díaz regime undertook widespread administrative reforms aimed primarily at creating an environment for economic growth. President Manuel González guided crucial legislation that transformed the conditions for business in Mexico. One of the most important pieces of legislation passed under González was the Law of Colonization of 1883. This legislation provided that the executive branch of government contract with private companies to survey *terrenos baldíos* (unoccupied lands owned by the government) and to es-

tablish colonies in the surveyed areas. The surveying companies were to receive one-third the land surveyed as payment for their services. Between 1881
and 1889 companies surveyed 80 million acres of land and received or bought
68 million, fourteen percent of Mexico's total land area. Opening up "vacant"
lands helped lay the basis for the commercialization of agriculture and added
impetus to the growing trend toward concentration of land ownership. (The
land parcels, of course, were not always vacant. Boundaries with communal
villages were often in dispute.) When combined with railroad construction,
the gigantic giveaway of public lands spurred foreign investment in export
agriculture.

A second critical law was the new mining code (1884), which permitted
private ownership of subsoil rights, overturning three centuries of Spanish
tradition and law. Mine operators for the first time actually owned their
mines. (Under previous laws, the state owned rights to subsoil minerals. Miners obtained concessions to exploit the mines.) The code also provided work-
able regulations and a simplified tax code. Laws passed in 1887 and 1892 eased
regulations and further reduced taxation. These innovations formed the basis
for the mining boom that followed. Foreign companies required subsoil
ownership in order to justify the large sums needed to refurbish old mines
or discover and work new ones.

In order to create the financial infrastructure for development, the government granted charters to national banks, most importantly to the National
Bank of Mexico. The González administration pushed through the Commercial Code of 1884, which set up the rules and regulations for banking. For
the first time in its history, Mexico had the basis for a modern banking system, a prerequisite for a growing economy.

The regime undertook far-reaching fiscal reform as well. The deficits that
had undermined five decades of Mexican governments continued through
both the first Díaz and the González administrations. In 1879 the government
operated with a 300,000 pesos monthly deficit (the peso exchanged for US$1
at the time). Over his four-year term González accumulated a shortfall of 38.5
million pesos. Corruption, which permeated the government, undoubtedly
exacerbated fiscal woes. Under the capable direction of finance minister José
Yves Limantour from 1893 on, the government balanced the budget. Limantour put Mexico on the gold standard in 1905, so as to eliminate the value fluc-
tuation that had plagued the silver peso for several years. The peso was then
devalued to US$0.50. By 1910 the Mexican government could borrow on in-

ternational financial markets at five percent, an excellent rate, and had reserves of 60 million pesos. Limantour had put the nation on sound financial footing indeed.

The Díaz regime adopted a number of additional measures to foster expanding markets and to encourage foreign investment. To facilitate the formation of a national market, the González administration abolished alcabalas, the taxes on interstate commerce (internal tariffs). The peso devaluation kept Mexican exports cheap in the face of declining prices on the world market.

Foreign Investment

Foreign enterprise financed Mexico's economic miracle. The amount of investment from abroad was startling. From 1884 to 1900 foreign investors poured almost US$1.2 billion into the country. In 1883 North American investment was a modest US$30 million. In less than twenty years it had risen by a factor of seventeen to US$501.6 million. Nine years later it had doubled to slightly more than US$1 billion. In 1880 British investment stood at 32.7 million pounds, rising to 90 million in 1910. At first most of this capital went into Mexican government bonds. By 1900, however, 86 percent of foreign funds went into direct investments in industrial or agricultural production, with only 14 percent in public debt. Nearly 90 percent of foreign investment was concentrated in railroads and mining.

Railroads

Mexico's lack of cheap transportation had long prevented the development of a nationwide domestic market and inhibited exports. Prior to the *Porfiriato*, the only extensive railroad ran from the capital to Veracruz; there were approximately 400 miles of track in the entire country in 1876. By 1910 there were more than 15,000 miles of railroad. The construction of this extensive network beginning in the 1880s stimulated Mexico's first economic miracle. The completion of two major north-south lines, the Mexican National and the Mexican Central, were largely responsible for creating a boom in agricultural and mineral exports. The railroads drastically cut the cost of transportation, which had long held back full exploitation of Mexican resources.

The government invested heavily in railroad construction. The Díaz administration paid subsidies in cash or in certificates from customs receipts, often borrowing to pay these debts. In addition, the government provided tax exemptions for essential equipment and supplies, land grants, and other concessions.

As it evolved, the railroad network was built with a distinct orientation toward export markets in the United States. Mexicans were initially quite wary of constructing north-south lines, because they feared repetition of the debacle of the war with the United States. Nonetheless, the major railroad companies constructed their lines north-south. These corporations were owned by U.S. investors, who sought to connect their Mexican rails with Mexico's major market north of the border.

Foreign corporations initially owned and operated all major railroads. The Mexican Central and the Mexican National were the most important. The Central ran from Mexico City to the U.S. border at El Paso, Texas. The National went from Mexico City through Saltillo and Monterrey to Laredo, Texas. The mighty Atchison, Topeka, and Santa Fe, one of the giant corporations that dominated access to the western United States, controlled the Central. Another giant, the Denver-Rio Grande, owned the National. U.S. railroad tycoon Collis P. Huntington controlled a third line, the International, which serviced various cities in the northeast. An English company, the Interoceanic, operated between Mexico City and Veracruz.

There were two major drawbacks in the construction of Mexico's railroads. (Both drawbacks were evident in the United States as well.) Because of the shenanigans that took place in the issue and reissue of stocks and bonds, the corporations that owned the railroads were often in financial difficulties. Railroads commonly earned small profits on operating revenues, only to suffer fiscal troubles resulting from high interest rates paid on indebtedness and from overvalued stock. In addition, the railroad network was not very carefully planned. While many areas remained unserved and isolated, others were overbuilt. Both of these weaknesses were costly.

After 1900 Díaz and his finance minister José Y. Limantour became quite concerned. At the same time, the threat of amalgamation of the railroad industry into the hands of one or two U.S. corporations (known as trusts) arose. As the movement toward trusts accelerated in the United States, both the Central and National were in dire financial straits, and thus vulnerable to takeovers. It seemed that these railway companies were likely to merge and create a rail monopoly in Mexico. To forestall this possibility, the Díaz government nationalized the main lines, most importantly the Central and Na-

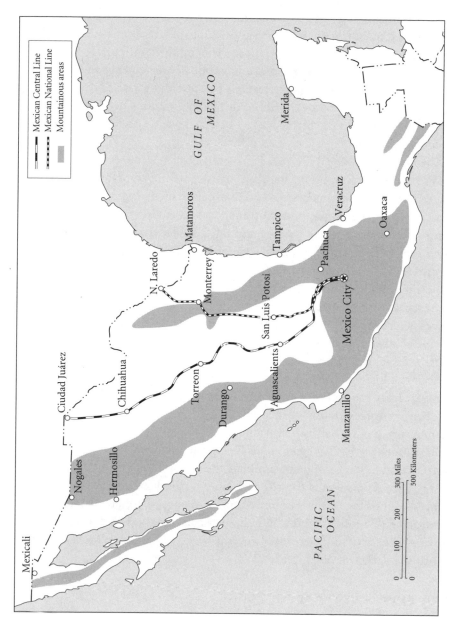

Map 3. Two Major Railroads and Physical Features, 1910

Legend:
- Mexican Central Line
- Mexican National Line
- Mountainous areas

GULF OF MEXICO

PACIFIC OCEAN

Mexicali
Nogales
Hermosillo
Ciudad Juárez
Chihuahua
Torreon
Durango
N. Laredo
Matamoros
Monterrey
San Luis Potosi
Aguascalients
Manzanillo
Mexico City
Pachuca
Tampico
Veracruz
Oaxaca
Merida

0   100   200   300 Miles
0   500 Kilometers

tional, through a series of purchases from 1902 to 1909. Ingeniously, Limantour saw to it that the nationalization appeared to be more of a bailout of foreign investors than an expropriation. The oddly configured company maintained two boards of directors, one public in Mexico City and another private in New York City. Foreign investors lost no money and foreign companies continued to operate the lines. At the cost of a considerable outlay of funds, Mexico retained what its leaders believed was a crucial aspect of national sovereignty.

The railroads changed Mexico. Torreón in Durango rose from the desert dust to become an important transportation center. It flourished as a depot for the Laguna region of Durango and Coahuila, which produced cotton and *guayule* (raw material for rubber) transported to markets by the railroad. Some old mining areas not on the main lines, such as Zacatecas and Guanajuato, faded. The north burgeoned, as mining resources were for the first time accessible via cheap transportation.

In addition to creating a mining boom, the railroads had an extensive impact on many other sectors of the economy. They enabled Mexico to greatly diversify its exports. In 1898 60 percent of its exports were precious metals, compared to 46 percent by 1910. In 1877–78 silver alone accounted for 60 percent of the value of all exports, and in 1910, 33 percent. By 1910 hemp, sugar, rubber, and livestock were also important exports. Railroads stimulated domestic market production as well. Cotton and other textiles expanded. Fast, inexpensive transportation opened up markets for processed food. Breweries doubled production between 1878 and 1910.

In contrast to the U.S. economic development pattern, however, railroad construction in Mexico did not stimulate the rise and expansion of heavy industry. Fifty-six percent of the gross revenues of all Mexican railroads in 1910 "leaked" out of the country to buy equipment abroad, to pay dividends, to remit interest on loans, and to purchase consumer goods for foreign employees. The forty-four percent of revenues that remained in Mexico went mostly to salaries for employees.

Mining

Mining led the Porfirian boom. Demand for silver and non-precious metals, such as copper and zinc, in Europe and the United States provided the markets. Western European and U.S. entrepreneurs seeking high returns on their investments found Mexico an attractive area, in part because they had faith in Díaz's ability to maintain peace and order. New technologies enabled miners to exploit their mines far more efficiently. The U.S. McKinley tariff of 1890 made it too expensive to import unrefined ore into the United States and therefore set off a boom in smelting in Mexico. Smelted ore was much cheaper to transport. Changes in mining legislation to allow for unencumbered development of mineral subsoil rights also lured investors. Finally, the railroads reduced transportation costs and permitted economies of scale in the mining industry.

Mining began its resurgence in the 1880s. A few risk takers plunged in before the actual construction of the railroads. U.S. businessman Alexander Shepherd set up in Batopilas, Chihuahua, deep in the Sierra Madres (where it is difficult to get to even today). He paid US$600,000 for a concession covering the mines in sixty-one square miles. Shepherd operated for more than a quarter century, digging millions of dollars worth of silver ore from his claims.

The real boom in mining claims occurred after 1892. That year there were 2,829 registered mine titles. The next year the total rose to 12,871. Silver production nearly quadrupled between 1877–78 and 1910–11; lead output more than tripled from 1891–92 to 1910–11; and copper output increased 8.5 times between 1891–92 and 1910–11.

Investors had built five smelters in Mexico by 1895. U.S. operators, such as the Guggenheim family, invested heavily in smelting during the 1890s. In 1901 the Guggenheims took over the American Smelting and Refining Company, known in the United States as the "Smelters' Trust," which in the first decade of the twentieth century virtually monopolized the smelting industry in Mexico. Only one major Mexican smelting operation competed with the trust: that of the Madero family of Coahuila and Monterrey.

In addition to the railroads, two technological innovations spurred mining: the general use of electric power and the introduction of the cyanide process. Electricity provided light, but more important, powered pumps, trams, and other crucial equipment. New processes made mining of gold and silver, in particular, much more profitable. These improvements reduced costs to the extent that it was profitable to rework old mine fills and dumps. The impact of the new technology was quite evident. In Guanajuato silver output had fallen by half between 1898 and 1904, but with the use of cyanide in refining and the installation of electricity, production more than doubled by 1911.

Table 1. Mining Production (kilograms and metric tons)

	1891	*1900*	*1910*
silver	1,087,261 kg	1,776,410	2,416,669
gold	1,477 kg	12,697	41,420
lead	30,187 MT	63,828	124,292
zinc	—	1,100 MT	1,833
copper	5,650 MT	22,473	48,160

Land Concentration

The combination of land expropriations by hacendados of communal village holdings and the vast giveaway of public properties under the auspices of the Law of Colonization of 1883 greatly concentrated land ownership during the Porfiriato. Hacendados had stolen the lands of communal villages for decades in independent Mexico. Individual states had outlawed communal landholding as early as the 1820s. The railroad boom of the 1880s, however, changed the balance of opportunity and power. After decades of stagnating land values, new access to markets in the cities, mining camps, and abroad stimulated hacendados to increase production of export commodities, which meant that they sought to expand their holdings. Until Díaz, instability and war had suppressed land values. With the railroads and peace, hacendados found ample reason to push small owners from the land. Moreover, hacendados and politicians no longer needed villagers to fight for them in incessant civil wars or against nomadic Indians or foreign invaders, so the battle for their traditionally held lands exploded anew.

Country people resisted. Uprisings broke out everywhere the railroads went. With the connivance of the Díaz regime, however, large landowners had gained the upper hand in this struggle. The second wave of expropriations that began around 1905 pushed villagers and small *rancheros* in some regions, notably Morelos and Chihuahua, to the point where they had nothing more to lose by resorting to arms.

Giveaways of public lands started in 1863 as a means to raise money for the cash-strapped Juárez government. Juárez distributed titles to more than 4 million acres. In 1867 Juárez modified the law to ensure that vacant land sales could not damage third parties (most likely villages). The new legislation also limited the possibilities of speculation. In 1877 there was a sharp upturn in the interest in vacant lands because of the large number of concessions for railroad construction granted by the government. In Sonora and Coahuila sales of vacant lands directly corresponded to the progress made by concessionaires in building the Sonora and Mexican Central Railways, respectively. Sales of vacant lands peaked in Chihuahua as the Mexican Central was completed in 1884–85. Mexican and foreign companies pieced together enormous holdings of 100,000 acres or more. Some, like the Hearst interests and the Palomas Land and Cattle Company, built ranches of a million acres. Luis Terrazas personally owned more than 10 million acres in Chihuahua (on which he grazed 500,000 head of cattle).

Industrialization

The boom era transformed Mexican industry. Artisan shops gave way to factories. Insular markets expanded to become international. Corporations owned by shareholders began to supplant family-operated companies. Entrepreneurs formed new industries like steel, oil, and cement. Several factors, however, limited Mexican industrialization: the relatively small size of the domestic market compared to its ability to produce resulted in overcapacity, which cut profits; the necessity to import equipment at high cost; and the low productivity of labor, which resulted from the minimal level of socialization to wage labor requirements attained by Mexican workers (see chapter 9). Despite the advantage of low wages, Mexican industrialists could not compete in the export market and in order to compete at home they had to rig the domestic market with government assistance. Mexican companies depended on artificially established and maintained monopolies or near-monopolies (oligopolies) that were protected by high tariffs and other government policies. Despite this strategy Mexican industry was only moderately profitable.

The small size of the domestic market was a result of both Mexico's relatively small population and severe inequalities in income distribution. Although the population had increased in the last half of the nineteenth century, most Mexicans were poor. Although per capita income had increased, wealth was concentrated in the hands of the very rich. There was only a limited demand for manufactured consumer goods. Poor transportation and communications also inhibited the creation of a nationwide domestic market.

The high cost and inappropriateness of imported technology further disadvantaged Mexican manufacturers. Imported equipment was very expensive. For example, imported textile machinery was 50 percent more costly to install in Mexico than in Great Britain. Often machinery did not fit Mexican conditions, for it was made to produce large quantities, but the market could not absorb this production. In the cement industry, for instance, the top companies produced at 30 to 43 percent of capacity during the Porfiriato. The steel industry exceeded 50 percent of capacity only once from 1903 to 1910. The most obvious solution to the problem of underutilization of productive capacity was to export surplus. Unfortunately, Mexican manufacturers could not compete against cheaper, higher quality products by manufacturers in Europe and the United States. Extremely costly investments went underused.

Despite relatively low wages, Mexican workers were not as productive as workers elsewhere, because they resisted socialization into the factory system. Mexican textile workers fought off factory discipline quite successfully well into the twentieth century. New England textile workers, for example, operated more than three times the number of looms. Mexican mills needed nearly three times the number of workers than in New England. The shortage of skilled labor allowed Mexican textile workers considerable leverage. They refused to increase their productivity without fear of being fired.

Mexican manufacturers could survive only if protected by tariffs or if the government provided subsidies. Tariffs, therefore, rose throughout the Porfiriato. All of the major manufacturing companies received various forms of tax exemptions. The government also limited competition by issuing only one such exemption per industry, thus guaranteeing a monopoly for the favored enterprise. Ultimately, Mexican industry consolidated into a few big firms that dominated specific markets. Monopolies or oligopolies dominated the steel, glass, soap, cigarettes, paper, dynamite, beer, and cement industries.

The lack of domestic financial institutions also disadvantaged Mexican industry. Despite the administrative and legal reforms instituted during the 1880s and 1890s, Mexico had only seven operating banks in 1897, none of which could legally loan funds for more than a year. The total number of banks reached twenty in 1910, and nearly all of them were small. Most functioned as short-term lenders that financed the real estate business. As a result, there was no "open" credit market. A small group of financiers, perhaps twenty-five in all, furnished the capital for most large industrial enterprises. Except for mining, U.S. and European investors were not interested in Mexican manufacturing. This small clique of financiers were all foreign-born merchants or investors who had no experience or knowledge of manufacturing. What they were good at was rigging the marketplace by using their extensive government influence.

Regional Differences

Monterrey, Nuevo León, epitomized the heady economic progress of the Porfiriato. At the confluence of two major railroads, the city became the major communications and transportation hub for northeast Mexico. It boomed as a smelting center for the newly resurgent mining industry. Foreign enterprise financed and operated the mines, smelters, and railroads. Nonetheless, a substantial network of domestic capitalists built a number of industrial conglomerates in such areas as cement, glass, beer brewing, and iron. Monterrey's population doubled, boosted by migrants who were among the highest wage earners in Mexico.

The economic history of Chiapas during the Díaz era is also illustrative of the effects of extensive foreign investment in transportation and export agriculture. From the 1870s foreigners in the region sunk their money into tropical commodities like hardwoods, rubber, sugar cane, coffee, and cacao. After 1890, however, the main emphasis was on coffee, the production of which spread out across the state. A new wave of investment after 1900 focused on coffee and rubber. U.S. entrepreneurs had poured almost US$3 million into Chiapas by 1909. Germans added another US$1.8 million. During this time the state built a transportation network consisting of the Pan American Railroad and a major highway. Telephone and telegraph lines connected the region's major towns. The railroad cut transport costs for coffee by half, stimulating a 100-percent increase in production from 1908 to 1910. Other commodities, such as corn, cotton, sugar, and cattle also found markets in Mexico City. In valleys where once there were no roads, no machinery, and laborers toiled with digging sticks, steam-driven sugar mills and steel plows appeared, and farmers sent their corn by railroad to the nation's capital. There are many indications of progress in the statistics. The value of rural and urban property, for example, increased by factors of seven and nine, respectively. Despite these impressive results, benefits from economic expansion went to only a few. Daily wages for workers remained the same for two decades. Labor conditions deteriorated in many areas into slavery in all but name.

The state of Guerrero, southwest of the capital, was an example of a region where the export economy did not generally intrude, and therefore its inhabitants endured fewer if any dislocations. Guerrero's rugged topography made transportation very difficult and costly. Guerrero primarily produced corn for local consumption. There were some tropical commodities cultivated along the coast, such as rice, coffee, tobacco, cotton, sugar, and sesame seed, but these were consumed locally. Entrepreneurs established a couple of small factories processing these local products. Only in the northern districts of the state, because of proximity to the Mexico City market and construction of a short railway line, did the economic boom intrude. The town of Iguala burgeoned into a commercial center. Ironically, just as political turbulence had provided maneuvering room for villagers and small farmers in the first years after Independence, the lack of accessibility also protected Guerrero's rancheros from the onslaught of land expropriations.

No region felt the impact of the export boom more than Yucatán. Nowhere were the contrasts between the burgeoning economy and the rewards for workers as stark. Production of the region's major crop, henequen, which yielded twine for baling wheat, skyrocketed fifteenfold in the last quarter of the nineteenth century. Colonial haciendas were transformed into modern plantations. The downside, however, was startling. Fantastically rich plantation owners (known locally as the *casta divina,* the divine group) lived lavishly in their palaces in Mérida, the state capital, deriving their profits from a modern form of slavery. The plantations had business arrangements with the police of Mexico City, who supplied them with "vagrants" from the jails and streets of the capital (usually drunks), whose terms of punishment were extended indefinitely, and with the national army, who sent Yaqui Indians captured in the fierce rebellion in Sonora. Moreover, although the henequeneros (planters) were all Yucatecans, the profits after 1900 fell to a small coterie led by Olegario Molina, which collaborated with the U.S. corporation International Harvester to virtually corner the market for henequen. Yucatán also epitomized the boom and bust economy. The boom hit its peak in 1902 with henequen at ten cents a pound, only to fall catastrophically to four cents in 1911.

After thirty years of economic miracle Mexico remained a nation of brutal contrasts. There were sharp differentiations between regions. The Huasteca area of Veracruz was hardly touched by Porfirian progress, while neighboring Tampico prospered with the impact of an oil boom. Throughout the nation the gap between rich and poor grew enormously. The palace of Riva Palacio (described in chapter 7) juxtaposed with the squalid vecindades (tenements) of Mexico City (described in chapter 1) was proof enough of that. There was an enormous outflow of resources abroad with virtually no gain in terms of better wages or living conditions for most Mexicans.

Export-led growth financed by foreign investment caused another disturbing development as well. Mexico's industry and finance were increasingly concentrated in the hands of a handful of economic groups, such as the French emigres of Mexico City, the Monterrey group, the Molina-Montes of Yucatán, and the Terrazas-Creel family of Chihuahua. These economic groups showed strong inclinations to extend their influence. They undertook various attempts at "trustification" in industries like food processing.

Unprecedented boom from the late 1890s to 1907 hid these weaknesses, but the depression that hit in the latter year exposed them to everyone, from notable to peon. Disillusionment set in. Political opposition inevitably followed. It is to politics and the fermentation of revolution that we turn next.

Chapter 9

EVERYDAY LIFE, 1877–1910: THE ONSLAUGHT OF CHANGE

C hanges in everyday life accelerated in the last quarter of the nineteenth and the first decade of the twentieth century. The vast influx of foreign investment into transportation, mining, industry, and commercial agriculture affected virtually every region of the nation. The countryside experienced the impact of the Reform Laws in full force, as elites took land from communal villages made more valuable by the spread of the railroad network. These land expropriations created a large pool of rural labor that kept wages low in the central plateau regions and in the Valley of Mexico. They also pushed country people to migrate to the cities, mining camps, and across the northern border to the United States to find better-paying employment. A significant portion of the population was ever on the move from shrinking landholdings to transient work and back. Throughout the period the enormous migration from countryside to city continued. Mexico City, hard-pressed at mid-century to provide livable conditions, had to accept 200,000 more migrants during the Díaz regime.

Economic growth brought considerable benefits to select areas and groups. It created a middle class in the countryside and in the cities. The number of independent small farmers increased in several regions, such as the states of Chihuahua and Hidalgo. In some parts of the nation working environments improved. The north, for example, offered better working conditions and higher wages, despite a higher cost of living. Expansion of the mining indus-

My great thanks to the work of Ana Alonso, Rodney Anderson, Carlton Beals, William Beezley, William French, Michael Johns, Gilbert Joseph, Jonathan Kandell, Friedrich Katz, John Lear, Tony Morgan, Piedad Peniche Rivero, Heather Fowler Salamini, and Allen Wells.

try and competition from U.S. employers kept wages high there. From the 1880s to the early years of the new century an urban middle class sprouted among the expanding bureaucracy of Mexico City and the opportunities for small-scale entrepreneurship in the north. For a time, the possibilities for upward mobility for some masked the deteriorating conditions of the lower classes.

For most Mexicans, however, the end of the century brought a new kind of misery with its origins in the burgeoning economy based on mineral and agricultural exports. The chasm between wealth and poverty deepened, as the rich grew richer and the poor grew poorer. The unfairness of disorder and underdevelopment experienced in earlier decades had given way to the injustice of peace and progress. By 1910 Mexico's export-led economic development financed by foreign investment had dislocated everyday life to the extent that it undermined the very foundations of the Díaz regime's legitimacy and authority. Ignited by a severe economic crisis in 1907 and a political crisis over Díaz's succession in 1910, these upheavals in daily life led to the overthrow of the dictator in 1911. One way that the Mexican Revolution of 1910 may be understood is that it was a locally-based, widespread popular attempt to reassert control over everyday life. The most vibrant issues of the era concerned local autonomy, as they had been during the years before the Liberal Reform. Country people pursued the freedom to control access to land, institute equitable taxes, and gain a fair hearing before the courts, in order to obtain once again what they regarded as their inherent right to control their own lives. Members of the urban middle class sought an even playing field to apply their skills and ambitions. Workers, unemployed because of the depression of 1907, sought steady jobs.

Transformations

Better transportation and communications brought an end to the relative isolation of much of the countryside and introduced market forces. Everyone from storekeepers to small farmers had to think in terms of broader competition. Landowners had wider horizons in the form of greater opportunities to sell to distant markets. Consequently, they introduced new crops, which required new work arrangements. In some areas, where labor was scarce, employers reimposed forced labor systems. In Yucatán and Tabasco, in particular, new forms of slavery emerged. Continuous pressure on land, ever less available to Indian communities, meant vast shifts in population. People whose families had farmed a plot for generations found themselves landless and in search of employment elsewhere. Migration to cities, to northern mining camps, and across the border to the United States began the process of alienation from the land and, to some extent, from traditional kinship support networks. The railroads enabled people to travel long distances from home inexpensively to find work and return. The entire male population of villages sometimes left seasonally to return at planting and harvest. In a Mexico on the move, traditional constraints loosened. Traditional attitudes such as male dominance (paternalism) eroded.

Commercialization of agriculture and industrialization changed the nature of work. The new forms of large-scale organization combined with technology to profoundly change the workplace. The more leisurely pace of the hacienda, village, and artisan shop gave way grudgingly to the discipline of the plantation, mine, and factory. Large employers struggled with workers' propensities for a slow pace and absenteeism. There was a deep clash of cultures between Mexico's rural people and the capitalist marketplace, and at times the conflicts led to violence. The proportion of the workforce in traditional manufacturing, much of it artisan based, declined. Skilled crafts, such as shoemaking, cigarette rolling, weaving, and corn grinding, lost out to machines in foreign-owned factories. On the positive side, there were new jobs. Machines required service, so mechanics were in demand. Transport (railroads, trolleys) and electric utilities created additional new opportunities and skills to be learned. Women found employment opportunities as seamstresses (and in related textile trades) and as factory workers.

The onslaught against working people proceeded more extensively than just in the implementation of the regimentation of the plantation or factory. Elites, allied with the middle class, sought to discipline the lives of their laborers as well. Bosses not only wanted them to arrive on time to work, but to stop drinking and gambling as well, because these activities did not fit their work ethic. The Porfirian era "persuasion" tried to produce a new Mexican, one who had no vices and docilely accepted the discipline of the workplace.

The cyclical nature of the new market economy also affected daily life. Booms followed busts and busts followed booms. Each wrench of the market struck hard, especially at the lower and middle classes, and redistributed wealth upward.

Elites changed as well, if only in their excesses. They sought to emulate their models of the modern world, the Europeans and North Americans, but they remained Mexicans. Conspicuous consumption marked their lifestyles. Their disdain for the lower classes intensified as the gap between rich and poor widened. They believed that the inherent inferiority of the lower classes, especially Indians, accounted for the dire circumstances of the poor. Porfirian elites brought the heritage of the hombres de bien (the elite that had dominated politics in the first decades after Independence) to an extreme. Fear of the lower classes transformed into the haughtiness and arrogance of racism.

The greater centralization brought about by the dictatorship also changed everyday life. *Jefes políticos*, appointed either by governors beholden to Díaz or by Díaz himself, governed local communities with an even stronger hand than during the Juárez years. They interfered in longstanding practices and arrangements. Corruption, once used by local people to influence government officials and, perhaps, ensure relative fair play, became institutionalized to the extent that these very same officials were no longer responsive to local grievances. Local political dominance meant control over taxes and access to land. Officials sold these privileges to the highest bidders.

Living Standards

The population grew more rapidly in the years 1877 to 1910 than in the first fifty years after Independence, and the nation was no longer able to feed its own people consistently. The government had to import corn in times of harvest failures during the 1890s and in 1907. With the exception of a brief period during the 1890s, staple (corn and beans) production lagged behind demographic growth throughout the era. There are conflicting interpretations as to why shortages occurred and what their impact was.

Most historians believe that export producers took land from corn production, which resulted in increased prices. Historians have generally thought that during the Porfiriato large landowners shifted from staple to export crops in order to make more money. The simultaneous expropriation of communal holdings further reduced the land area planted in corn. The decline of staple production then, according to this analysis, led to increased prices for corn and beans at a time when wages were stagnant. Rising prices and stagnating wages meant that real wages (wages' actual purchasing power) declined, which badly eroded living standards.

Other observers point to evidence indicating that farmers did not increase staple planting in response to lower market demand. A more prosperous population had increased its consumption of meat and reduced its consumption of tortillas and frijoles. A significant increase in the production of chile at the end of the century might suggest increased consumption of meat, for chile was used as a condiment in meat dishes. But meat consumption increased only 4.2 percent from 1897 to 1907, hardly enough to account for a drop in corn production.

It seems most probable that the Mexican diet changed to incorporate a greater variety of fruits and vegetables and to substitute wheat-based products for corn. The fact that consumption of other foods and drinks increased 34 percent per capita between 1897 and 1907 and that wheat production also increased by 7.1 percent per capita in the same period seems to bolster the theory of a more varied diet. If staple production stagnated at a time when the population was growing, these two factors alone might have accounted for shortfalls leading to higher prices.

Staple production may not have declined, and prices did not rise uniformly. Statistics are somewhat unreliable as a result of several factors. First, there were wide regional variations. It appears that while prices rose quite sharply in Mexico City and in the north, this was not the case elsewhere. The cost of necessities in the Federal District doubled from 1898 to 1908. Wheat prices rose by half. After 1900 it was impossible for urban workers to support their families. The only way to survive was for everyone, including wife and children, to work, and even this might not have been sufficient. But, of course, Mexico City was not all of Mexico.

Second, crop statistics also depend on what time of year observers compiled them. Corn prices, for example, were cyclical according to season: prices were high before the harvest and low after it. Weather might affect harvest one year and not the next, depending on the amount of rain or whether there was an early frost.

Third, price measurements were not always the same. Standards often varied from region to region. To further complicate the analysis, the cost of corn was not always a matter of concern to workers, because rations or subsidized corn from their hacendado employers may have shielded at least resident hacienda laborers from price increases. The status of real wages also varied regionally. Although industrial wages in the central region dropped thirty-eight percent during the Porfiriato, this was not the case in the mining regions of the north.

The preponderance of evidence indicates that a vast majority of Mexicans both in the countryside and the cities struggled to survive throughout the Porfiriato, despite economic growth. The years from 1907 to 1910 were particularly difficult, because of the combination of drought and depression that struck much of the nation. The lost harvests of 1907, 1908, and 1909 (which clearly indicated the inability of domestic farmers to feed the population) sent prices for basic foodstuffs soaring. The worldwide depression beginning in mid-1907 caused massive unemployment in the cities and mining camps. Employers lowered wages in response to falling demand for their products. The disaster of 1907 fell particularly hard on those segments of the population, such as northern miners and the emerging middle class, who had prospered during the previous decade, at least in a relative sense. The latter reacted with anger to their sudden loss of income and status. Not surprisingly, they formed a solid base for the opposition to Díaz in 1910.

The Countryside

Until the Díaz era, when property values shot up in response to the expansion of the railroad network, national and state governments only sporadically enforced the Reform legislation that made it illegal for villages to hold land collectively. Access to markets in the cities and abroad stimulated production and rising prices and profits gave incentive for politicians and large landowners to expropriate communal holdings. In many regions communal villages lost their lands entirely, which devastated the traditional structure of rural society. Rural males' status and honor depended on collective or individual ownership, sharecropping, or tenancy. Expropriation created a large number of landless, unemployed peons whose presence in the labor market depressed wages. In some regions cheap, temporary labor became more readily available than ever, creating a relatively mobile workforce. For sharecroppers and tenants land use arrangements were unfavorable and, because hacendados growing export crops allowed them the use of only the most marginal lands, they inevitably grew ever more indebted and less mobile.

Land expropriations occurred in two great waves. The first, which took place during the 1880s, resulted from the construction of the major railroad lines, the Mexican Central and the Mexican National. Land values skyrocketed with the barest whisper of a rumor that the railroad was to pass through an area. The second wave occurred in the first decade of the twentieth century, when Mexico experienced a boom in the construction of feeder or secondary railroad lines. This led to violent resistance in several regions.

In central Mexico the inhabitants of the communal villages (pueblos) that lost their lands during the Díaz era had to look to the neighboring haciendas for their livelihoods. The majority continued to reside in their villages. And the pueblos maintained autonomy, at least in part. Some villages held on to a small part of their lands, but not enough land to feed their inhabitants around the year. Others lost all their lands. There were cases, such as the Hacienda de Cantabria in Michoacán, when the hacienda imported resident peons and most of its sharecroppers from elsewhere. Because hacendados wanted loyal workers and refused to hire workers displaced by the hacienda's expansion, most villagers had to go far from home to other haciendas in order to find work. Thus, Mexico had a substantial population of rural people who once individually or collectively had owned their own land, but who now faced unemployment, transiency, temporary work at low wages, or highly unfavorable sharecropping or tenancy arrangements. The villagers protested and took legal recourse against the expropriations. Many, frustrated at the actions of unfair courts and bureaucracy, joined with leaders like Emiliano Zapata to rebel in 1910.

The processes of commercialization and expropriation altered the countryside. Perhaps Yucatán furnishes the best example of how world market forces and national and local politics came together to affect everyday life. In the late nineteenth century Yucatecan haciendas, which had earlier produced cattle and corn, transformed themselves into henequen plantations connected to markets in the United States. Commercial production resulted from two technological innovations: the first a process that extracted large quantities of fiber from agave (henequen) leaves using an implement called a "rasper," and, the second, a mechanism that turned the fibers into twine strong enough to bind grain gathered by automated grain harvesters. The widespread use of mechanical harvesters in the United States set off a boom in the demand for henequen. Yucatán's new henequen plantations required a much different labor system than their predecessors. They needed a year-round labor supply to weed the fields and then cut and carry the agave leaves to processors for extraction. The "delicate balance that had existed in the pre-1850 labor system between the cattle producing haciendas . . . and the peasants in the free villages that surrounded them" had to change because of the new demand for workers.

In the old days village labor was always plentiful and available as needed. Before the henequen transformation, there were three types of labor on the hacienda: resident labor, renter/sharecroppers, and luneros (those who labored Mondays on the hacienda in return for milpa plots). Enabled by technological improvements to produce on an even larger scale, and in need of a stable, year-round labor force, commercial henequen producers undertook to strip neighboring villagers of their lands. In cahoots with state political authorities, the planters saw to it that the government implemented the Reform Laws to deprive the villagers of their lands. Loss of their subsistence plots left Yucatán's country people with no alternative but to toil on the plantations. The henequeneros also devised a number of ploys to keep peons indebted and tied to their estates.

In order to ensure a plentiful, cheap labor supply, plantation owners meddled in the institution of marriage, which was at the very center of Maya life. A Maya male could achieve adulthood and obtain land only when he married. The henequeneros took control of the process of finding suitable matches. As one Maya recollected:

> The rich control their workers. You are a young man and they say you must marry. They take you to the master and then they get all the unmarried women, line them up and then say to you, there they are, now choose your wife. You choose the one that you like best and say, 'this one'. . . . On the hacienda there is no such thing as love. . . . The patrón arrives and tells you, this man will be your husband. Then they give you your household utensils. . . .

The henequeneros kept their Maya laborers deep in debt by advancing the money to pay for crucial family events, such as weddings, burials, and fiestas — the rites that made the Maya man a man in the eyes of his family and community.

The hacendado actually assumed the role traditionally played by the groom's family to provide gifts, money, and food to the bride's family. In addition, when the male married, he received a milpa, a house with household goods, and the guarantee of full employment. The hacendado eventually received in return the offspring of the Maya couple for employment in his fields. The women served as housekeepers. Hacendados and Maya understood obligation in different terms. The hacendado regarded debt as a financial obligation that ensured a stable workforce and as a part of the cost of doing business. The Maya saw the arrangement as an obligation to the patrón in exchange for his loyalty.

By 1900 hacendados had reinstituted debt peonage, physical abuse, and, in some instances, slavery. So endless was the demand for labor that the Mexican government sent to Yucatán kidnapped "vagrants" from Mexico City, political dissidents (as defined by local bosses) from all over the nation, and Yaqui Indians captured in rebellion from Sonora.

If there was any region for which we could argue that a substantial portion of the rural population experienced improved conditions, it was the north, although good times lasted only until 1907. In the north the scarcity of labor forced hacendados to compete for workers with neighboring mines and employers in the United States, who paid twice the wage rates in Mexico. Agricultural wages in the north were the highest anywhere in Mexico. Sharecropping arrangements were also more favorable. In the south and center of the nation sharecroppers had to turn over two-thirds of their crop to hacendados, compared to only one-third to one-half in the north. Some enlightened hacendados such as Francisco I. Madero, who was to lead the Revolution in 1910, offered other incentives, including medical care and schools, to attract labor. In general, the closer to the U.S. border the higher the wages and the better the working conditions. The farther from the border and mining camps the harsher the conditions.

With the exception of the north, circumstances for hacienda workers deteriorated during the Porfiriato. Those resident peons who maintained access to land and gained salary advances were the best off. Real wages (actual purchasing power) in some areas actually declined, because, while nominal wages remained the same, the cost of living may have increased as much as thirty percent. At least these resident peons enjoyed basic security. Permanent residents who lost access to land joined a group that included tenants and sharecroppers, contract workers, and indebted temporary workers, whose situation deteriorated both in real and relative terms. Others were forced to accept less favorable arrangements. Debts often constrained their movement.

There were proportionately more permanent workers on northern livestock haciendas than elsewhere in Mexico. Probably the best off of these were vaqueros (cowboys). Because their services were in great demand in the United States, vaqueros obtained very high wages, between 7 and 8 pesos a month in Chihuahua in 1902 and as high as 15 pesos per month in 1913. A foreman (*caporal*) could earn as much as 30 pesos a month. There were also considerable possibilities for upward mobility on northern haciendas, for it was not unlikely that a cowboy who stayed on one ranch for a while would earn a promotion to a supervisory position, since haciendas required a caporal for every seven or eight cowboys. Even in the north there was a down side to economic expansion. With the exception of cowboys and shepherds, most workers in the north lacked job security. In boom times, employees could move easily from job to job. But the economy was cyclical. The temporary workforce, which toiled in both mining camp and on haciendas, was subject to layoffs. Misery was the predictable result of unemployment.

Hacienda and plantation workers in the south—in Yucatán, Veracruz, and Tabasco, for example—endured dismal conditions even at the height of the boom. In Yucatán, despite new technology, planting and harvesting henequen remained backbreaking and dangerous. The agave leaf was cut with a knife, the end spine removed, and then the side spines taken off. The sharp blade was always a threat to the peon's life and limbs. After preparing the agave leaves the workers then gathered and tied them in bundles and carried them to a tramway.

We have plantation records that tell us how the labor system on the henequen plantations functioned. Gender, age, and marital status determined one's role in the production process. At the top were married men who were fully employed at the hardest tasks, such as cutting, rasping, and weeding. Women worked as supplements to their spouses; they were not directly employed by the hacienda and often went unpaid, though they worked alongside their men. They were commonly required to perform unpaid domestic service for the hacendado as well. Single men weeded and transported the refuse from the rasping. Boys hung the fibers to dry in the sun. Married male workers earned the highest wages, between 3.5 and 6.5 pesos per week. This was not by any means adequate to fulfill the needs of their households. Milpas, which permitted a family to grow some of their food, went only to married males.

The coffee plantations of Veracruz were no better. Men readied the land for coffee trees by burning the forest and prepared the seedlings and transplanted them. They pruned the trees every year. Women weeded and harvested. After the harvested beans dried on large cement terraces, women picked over the coffee beans by hand, classifying them before the product was packaged. In the final stages skilled male workers operated steam and electric processors to de-pulp, wash, skin, and polish the beans. The women took the most labor-intensive, lowest-paying jobs, spending twelve hours a day in a room hunched over a table in their wooden clogs, sorting the beans and depositing them into different chutes to be packaged. However hard the work, women preferred this work to the fields. It was not unusual in areas where labor was scarce for planters to hire entire families, including the children.

In another new coffee region, Chiapas, families obtained a plot of land from the hacendado for subsistence crops, in return for which both males and females worked all year round on the coffee estate. Rural workers in Chiapas earned between 50 and 62 centavos, substantially higher than the 37 paid elsewhere. Planters paid female rural workers one-third to one-half the wages of males, and because there was a surplus of female workers, employers did not raise their pay. From 1897 to 1910 men's wages rose from 50 to 75 centavos per day, but women's stayed at 25. In the processing plants women earned 50 centavos, twice what they earned in the fields.

Throughout Mexico for rancheros and village farmers who held on to their land, life remained much the same as it always had been. Mexican elites often mocked rural Mexicans for their resistance to modern labor-saving agricultural implements. But country people understood the limitations of their environment much better than did these haughty outsiders. Take, for example, the Mexican Indians' preference for the old plow of their ancestors. It consisted of a long tree branch with a crook, sometimes faced with iron to penetrate the topsoil, pushed by an ox. Country people rejected the modern plow, which would not last very long in the rocky soil pervasive in much of Mexico. The modern plow clanged against the rocks, while the old wooden plow slid off and continued on. Just as important, deep and wide furrows were not necessary, for farmers only had to scratch the surface to create sufficient depth for corn seed. The steel plow dug up too much topsoil, leading to erosion in the wind and rain.

Village and ranchero cultivators almost certainly lacked the capital for other innovations. The most common irrigation method was to dip pottery jugs in streams and pour water in ditches. Mexican farmers did not rotate crops. Some practices were downright unhealthful. Some farmers threshed grain by letting animals trample it in a corral for two or three days. Unfortunately, dirt and filth mixed in with the wheat.

For small producers, such as rancheros, tenants, or sharecroppers, insecurity was an inalterable fact. Dryland farming (without man-made irrigation) everywhere was precarious at its best. In the arid north the rain could stop for years at a time. By the end of the nineteenth century small agriculturalists were evermore dependent on outside income to subsist. We can see these uncertainties in the coffee districts of Veracruz. A large number of smallholders (less than 20 acres) overpicked their coffee trees and grew other crops under the trees, such as tobacco and corn, to maintain themselves and their families in the face of the rising cost of living. They found that their yields declined, because they had to supplement their incomes working elsewhere and, consequently, inadequately cared for their plantings. Small coffee producers were at the mercy of processors, who prepared the commodities for sale and determined the price the farmers received for their product.

During the Porfiriato, especially in its last decade, the Mexican countryside was under enormous stress. The traditional world of the rural mestizo and Indian crumbled beneath the onset of the commercialization of agriculture and the commodification of land. The ruling elite, having cast aside the restraints of the Church, turned on the country people, particularly the Indian, as the last great impediment to progress. The differences between rural people and the modernizers were essential. To the rural Mexican (in the ideal) work provided pleasure in doing the actual task, the camaraderie of labor with friends and neighbors, and a feeling of accomplishment. Work strengthened family ties and community solidarity through shared tasks and celebrations. Rural Mexicans rejected the modern sense of time and money. No one rushed to finish a pleasurable task. (Of course, not all tasks, especially those assigned by employers, were pleasurable.) There was no reason to save money, for in many villages the accumulation of capital would have violated custom and alienated one's neighbors.

As the rural population grew, the Porfirian economy made land a market commodity, industrialization undermined rural home crafts production, and mechanization reduced the demand for labor, resulting in severe social dislocations, such as landlessness. Country people reacted in several ways to these transformations and pressures. At first, rural people sought solace, if not salvation, in their traditions. Then they resisted the modernizers in quiet everyday ways. They sought to maintain the distinctive rhythm of their lives dictated by the agricultural and religious calendars. Some observers believe that the growing tensions among rural communities caused them to turn on themselves. In many cases village society was downright fractious in the best of times. Class differences split villages. Vicious gossip, vengeance, spite, and pettiness were integral to daily existence. Fights among local groups, called *camarillas*, who vied for control over local resources, grew more heated. There was a substantial increase in violent crime.

Some Mexicans began to question the relevance and usefulness of both the Catholic Church as an institution and religion itself. Protestantism, spiritism, and messianic movements challenged the traditional Church. It was no accident that areas where these alternatives made the greatest inroads engendered upheavals in the 1890s and 1910. Eventually in 1910, in many areas the people of the villages and the rancheros would take up arms to fight to reestablish control over their daily lives.

The Mines

Miners earned the highest wages in Mexico, but their work was dangerous, the cost of living in the mining camps very high, and employment insecure. Throughout the Porfiriato, in the mines the best jobs, skilled and supervisory, went to foreigners. Miners were in the formative stages of transformation into a working class. Many worked part-time in the mines and still maintained property they cultivated or engaged in other part-time employment on the haciendas as well. After 1900 many miners spent time working in the United States.

The work was enormously difficult. In a typical silver mine, workers first dug a short tunnel into a hillside and then excavated straight down. They

Mining camp

climbed in and out of the shaft on eight- to ten-foot notched logs. They cut the shafts to follow the veins. Drillers (barreteros) were the top of the underground hierarchy. They earned the highest wages, as much as 3 pesos a day. In the shaft drillers used steel-tipped iron rods to tear loose the ore. Other less skilled workers then hauled 150- to 200-pound bullhide sacks up the log ladders to the surface and emptied the sacks in a dump. If there was no stamp mill, workers crushed the ore and then put it into a trough, where water poured over it. Workers hauled the water. They then sacked the washed ore in 200-pound bags. The mine shipped the bags to the smelter. Workers who hauled ore earned 18 to 20 centavos a day.

Although working conditions varied substantially according to the region, there were common trends across the mining sector. New technology greatly changed the workplace. The introduction of new machinery, such as pneumatic drills and electric-powered machinery, led to increased disease and accidents. The change from drilling with a bar and sledge and blasting with black powder to pneumatic drill and dynamite, the use of hoists, and new drainage and ventilation equipment demanded a new kind of worker. Experience, intelligence, and judgment were less important than obedience and diligence. The demand for unskilled labor rose. Unskilled labor (peons) came to comprise two-thirds to three-quarters of the workforce. They were shovelers, rock breakers, ore sorters, car men, and helpers who had come from rural areas. Skilled workers continued to drill the ore, install timber, and operate and maintain machinery, but they generally had far less independence. Miners often worked in gangs called *cuadrillas* under contractors, and earned their pay by task rather than as daily wages.

Earlier barreteros working in pairs with picks, wedges, sledges, bars, and black powder controlled their own crew, hiring unskilled labor to work with them. They bid on specific tasks. In the old days drillers pounded steel bars into rock with sledgehammers that weighed four or eight pounds. They held the iron rod in one hand and swung the hammer with the other. The heavier hammer required a two-man crew with one holding the bar and the other wielding the hammer. Often members of the teams were relatives who supported each other. Although air drills supposedly replaced fifteen to twenty men and were in common use after 1900, the days of the hand drillers had not quite passed, for many mines employed both new and old methods. The contract system transferred risk to the workers, for any delays (caused by any circumstances ranging from absenteeism among the crew to cave-ins) reduced income.

It was common for several work arrangements to operate simultaneously. Mine owners could contract out a single part of the process or the entire operation. Most owners favored piecework (the employer paid the miner for a specific task or amount of ore excavated), which spurred productivity. Whatever the case, as time went on miners were much more regimented, with foremen supervising almost all activities. The mine owner might contract with a barretero, who hired his own crew, or with pairs of barreteros who received payment for the amount of area drilled. In some mines owners complained their workers stole precious ore. The guards at the Real del Monte searched the men three times each day for hidden silver ore. Smuggling was an art form. There were stories of miners who concealed ore between their toes and in hammers with hollow handles.

In boom times, there were never enough workers. But the busts in this cyclical industry were catastrophic. The situation in Hidalgo de Parral, Chihuahua, was indicative of the ups and downs miners endured. From 1897 to 1903 Parral experienced unprecedented prosperity as mineral prices rose, causing the population to increase from 11,250 to 16,382 between 1895 and 1900. Beginning in 1903, however, conditions deteriorated. There were times when forty percent of the population was forced to abandon the district in search of employment. By the end of 1906, 5,000 people had departed and by 1909 only 9,000 people resided in Parral.

The economic boom sent people to where the jobs were and, as a result, 300,000 Mexicans settled in the north between 1877 and 1910. Most of these people were displaced rural workers, ruined artisans, or adventurers hoping for better opportunities. They swelled Monterrey from 14,000 residents in 1877 to 78,000 in 1910, and transformed Torreón from a tiny village to 43,000 by 1910. The north was for many transient workers only a stopover, for their preferred destination was the United States where employers offered double the pay. After 1900 between 60,000 and 100,000 Mexicans crossed the border every year to work on farms, on the railroads, and in the mines. One has a picture of the people of the northern states always in transit, between farm and city, city and city, farm and border, farm and mine, mine and mine, mining camp and mining camp. People would leave their employment to return home for planting and harvest. Many ranchos were abandoned for much of the year, only to teem with activity when crops called.

This pattern, of course, was unacceptable to the mine owners, who sought more reliable employees. They used a number of strategies to attain a regular workforce. They paid high wages, tried to hire men with families, and gave bonuses to employees who worked regularly. During the first decade of the twentieth century, Cananea, an enormous North American-owned mining complex in Sonora, increased the average number of work days a month when it instituted bonuses for attendance. Northern employers attracted workers by offering subsidies for commodities at the company store, housing, schools, and medical care. After 1900, some of the larger companies, such as the American Smelting and Refining Company (ASARCO), committed substantial investment to safety improvements. A few mine owners, like Alexander Shepherd of Batopilas, Chihuahua, kept his workers by maintaining personal relations with them. He acted much like a Mexican patrón or father figure, who "took care" of his employees. Even ASARCO managers exhibited personal interests in workers and their families in an effort to maintain their loyalty.

Pachuca, a mining town

Once the miners settled, employers sought to inculcate them with the capitalist work ethic through campaigns against gambling, drinking, and other vices. The Mexican middle class was a willing and enthusiastic participant in these morality campaigns. The goal was to convert the transient mass of workers into peaceful, hardworking, patriotic, if not quiescent, people. If other methods failed, companies were not averse to using coercion to maintain labor discipline. In many mining camps they provided financial support for the local police. Each mine had an agent who maintained order.

However dangerous and insecure their employment, miners nonetheless carried on their lives in the mining camps. Many of the mining and timber companies encouraged men to bring their families in the hope that these attachments would reduce transiency. The companies provided housing, schools, and hospitals to tie them down. Women in the camps worked as domestics, petty merchants, factory workers, and prostitutes, but rarely in the mines and never below ground. Miners, always a rowdy bunch, found entertainment, not only with the prostitutes, but with gambling and billiards. Occasionally, the circus arrived with magicians, a particular favorite.

Mexico City

More than anyplace else in Mexico, the capital experienced the down side of life during the Porfiriato. The city's population doubled between 1869 and 1910 from 230,000 to 470,000 inhabitants. Half of its people were born elsewhere and came to the city to look for a new start. The burgeoning economy and the accompanying expansion of the national government provided numerous opportunities for employment. Surely migrants found a better world than they had left. But their expectations were inevitably too high.

Traditional rural kinship networks that had supported the migrants eroded in the city. Political alienation soon arose in the new world of industrialization. The Porfirian urban elite had no inclination to accommodate either high expectations or disappointed dreams, clinging instead to paternalism and cooptation, previously the bases of social relations. The Díaz regime certainly did not provide the necessary education, welfare facilities, or recreation for the new (or old) residents. Capitalinos (residents of Mexico City) could take their solace in their cultural and religious traditions. Certainly there was not much room for optimism in their lives. To visitors Mexico City gleamed with modernity. But it was a glistening facade covering a squalid underworld. It was a city of starkest contrasts between rich and poor, old and new.

During the Díaz era, the great city absorbed most of the nation's resources and generated much of its wealth. The national government spent most of its discretionary funds in Mexico City. The capital received eighty percent of the nation's outlays for streets, electricity, and sewer systems, as well as the lion's share spent on libraries and schools. Government employed two-thirds of the city's professionals. One-third of the nation's small manufacturers, such as in textiles, shoes, and cigarettes, operated in the capital. Almost a quarter of nation's retail purchases took place along the axis from the Zocalo to the Alameda Park.

Like other Latin American cities such as Buenos Aires and Rio de Janeiro, the turn of the century brought a fundamental physical transformation of the capital. It began a relentless push toward the mountains that surrounded the valley on three sides. In 1900 Mexico City had not yet filled the vast valley. There were many Indian villages and several towns, such as San Angel, Coyoacán, and Tlalpan in the south, Tacubaya in the southwest, and Azcapotzalco in the northwest, which were independent entities. These are all parts of the city today. In the 1890s these towns became the sites of the region's industry, including textile, paper, tobacco, and shoe factories.

In 1900 the capital was a city of outsiders with 66 percent of its residents born elsewhere. The drain of people from the central plateau was striking. The population of the city of Guanajuato in the Bajio region, for example, dropped from 52,000 to 36,000. The population was relatively young with 56 percent

Table 2. Population, Selected Years, 1803 to 1910

Year	Mexico	Mexico City
1803	5,800,000	138,000
1852	7,663,000	170,000
1869	8,813,000	230,000
1884	10,000,002	300,000
1895	12,570,000	330,000
1900	13,606,000	369,000
1910	15,160,000	471,000

between 16 and 45, whereas nationally this age group accounted for 45 percent of the population.

Similar to the first half of the nineteenth century, women made up a slight majority of the overall and migrant populations, at 53 percent. Demands for labor in domestic service and manufacturing, which predominantly employed females, created unprecedented employment opportunities, making Mexico City a magnet for women.

Because Mexico City was the center of government, finance, and commerce, it required a substantial white-collar population. As the government expanded under Porfirio Díaz, the demand for bureaucrats and professionals increased. The number of government employees in the city reached 5,000 in 1900, a 75-percent increase from 1895. There were an additional 5,000 to 6,000 military personnel, about 20 percent of whom were officers. Teachers numbered over 3,000. There was a growing need for lawyers, engineers, and doctors, many of whom went to work for the government. The number of lawyers increased by 79 percent, engineers by 127 percent, and professors by 90 percent.

The middle class burgeoned, comprising 22 percent of the workforce, a 62-percent increase since 1895. Its members emulated the rich, including a considered disdain for the lower classes. They were ambitious, for they aspired quite openly to higher status. One measure of social standing was the number of servants in one's household. The middle class, as it prospered, demanded ever more domestics.

The physical transformation of Mexico City began under Maximilian. He laid out the boulevard linking the downtown area to Chapultepec Park, which eventually was named the Paseo de la Reforma. The avenue starts out from the statue of Charles IV of Spain, approximately a mile from the Zocalo, and extends for somewhat over two miles to the park. Along the way is a magnificent promenade, measuring 170 feet in width, including sidewalks and street. The Paseo has six circular parks 400 feet in diameter, each of which now has a monument.

During the Porfiriato the Paseo was the boulevard of the rich. Beginning in the 1890s, the great avenue stimulated the movement of the wealthy and middle classes from the area between the Zocalo and the Alameda Park, known as the Plateros district. The rich maintained their offices and continued to shop in Plateros, but shifted their residences to the affluent neighborhoods to the west along the Paseo. Most of the affluent lived in two-story homes along Bucareli Street, the Paseo de la Reforma, and in the Colonías Cuauhtémoc,

Roma, and Juárez. Many of the streets in Cuauhtémoc were named after European cities so much admired by the Mexican upper class. In all of these suburbs the environment was healthier, for the districts enjoyed modern drinking water and sewer systems. So popular did the new neighborhoods become that land prices along Reforma increased sixteenfold between 1880 and 1900. The wealthiest areas had treelined streets and single-family dwellings, with occasional apartment buildings. Stores occupied the corner lots. Streetcar lines were built to service the suburbs, enabling domestics access to their employers. Homes of the rich were ostentatious. The small middle class and some skilled workers lived west and northwest of the upper end of the Reforma in San Rafael and Santa María. These areas consisted of mostly modest single-family dwellings owned by their occupants.

Despite the movement of the affluent residents to the farther reaches of the city, the Plateros remained vibrant with activity. Several large department

Zocalo or Plaza in Mexico City

stores, such as the Port of Veracruz and the City of London, occupied the southwestern corner of the Zocalo. A few blocks west of the plaza stood the House of Tiles, the location of the famed Jockey Club, the "in" club of the rich, where each day in the late afternoon the surrounding streets were filled with beautiful, well-dressed women in their elegant carriages. The endless line of carriages brought traffic to a halt, while the city's dandies loitered, ever on the lookout for a new acquaintance of high standing. It was quite a show!

Just down a block, a safe distance from the slums and near downtown, the Alameda Park was a refuge for the upper and middle classes. Friday and Saturday nights the well-to-do rented shaded seats and listened to police band concerts. The municipal government installed electric lights in 1892, making the evenings more secure as well as more pleasant. On Sundays men and women put on their finery for yet another fashion show at the park. The men wore vests and black jackets and felt hats. The women wrapped their shoulders in colorful shawls, and donned their best jewelry.

The sharp, grim contrast between rich and poor was breathtaking. Even the newspapers, generally insensitive to such matters, noticed the differences: "central avenues with their luxurious stores" juxtaposed to the "muddy - pigsties . . . of our sickening tenements on those open sewers we call streets. . . ." In 1886 the municipal council bemoaned "this cesspool we call a city." It was without doubt one of the most unhealthy places in all the world in 1910. These descriptions referred to the slums spread out along the eastern border of city. They lacked sewers, drinkable water, and paved roads. One reporter wrote in 1896 of the "gloomy and festering vecindades (tenements) of the walking dead." The next two decades saw no improvement. The area east of the Zocalo doubled in population from 1880 to 1900. One-third of the population lived on fifteen percent of the land, crammed into "barrios full of squat, dirty, and cracked houses that reek of misery and putrefaction. . . ." Open drainage ditches carried the poor's filth. The smell was overwhelming. The only relief came in the rainy season, when precipitation carried away the waste. Tenements stuffed sixteen to twenty people in a room. As a result, typhus festered in half of all the poorly ventilated, overcrowded buildings. In the far south in the marshlands new slums arose. There garbage dump dwellers picked through the stench and rot to salvage food and clothing.

Each of the dozen or so poor barrios had its own community with stores, a church, and often its own particular group of inhabitants. However distinct their local flavor, they had squalor in common. When floods arrived, the barrios turned into "rivers of dirty, greasy, and pestilent water. . . ." Because the eastern districts were the lowest, flooding was worst there.

Not surprisingly, the mortality rate, at 42.3 per 1,000, was among the highest in the world at twice that of Buenos Aires, Argentina, and Rio de Janeiro, Brazil, and even higher than in Madras, India, and Cairo, Egypt, two of the world's most notoriously unhealthy cities. The death rate had increased by 60 percent between 1878 and 1890. Despite extensive expenditures on potable water and sewage systems, in the years after 1900 more than 8,000 children died every year. Typhus epidemics struck in 1901, 1902, 1905, and 1906.

Although the city spent millions to improve drainage, flooding continued a desperate problem. During the 1870s, the government repaired existing drainage systems that took runoff and waste to Lake Texcoco. It also built new canals to channel water from creeks in the north and southeast. Nonetheless, the floods in 1886 turned the city into a "veritable lake," which destroyed 500 houses. In the 1880s residents tried to raise the streets, but this only exacerbated the impact of flooding in lower areas.

Huge drainage projects successively failed. In 1889 the city undertook to construct a monumental drainage system. The main element was a Great Canal that flowed north for thirty miles and drained the swamp east and north of city, took away waste, and regulated the level of Lake Texcoco. Constructing the canal required cutting a six-mile tunnel underneath the surrounding mountains to take water out of the valley. Despite completion of the new canal network in 1895, the entire eastern half of city flooded two years later. Even when the entire project was finished in 1900 at the cost of 15.9 million pesos, the floods continued. More flood control was added in 1908 and 1909, but this did not prevent another major inundation in 1910. A new water system to flush sewers to ensure proper cleansing was added, but this did not help the parts of the city without sewer systems. The city literally stunk.

With its under- and unemployment, wretched living conditions, and disease, Mexico City was the capital of shattered dreams. It is unsurprising that the poor sought solace for their hopelessness and an outlet for their rage. They turned first to alcohol. Consumption of pulque, the most popular alcoholic drink among the poor, was enormous: 41,000 tons in 1875, 100,000 tons in 1883, 300,000 tons in 1910. Per capita intake of pulque actually doubled during the Díaz era. In 1864 there were 64 *pulquerías,* 817 in 1885, and 1,200 in 1905. There was a pulquería for every 300 residents. The typical pulquería was a one-room saloon on a corner lot with a colorful name, like "Fountain of Love" or "The Remedy of Heartache," and wild, colorfully painted walls on the inside. Evidently one could not just have one pulque and go home. Drunkenness and rowdiness were endemic. Eighty-five percent of the people occupying jail cells in Mexico City were held as drunks. In 1893 26,000 people were incarcerated for their behavior while drunk. In 1902 there were 90,000 arrests for drunkenness.

Not unexpectedly, the capital was always in a state of "perpetual slow boil." The noise was maddening and the smell unbearable. The city was ever ready to explode into violence. It was dangerous to walk the streets. Two-thirds of the crimes were knifings, shootings, or beatings. Most crimes were committed by the poor against the poor in the eastern slums. After a government crackdown in 1897, there were 10,000 arrests a year, mostly for loitering, begging, or smelling badly. Local authorities assigned petty criminals, called *rateros,* to the drainage projects or other public works. They dispatched others to Yucatán's henequen plantations or tobacco farms in Oaxaca's Valle Nacional as slave labor. Deportations continued to the end of the Díaz era.

Prostitution was common. A 1906 study claimed there were 10,000 prostitutes in Mexico City, no less than five percent of all women residing in the city and a remarkable ten percent of women aged 15 to 30. There may have been thousands more prostitutes who were not counted, because they worked unregistered at the trade in the streets. City officials established brothel zones and required regular medical checkups.

Maintaining control of the streets was a constant strain. The police exacerbated the problems of violence and crime, for like the *rurales* (rural police), they were "recruited from the most ignorant and abject among us. . . ." They received improved training during the Díaz era, but drunkenness, absenteeism, and insubordination were rampant, as were graft and petty extortion.

The Porfirian project to create a disciplined workforce obviously encountered stiff resistance in the capital. Through the police Díaz's officials tried to exert social controls, but the population, heavily comprised of rural migrants, was uncooperative.

The reaction of the upper and middle classes to this grim picture was by no means sympathetic. One traveler accurately reflected their view in this description of the rabble:

> . . . [The] poor masses . . . were known colloquially as léperos. . . . They went barefoot or wore sandals, were unwashed and often tipsy, capped with straw hats and wrapped in rebozos. . . .

One newspaper declared that "it is necessary to keep a strict watch over them, so that they do not get out of control and make trouble. . . ." The fear and hate inherited from the hombres de bien continued among the Porfirian elite. Almost benevolent in comparison, worried members of the middle and upper classes periodically headed quite unsuccessful temperance movements.

The number of factory workers rose to 10,000 in 1910, a 400 percent increase from 1895. One-third were women. The introduction of electricity in the 1890s enabled entrepreneurs to build factories in the city proper on the southern and eastern edges, whereas previously they had built them in the outskirts where water power was available. The factories were relatively small. The largest textile factory had 1,000 workers. Seven others employed more than 200 people. The largest factory was the Buen Tono cigarette plant with 2,000 employees, mostly women. Women comprised 20 percent of Mexico City textile factory employees and over half of all workers in cigarette factories. Although growing in numbers, factory workers comprised only 4 percent of the workforce in Mexico City in 1910, about the same number as government employees, including the military.

As light industry expanded, the nature of work changed. By the 1880s craftsmen, who had dominated this sector until then, were nearly obsolete. Machinery replaced artisans, whose ranks fell sharply from 1895 to 1910 at a time when the population increased. Shoemakers, as a case in point, were once the most numerous artisans in Mexico City. By the end of the Porfiriato workshops had become factories with hundreds of workers specialized in tanning, cutting, or assembling. Many shoemakers stopped making shoes, earning their sustenance repairing them. In *tortilla* milling, printing, and metalworking, the scale of production grew larger, which resulted in a process of de-skilling and concentration of production. Factories created a few new crafts. The number of mechanics more than tripled from 1,200 to 4,000 from 1895 to 1910; in 1910 mechanics outnumbered shoemakers.

The most significant jump in employment was in light industry. The manufacture of clothing, for example, expanded rapidly. From 1895 to 1910 the number of seamstresses in Mexico City rose by 34 percent and dressmakers by 174 percent. Factory owners paid seamstresses on a piece work system at very low rates. The department store El Palacio de Hierro employed about 1,000 people in its stores, many of whom were clerks, and 600 seamstresses in its sweatshop on the outskirts of the capital.

As in previous decades, domestic service remained the largest source of employment. The number of domestic workers increased from 43,000 in 1895 to 66,000 in 1910; they comprised almost 30 percent of the workforce. Approximately 35,000 women, 43 percent of all employed women, worked as domestic servants. These percentages were almost identical to those of 1848. Continued high demand for domestics was closely related to the expansion of the middle class, who associated status with number of servants. At best, these jobs acculturated young women from the countryside, allowing them to progress to factory work and, perhaps, marriage, while simultaneously providing low-cost respectability for the middle class. At worst, the women were stuck in an exploitative situation with little more than room and board and with few prospects for the future other than rape or seduction by their employers.

The factories were not uniformly dismal and exploitative. Some employers realized the value of better working conditions, auxiliary support services, and entertainment. The Robertson brothers, of Scottish descent, owned the Miraflores textile mill in Chalco that was a "model" settlement. There was a well-equipped school, music training, a theatre and well-paid teachers. Another textile mill called La Fama in Tlalpan had two schools, a doctor and pharmacy, and a band. Many mills had chapels on the grounds. El Buen Tono tobacco company was well known for good working conditions: it furnished housing for employees and boasted a profit-sharing scheme. The tobacco company's owner was known to encourage women to work. The Excelsior shoe factory, the leading mechanized factory in the capital, had a gymnasium and pool for employees, helped with housing, and was known for treating employees well. The three giant companies that dominated the tobacco industry ran films at night in their factories. La Tabacelera showed circus and opera in a 1,400-seat theatre. Entertainment was an acceptable expenditure for the tobacco companies, but evidently education was not, for there were only two schools for tobacco workers in the entire country. However hopeful these innovations, they were clearly exceptions. They were paternalistic offerings subject to the whims of employers.

Labor Organizations

Mutualist societies and labor unions were one method for urban workers and miners to exert influence over their everyday lives in the face of the overwhelming economic and political power of their employers. The first mutualist society in Mexico was probably formed in the 1850s or 1860s, and by the 1870s there were several in Mexico City among artisans. For the most part the early mutualist societies looked after their members by setting up funds for medical expenses, unemployment compensation, and retirement pensions. Few, if any, stridently opposed oppressive conditions in the workplace.

Labor organizing blossomed in the 1870s among artisans and textile workers. Despite an overwhelming inclination toward moderation, there were at least twenty-seven recorded strikes from 1865 to 1880, almost all in textiles and mining. Wages were the main issue. During the ensuing decade, as labor unions gradually supplanted mutualist societies, there were fewer strikes. The most notable occurred in Pinos Altos, Chihuahua, where miners protested against payment of their wages in scrip redeemable only at the company-owned store. Federal troops were sent in to restore order. In the 1890s the number of strikes increased, but, according to Rodney Anderson, the focus shifted from wages to "discontent with the nature of work itself." Workers resisted longer hours (possibly because of the installation of electric lighting) and the introduction of factory discipline.

By the turn of the century industrial labor unions emerged in three crucial sectors: railroads, textiles, and mining. Each would experience major strikes in the first decade of the twentieth century. Employers in these industries instituted rather objectionable new practices and accelerated earlier attempts to instill discipline. New technology was accompanied by a harsher regimen. In some cases factories lowered wages in order to pay for new technical innovations. One textile worker wrote of "the outrages of which we are the victim." Miners and railroad workers in particular had experienced a wider world of labor relations across the border in the United States, which led them to protest their plight.

In 1906 major strikes were launched in the textile industry at Puebla and Tlaxcala, the copper mines at Cananea, Sonora, and by mechanics on the railroads. According to Rodney Anderson they struck over "eroding wages, hazardous working conditions, ill treatment by foremen, and favoritism shown to foreign labor over Mexican workers."

Unions, whose members were most concerned with local issues of wages and working conditions, came into direct conflict with wider interests at the national level, because the strikes took place against foreign-owned companies and because the national government had to intervene in the confrontations using troops to defeat the strikers. Violence occurred in the textile factories and mines. The bloody events at the Río Blanco textile factory in Orizaba in early 1907 taught workers that the government would be un-bending.

The commercialization of agriculture and industrialization profoundly al-tered everyday life at the turn of the century. These changes would, in turn, inevitably affect politics. Mexicans, some whose backs were to the wall, sought to regain a modicum of control over their daily existence. As seen in chapter 10, when combined with a series of economic and political crises between 1900 and 1910, this push provided the force to topple the Díaz dictatorship.

THE POLITICS OF ORDER, 1877–1910

Porfirio Díaz was president of Mexico for thirty-one of the thirty-five years between 1876 and 1911. He ruled over an era of unprecedented peace, political stability, and, as we have seen, economic growth. There were neither foreign wars, nor widespread civil conflicts. Díaz built his regime with a shrewd combination of consensus and repression. He put together a complicated mosaic of arrangements with various regional groups, which ensured general domestic tranquility and gradually expanded national government authority. Díaz pushed aside ideology in favor of a raw pragmatism, which yielded a strong centralized regime. The general insisted on all the trappings of democracy: he scrupulously followed the Constitution of 1857, seeing to it that Congress amended it to permit his reelection in 1888 and thereafter. Throughout the Díaz era, the nation held regular elections for posts ranging from municipal councils to the national Congress. However, as revealed by the economic and political crises that occurred between 1907 and 1910, it was a dictatorship built on quicksand. When challenged by a multi-class opposition coalition and armed insurrection in 1910, the Díaz regime collapsed.

The Pax Porfiriana (Porfirian peace) did not come either immediately or easily. We can divide the Porfiriato roughly into three periods. The first period encompassed Díaz's initial term, 1877 to 1880, and the presidency of Manuel González, 1880 to 1884. During this time, Díaz struggled to find reliable allies, to reestablish relations with the major foreign powers, and to build a favorable environment to attract foreign investment for economic development. The second period included the years 1884 to 1900, when Díaz consol-

---

Unending thanks to the work of William Beezley, Don Coerver, Daniel Cosío Villegas, Romana Falcón, Charles Hale, Alicia Hernández Chávez, Evelyn Hu-DeHart, Gilbert Joseph, Friedrich Katz, Alan Knight, Enrique Krauze, Stanley Langston, Douglas Richmond, Paul Vanderwood, Stuart Voss, and Allen Wells.

idated his rule. During this era, he defeated or bought off nearly every regional political opposition group, changed the laws to make them more favorable toward business investment, and put the nation on firm financial footing. The third comprised the years after 1900, when the foundation of the dictatorship cracked badly under the weight of social change and aging, corrupt leadership.

The regime rested on three crucial underpinnings. Díaz was his own chief political asset. As a war hero, patriot, and representative of a new, rising generation of Liberals, the general had enormous credibility with a wide spectrum of the population. He proved to be an unequalled deal maker, and was simultaneously feared and admired. He exercised authority over matters large and small. Letters to him read similarly to those addressed to Spanish kings during the colonial era. People from all walks of life wrote to him with complaints or information. Few blamed him for the inadequacies of the regime. All looked to him for wisdom and fairness. At least in the early years of his regime, he personally met with his people on a regular basis.

The second political resource was the fast-expanding economy, which provided rewards for those who allied or otherwise cooperated with Díaz. There were jobs, concessions, subsidies, tax exemptions, and contracts for those who were reliable. As long as the economy grew, the dictator had ample rewards at his disposal to maintain his political arrangements. It was no coincidence that the major challenges to his rule occurred during economic downturns. In the early 1890s, for example, a worldwide financial crisis plunged Mexico into depression, as markets for its mineral exports slumped badly. Several rebellions erupted as a consequence. The depression of 1907 led to his downfall.

The third of these political resources, coercion, or the threat of coercion, was as important as the rewards. Díaz was more than willing (as had been Juárez before him) to eliminate his opponents, if the need arose. When early in his rule a subordinate asked him what to do with captured rebels, Díaz told his lieutenant to "kill them in cold blood" ("*Mátalos en caliente*"). The dictator used the rural police (rurales), established originally by Juárez, to terrorize the countryside. (People feared being captured by the rurales, who inevitably shot their prisoners when they allegedly tried to "escape" from custody. This was known at the time as the *ley fuga*.) Over the years, coercion became more myth than reality, but as long as Mexicans, rich and poor, feared the regime and the consequences of opposition, the Porfiriato endured. The second and third crucial political assets can be summarized by the regime's motto, "*pan o palo*" ("bread or the club"). All three of these—Díaz himself, a growing economy, and the coercive apparatus—functioned together in delicate balance. In 1910 all would come apart.

The First Presidency of Porfirio Díaz, 1877–80

Two political promises limited the new president. Most important, because Díaz had rebelled against Juárez and toppled Lerdo when they had sought reelection, he vowed not to succeed himself in 1880. In addition, Díaz the rebel had pledged his support of municipal democracy. This promise constrained his ability to consolidate his hold on the countryside. Nonetheless, the general set about to reestablish order. In his first term Díaz was conciliatory for the most part, though he was not afraid to use force. He did not repress opponents in Congress. The press operated freely. It was not until the 1890s, after he had served for a decade as president, that he was able to completely muzzle the opposition. When he could, he removed regional bosses, who had allied with Lerdo, but he did not ruin them. They kept their land and wealth and the definite prospect of increasing both. Díaz also followed a conciliatory policy toward the Church. Although he did not repeal the Reform Laws, he permitted the Catholic Church to publicly practice religion and to clandestinely obtain property.

At the time of Díaz's first election, Mexico was an international outcast without formal diplomatic relations with either France and Great Britain, as a residual from the Tripartite Intervention in 1861. Extensive and dangerous differences remained with the United States as well. The conflict with the United States resulted from the inability of either country to maintain order along the border. Bandits and nomadic Indians attacked on both sides, using the international boundary as a shield from pursuit. Neither nation was satisfied with the other's diligence in patrolling the borderlands to rein in these marauders. The United States also objected to the Mexican duty-free zone along the border, which Díaz had introduced to attract commerce and investment, because it had engendered widespread smuggling. These areas of contention caused the United States to refuse to recognize the Díaz government in 1877. At one point, when both sides sent reinforced troop detachments to the border, war seemed inevitable. Fortunately, cooler heads prevailed and both sides backed down.

In 1878 the United States finally recognized the Díaz government. Recognition was crucial for Mexico, because foreign investment from the United States was to be the cornerstone of the Porfirian development strategy. Without diplomatic relations between the two nations, few U.S. investors would risk their money in Mexico. Although his popularity benefited from this brief war scare with the United States, Díaz would not risk the wrath of the northern colossus for a quarter of a century. Another diplomatic accomplishment was the reestablishment of relations with France in 1880. This enabled Díaz to lay the groundwork for European investment, which he hoped to use to counterbalance the economic influence of the United States.

The Presidency of Manuel González, 1880–84

Don Porfirio's next dilemma was to choose a successor, who was strong enough to maintain order, but sufficiently weak so as not to challenge him over the long run. General Manuel González proved an almost perfect selection. His administration provided much of the legislative base for subsequent economic development with new laws that encouraged foreign investment and transferred public land to private hands. He also negotiated resumption of diplomatic relations with Great Britain (1884). During his term U.S. companies built the two north-south railroad lines and the Mexican army and militia finally defeated the Apaches in the north, opening the way for a deluge of foreign investment.

González had been a soldier since fighting in the war with the United States as a teenager. In the late 1850s, he fought on the Conservative side in the War of the Reform, but later was with Porfirio Díaz against the French. He was badly wounded during the Porfirista rebellion of Tuxtepec in 1876. After a long recuperation he served as governor of Michoacán. In 1878 Díaz selected him as minister of war. The stern González—whose scarred face and missing arm showed the proof of his bravery and patriotism—was an attractive candidate, because as a military officer with an excellent record he commanded respect from the army at a time of political unrest, and because he was loyal to Díaz. From his days as Díaz's chief of staff during the French Intervention, the two men had been close, personal friends.

González did not steer far from the course Díaz had set. He continued the policy of conciliation with the Church. He remained on good terms with the army, but subtly undermined its political influence. He instituted the practice of recalling generals to active duty, so as to prevent them from returning to their regional popular bases at home and building their own independent political fiefdoms. González showered attention and special privileges on the officer corps, but at the same time began the slow reduction of military expenditures.

The stand-in president guided crucial legislation (discussed in chapter 8), which transformed conditions for business in Mexico. The new legislation formed the basis for the commercialization of agriculture, the full exploitation of Mexico's mineral resources (most importantly by foreign investors), the creation of a national domestic market, and the establishment of a modern banking system.

Despite his impressive accomplishments, contemporaries gave González little recognition. The combination of a long, drawn-out investigation of his business dealings by the Congress and a bitter divorce litigation thoroughly ruined González's reputation in the late 1880s. There is little doubt that González presided over widespread corruption, though probably no more so than had (or would) Díaz. But González served Díaz's purpose well. He carried out a number of onerous tasks necessary for the long-term strength of the regime. He saw through a considerable amount of unpopular legislation, which formed the foundation of Mexico's economic growth. The increasing disrepute of his administration in its last years contributed to Díaz's aura as the savior of the nation.

Porfirio Díaz and Consolidation of the Dictatorship, 1884–1900

In his consolidation of power, Porfirio Díaz employed several crucial tactics. He erased the contentious political rivalries between competing factions and ideologies, such as moderados, puros, and Conservatives. He modified decades of obstructionist regionalism, and he diminished the army as a spawning ground for political challengers. He also created and maintained a myth of invincibility that scared off potential opponents, and he proved adept at keeping rivals divided and off balance.

IDEOLOGY

After his election in 1884, the president ended many of the old ideological divisions that had torn the nation apart for a half century. By the late 1890s few took heed of the past differences between Conservatives and Liberals. Discredited Conservative families, some of whom had collaborated with Maximilian and the French, reappeared as Díaz allies. The government and Church reconciled. In this era the old Liberals, both puros and moderados, either died peacefully or grew rich and complacent. Díaz's motto, "*mucha administración y poca política*" (much administration and little politics), clearly illustrated his pragmatism. Díaz also put an end to the lively (and at times courageous) independence of the national congress. After 1884 he prevented the election of any opposition. By 1888 the Congress was a rubberstamp institution. Díaz's handpicked Congress then changed the Constitution to allow his reelections in 1888, 1892, 1898, 1904 and 1910. He also brought the press—until then quite feisty—under his thumb.

Loyalty superseded ideology. His allies could abuse their powers, enrich themselves, and rule incompetently, as long as they kept the peace, did as Díaz told them, and never acted disloyally. Any hint of betrayal, however, and he tossed them aside. Díaz ordered General Bernardo Reyes, long-time governor and boss of Nuevo León, into exile in 1908, despite decades of impeccable loyalty and service, after rumors arose of Reyes's ambition to succeed Don Porfirio as president.

SUPPRESSING REGIONALISM

To carry out his strategy of centralization, the president required loyal allies, especially at the state level. The dictator did not ever entirely trust his allies either, for he was no fool. He preferred to bring in governors who had no kinship or business ties to the regions they ruled. It was inevitable that over the course of time, as many served in office a decade or so, almost all these officials established such links. To counteract these relationships and to further ensure that regional bosses would not challenge him, Díaz installed separate military zone commanders to counterbalance the political power of the governors. The zone commanders did not have local ties. Governors and military zone commanders kept an eye on each other for Díaz. The ideal was to have a governor and a military commander, both of whom owed their power base to Díaz and who were somewhat hostile to each other, though not to the extent that they threatened the peace.

The dictator used a variety of strategies to rein in regional notables, depending on the local situation. In some instances, he used to his advantage the bitter rivalries existing among factions (known as *camarillas*) in the states.

Díaz set competing groups against each other in order to undermine the power bases of the regional bosses. Díaz usually chose the side that would be most beholden to him and thereby would be his most loyal allies. Díaz rarely crushed the groups out of favor, however, preferring to buy off their members with lucrative economic concessions, such as tax exemptions. Evaristo Madero and his family of Coahuila headed one of the groups Díaz excluded from political influence during the 1880s. Nonetheless, they became one of the richest Mexican families of the era with enormous holdings in land, industry, and mining. In other cases firmly entrenched bosses were either won over or left alone. A few regional bosses resisted Díaz's incursions. The most successful of these was General Luis Terrazas in Chihuahua, who stalemated the dictator after a quarter-century struggle.

Díaz brilliantly used fractionalized politics in the states to his advantage. In the case of Sonora the wily dictator allied early with a new political group that pushed aside Ignacio Pesqueira, the boss who had dominated the state since the 1860s. Porfiristas Luis Torres, Ramón Corral, and Rafael Izábal led this very young, ambitious camarilla. In the tough politics of Sonora, based on the bitter rivalries between notables of the major cities—Alamos, Guaymas, and Hermosillo—the three men realized quickly they could not win on their own. They needed an ally in Mexico City. Díaz wanted to curtail the old Liberal war-horses like Pesqueira, especially in distant Sonora, known for its resistance to outsiders. The dictator did not seek allies with independent power bases. Torres, who was not a native Sonoran, Corral and Izábal as young intruders without strong local support, fit his requirements. The Triumvirate, as they were known, no better than evenly matched with rival factions, struck a deal with Díaz in 1880 and sold themselves heart and soul.

For their support, Díaz rewarded the Triumvirate extensively. Federal troops put down the Apaches in 1886, for example, ending a century of bloody war. Díaz also backed the Torres group's plans to settle and farm the Mayo and Yaqui Valleys. Federal military presence was necessary for the camarilla to force these Indian peoples from their ancestral lands. In addition, the national government promoted the construction of a much needed railroad. As a result of these measures, Sonora's economy boomed. The Triumvirate practiced the policies on the state level that Díaz had perfected nationally. They coopted their opponents, going so far as to offer them employment in the state government. The Triumvirate and the other notables who cooperated with them grew rich. The three men, who had risen from modest beginnings to accumulate substantial fortunes, intermarried with the most important political, commercial, and landholding families in Sonora.

In Yucatán Díaz played off three strong factions. Carlos Peón Machado (governor in 1894–97) headed the first group. He had enjoyed ties to Díaz's father-in-law Romero Rubio, but lost out after Romero died in 1895. General Francisco "Pancho" Cantón (governor in 1898–1902) led another faction. Cantón had once been a traitor, supporting Maximilian. Olegario Molina (governor in 1902–10) represented the upstarts. As in the case of Sonora, the federal government waged a brutal war against Indian peoples who occupied land wanted for development by regional notables (see chapter 2). Cantón headed the military campaign that pacified the region by 1902. Díaz then abandoned Cantón, who had served his purpose, and replaced him with Olegario Molina.

Chihuahua was the most obvious instance in which Díaz failed to oust an old rival. Luis Terrazas, who had fought by Juárez's side in the darkest hours of the French Intervention, and his son-in-law Enrique C. Creel, led a Liberal faction in the state of Chihuahua, which stalemated the dictator by means of its enormous economic holdings. The Terrazas family opposed Porfirista rebellions in 1872 and 1876, temporarily lost out to a Porfirista faction from the mid-1880s to 1892, endured eight years of a Díaz-imposed outsider as governor, and then reconciled with the dictator in 1900. In the end the Terrazas were too strong for Díaz to subdue. Even while in opposition, the Terrazas enriched themselves with Don Porfirio's blessing.

Díaz believed that in order to restore tranquility and institute economic development, he would not only have to reject the Liberals' decades-long adherence to federalism, but would also have to set aside the principle of local autonomy. As we have seen, through mid-century most villages had enjoyed a great deal of autonomy and elected their own councils and mayors. These officials allocated access to land, levied taxes, resolved conflicts, and determined who would join or be exempted from military service. As seen in earlier chapters, local autonomy increased after Independence, because the federal government was too weak to impose on the prerogatives of local authorities. Moreover, local entities were important allies for elite factions at the state and national levels. Díaz took on the task of reining in local autonomy through the office of the jefe político (district boss). Over time the jefes would become the linchpin of relations between localities and the central government, enabling the Porfirista regime to take firmer control in the provinces. In brief, the jefes were the essential instruments of Porfirista nation building.

The *jefetura política* came into being in the last years of colonial rule after 1812, and was always intended to rein in the countryside. During much of the nineteenth century, however, jefes acted more as agents of powerful regional groups than agents of the central government and were therefore advocates of local autonomy. In many areas jefes obtained their offices by popular vote until the 1880s, after which state governors appointed them almost everywhere. The jefes were critical intermediaries between higher political powers and the localities, between landowners and landless, and between the powerful and the powerless. They exercised executive, legislative, and judicial functions and they used these to become involved in all aspects of life in every area of their jurisdiction. They used patronage and client networks to maintain their influence. The jefes tried to shape people's thoughts, customs, and behavior. It was their job to give the regime everyday legitimacy, which required the use of every tool from corruption to coercion.

It was through the jefes that the regime of Porfirio Díaz impinged on the everyday lives of families through interfering in private property, private activities, and homes. At times the intrusion into private life was extensive. In Coahuila, for example, there were regulations that governed small social gatherings, such as dances. Hosts had to request permission from local authorities to hold gatherings and pay a tax to sponsor them. The jefes oversaw the church, hospitals, and jails. They were also the police. Jefes were supposed to mediate conflicts in order to prevent violence. They could deploy soldiers or police and determine how they were to be organized and used. Jefes involved themselves in promotion of private enterprise and development. They often controlled the extent and collection of local taxes. They could suspend municipal authorities. Abuses, of course, were common. The changeover from elected to appointed jefes was a body blow to the concept of local autonomy. When the jefes became beholden not to their locality, but to higher authorities in the state capital or in Mexico City, local autonomy was doomed.

The intrusion of centralized authority and the decline of local autonomy struck hardest, perhaps, in the northern tier of states comprised of Sonora, Chihuahua, and Coahuila. In the north the end of the Apache wars in the mid-1880s transformed the balance of politics. The villagers and *rancheros*, who had fought side by side with the notable families for six decades (or more), were no longer needed as soldiers and allies. Díaz's consolidation of power left the villages without notable factions to play off. The villagers were clearly vulnerable now to the implementation of centralism and its inevitable accompaniment, the enforcement of the Reform Laws. In Chihuahua the state government carefully took apart the locally-based military organizations that had defeated the Indians. The state government instead set up a professional police force and invited in detachments of federal rurales to keep peace.

Worse still, the country people of Chihuahua and elsewhere not only had lost their status as valued allies, but elites now openly regarded them as impediments to progress. The Porfiristas no longer wanted brave soldiers, but instead they wanted rural people transformed into a docile labor force. The country people of the north would have none of it. Their entire system of values was at risk. Male status depended first and foremost on prowess as soldiers and on skills as independent farmers. Rural northerners clung stubbornly to what they had been. The march of order and progress sharply constrained local autonomy. The Chihuahuan Constitution of 1887, for example, ended the democratic election of jefes políticos. In 1904 further revisions reduced local elections for other positions to mere rituals to affirm selections made elsewhere. At the same time they lost their positions as honored soldiers and the national government severely limited the autonomy of their villages (as seen in chapter 9). Moreover, their land was under siege as notables and foreigners stole it. Northern country people did not accept this fate without resistance. From the mid-1880s through the early 1890s there were several rebellions in the sierras (foothill regions) of Chihuahua, the most famous of which occurred in Tomochic in 1892. These same villages would rise again over the very same issues in 1910.

LIMITING THE ARMY

Because he was a general who had overthrown an elected president, Porfirio Díaz well understood that the army had dominated Mexican national government and politics since Independence and that the most serious challenges to his rule would come from his fellow generals. He systematically eroded the influence of the generals in politics, encouraging them to grow fat and indolent. From 1885 to 1903 Díaz reduced the number of state governorships held by generals by more than half to eight. Paradoxically, Díaz increased the military budget and modernized the army's armaments and training, while at the same time shrinking it in size and allowing it to sink into a morass of corruption. He reduced the number of generals by twenty-five percent. By 1910 the army had only 20,000 soldiers, of whom a mere 14,000 were actually available for anti-guerrilla campaigns in 1910. The most notorious practice of the Díaz era was for commanders to collect the salaries of nonexistent soldiers (accounting for the discrepancy of 6,000 troops). State auxiliaries did not escape the butcher knife either, for the dictator viewed them as the true bastions of regionalism. In retrospect, paring the military was dangerously risky, for while it cut down the number of possible rivals and limited potential armed opposition in the provinces, it did not allow Díaz to respond on more than one front at a time when challenged.

DON PORFIRIO THE INVINCIBLE

The coercive power of the state depended more on show than substance. Díaz constructed a myth of invincibility in part from his own record as a heroic general and in part from the two crucial instruments of repression, the army and the rural police (rurales). As previously discussed, the army was most important to Díaz as a symbol. The army's officers trained at Mexico's new military academy and in Europe, and its armaments were the newest technology imported from abroad. For most of four decades no one challenged the myth of the army's power. The rurales were much the same. One elite unit of so-called rurales toured with performances of derring-do, contributing to their reputation as the world's greatest horsemen and courageous lawmen. In fact one-third of them never rode horses. Those who had mounts rode starved, lame, overworked, untrained animals. Rurales were variously former outlaws who continued their previous activities, but in a more orderly manner, or unemployable artisans from the cities. Public relations made them formidable. When the truth revealed itself in 1910 and 1911, the dictatorship crumbled.

The Díaz regime never depended entirely on its coercive power, though in its early days the army and the rurales were crucial institutions. In place of coercion, widely practiced corruption underlay the dictatorship. Fraud, graft, and nepotism were the watchwords of the era. The *mordida* (bite) or bribe fueled all workings of business and politics. Self-interest and personal gain were paramount. The system functioned with few hitches for a quarter century.

DIVIDE AND RULE

Díaz survived by the principle of divide and rule. Despite the iron grip he exerted on politics, rivalries were inevitable. The intense factionalism that characterized national politics since the 1820s was not easily suppressed for very long. Consequently, Don Porfirio turned potentially dangerous compe tition to his advantage by ensuring that vying groups expended their energies against each other, rather than plotting against him. There were only two major factions on the national scene after 1890: the científicos and the old generals (who became known as Reyistas after their leader General Bernardo Reyes).

Led first by Manuel Romero Rubio, the minister of the interior and Díaz's father-in-law, and then after 1895 by José Yves Limantour, the finance minister, the científicos comprised bankers, prominent landowners, government officials, and technocrats. They arose initially in 1891, when middle-class Díaz supporters formed the new Liberal Party whose ideology was based on positivism. (Posivitism was an empiricist philosophy aimed at understanding and reforming society developed by Frenchman Auguste Comte in the nineteenth century, which privileged Mexicans translated into a racist doctrine.) The Liberals hoped originally to broaden the base of the regime and restrain Díaz. They also sought an orderly transition from his rule. But the dictator rejected the notion of political parties. From the failure of the Liberals the científicos emerged as a group of entrepreneurs with a vision for Mexican development based on foreign investment at the core and progressive ideas about education, sanitation, and preventive medicine. The científicos had very limited political power. With the exceptions of Olegario Molina, the political boss of Yucatán after 1900, and Enrique C. Creel of the powerful Terrazas family of Chihuahua, most were Mexico City based and had little or no support in the provinces. Because of their elitism and well-known greed, they were very unpopular. They relied entirely on Díaz.

The old generals group was made up of traditional regional strongmen, former military officers, doctrinaire liberals, and some bureaucrats, who were very critical of the científicos. In the 1880s Manuel González, the former president, was their main leader. Bernardo Reyes succeeded him after 1900. The Reyistas, as they were called after 1900, were more of a threat to Díaz because of their connections to the army and their access to regional support. Reyes, for example, ruled over Nuevo León for many years and was quite popular there.

During the last ten years of his regime, Díaz's policy of divide and rule weakened. He seemingly abandoned his complex system of checks and balances that had kept any one group from gaining too much power, and after 1900 he was less willing to maintain the precarious balance in the states. Both the Terrazas-Creel and Molina camarillas, for example, came to thoroughly dominate their respective states, leaving considerable bitterness among the other factions. Rumblings of discontent were heard from a new generation, which wanted more influence.

Díaz lost control of the balance between the científicos and the old generals as well. Pressed hard to designate a successor, the dictator finally, in order to reassure científicos and foreign investors, selected Ramón Corral, a científico from Sonora, as his vice president for the 1904 election. He removed Reyes from his post as secretary of war (1900–04) and sent him to be governor of Nuevo León. At the same time, Díaz backed científico factions in Sonora and Coahuila against the landowning elite of those states. Soon-to-be revolutionaries José María Maytorena and Venustiano Carranza were the leaders of their respective states' disaffected groups. He also supported foreign interests in the north against local elites, most notably against the Maderos in the Laguna region. (The Maderos, of course, would lead the 1910 rebellion.)

The strongest challenges to the dictator took place during the early 1890s when plummeting mineral prices, caused by a worldwide depression temporarily derailed Mexico's economic miracle, and a series of harvest failures upset the political balance. Rebellions occurred in the states of México, Yucatán, Tamaulipas, Guerrero, and Chihuahua. In the most famous instance, Tomochi, a small village in Chihuahua, held off the Mexican army for months. By the mid-1890s, however, Porfirio Díaz was again secure in power. Many of the issues the rebels raised, such as local autonomy, undue foreign influence, and the reelection of Díaz, would surface again in 1910. As the dictator turned from constant battles against regional strongmen and adversaries to the tasks of building a new state, he became less responsive to public opinion. No longer a man of the people, he powdered his face to play down his Indian heritage and dressed in fancy uniforms. Díaz had lost touch.

The Dictatorship Unravels, 1900–10

Four crises evolved simultaneously in the first decade of the twentieth century. The most immediate crisis was the succession. As mentioned previously, Díaz was wary of his most capable subordinates, shrewdly played them off against each other, and disposed of them when they showed independence or ambition. When he finally permitted the establishment of the office of vice president in 1904, he made sure that its occupant would prove no threat by anointing the most unpopular of his henchmen, Ramón Corral of Sonora, to the post. There were only two men with sufficient public stature to succeed Díaz: General Bernardo Reyes, the political boss of the northeast, whom Díaz dispatched into exile as soon as he displayed even the most timid notion of a run for the presidency; and José Yves Limantour, the brilliant finance minister, whose candidacy was troubled by questions about his citizenship. Critics claimed he was not Mexican by birth. (He was born in Mexico of a French father.) As Díaz approached his eightieth birthday, the issue of succession grew more anxious. There was little likelihood that he would live out his six-year term.

The second crisis emerged from the economy. The depression of 1907 resulted in plunging export prices and widespread unemployment, striking hard at the gains of the Porfirian economic miracle. To make matters worse, the Faustian bargain Díaz had made with U.S. investors, began to threaten Mexican sovereignty as well as to restrict the dictator's maneuvering room. Crucially, the Porfirian political structure depended on a growing economy to supply rewards for cooperation. Depression deprived the dictator of the grease for the wheels of his regime. The depression also adversely affected the emergent middle class in the north, which led the protests against Díaz's closed system.

Third, the carefully crafted mosaic of arrangements with regional elites cracked, partly because of conflicts over economic interests and partly because long-subdued factions sensed weakness and sought to take advantage. Notable families like Maytorena in Sonora, González in Chihuahua, and Madero and Carranza in Coahuila had nursed their grievances for two decades or more. Pushed by economic reverses they blamed on the Díaz government, they jumped when opportunity presented itself. Other potential opponents lurked in the regions where Díaz had allowed one faction to become too powerful. In Yucatán and Chihuahua, for example, the Molina and Terrazas camarillas, respectively, had emerged nearly omnipotent with Díaz's seemingly meek compliance.

Finally, crisis from the lower classes, who had watched nearly powerlessly while the Porfirians had wrenched control of their everyday lives from them in the succession of reforms we have documented, came to a boil. Economic depression, overbearing elites, and an overwhelming sense of unfairness pushed them to the point of rebellion. They needed only for the dictator to falter ever so slightly. The major supports of the regime were crumbling and in crisis: Díaz himself had outlived his usefulness; the economy had abruptly stopped generating the revenues that kept the Porfirista machine running; and the coercive apparatus of the state was corrupt and incompetent.

Creelman

Porfirio Díaz, perhaps self-satisfied in his success, made a critical mistake, when in an interview with U.S. journalist James Creelman in 1908, he announced that Mexico in his mind had at last come of age. It was time for a new, democratically elected leader to take the nation into the new century. This statement set off a wave of speculation in Mexico. Most observers scoffed at the pronouncement. They believed Díaz would never retire. No one dared express the ambition to succeed Díaz, for to do so might lead to exile or worse. The camarilla around Bernardo Reyes tried to push him to organize a presidential campaign, but Reyes hesitated, too accustomed to his prerogatives as the boss of the northeast and too comfortable in the role of the dictator's subordinate. Reyes's supporters had hoped to put together an alliance of dissident upper and middle class groups with rebels in the army—the same coalition that had placed Díaz in power in 1877. Reyes was the key to this scheme, for he was the coalition's link to the army. An angry Díaz shipped Reyes abroad just for thinking about succession. Reyes submitted meekly and went off into exile. This meant that the only way to overthrow Díaz was to link up with lower classes and for most of the elite opposition this was unthinkable.

Although not at all clear at the time, Díaz had upset the delicate balance of his regime with his vanity. Northern hacendados, dissatisfied with a series of government decisions against their interests were, in fact, willing to stir up the lower classes to their advantage. They did not fear the lower classes in the countryside, perhaps because they earlier had fought together as allies against nomadic Indians and in the civil wars of the mid-nineteenth century. From the ranks of the northern landowners arose Francisco I. Madero to challenge Díaz in the election of 1910.

The Revolution of 1910

The Revolution of 1910 resulted from the confluence of the four crises we have discussed: succession, economic depression, the resurgence of dissident regional elites, and the growing oppression of country people and the working class. The effects of the depression were particularly important on the emerging, northern middle class, which provided much of the leadership for the uprisings. Unemployed workers, many from the ruined mining camps of the north, joined the revolutionaries. Crucial, too, was the cracking of the mosaic of political deals between regional notables and the Díaz regime and the process by which rancheros in the north and villagers in the center reached the point where they rebelled in alliance with the discontented elements of the middle class, desperate workers, and dissident elites. All of these factors combined to produce a vertical class alliance, particularly in the north, which openly opposed Díaz in the presidential election campaign of 1910 and then led the rebellion. A charismatic leader, Francisco I. Madero, held together the widely disparate multi-class alliance.

The decade between 1897 and 1907 brought unprecedented economic opportunities for upward mobility in the north. A middle class, consisting of small mine owners, landowners, and merchants, as well as shopkeepers, tradesmen, non-elite professionals, foremen, teachers, and shift bosses, greatly increased in numbers. Nonetheless, they grew increasingly frustrated by the constraints on their political and economic ambitions imposed by the Porfirian system. Elites enjoyed privileged access to credit and favored treatment by the government.

Prosperity eased the pain of injustice for a time, but the depression in 1907 drove the middle class to desperation. In Chihuahua, for example, the effect of the downturn was devastating. The number of small-scale enterprises dropped by thirty-five percent. Many were bankrupted.

These ruined or threatened middle-class entrepreneurs became leaders of the Anti-reelectionist movement, organized in 1908 to protest Díaz's decision to seek another term. They were also active in several gubernatorial campaigns between 1908 and 1910, where they opposed Porfirista henchmen. We can see the progression of the middle class from discontent to disillusionment, and finally, to revolution in the career of Silvestre Terrazas (a distant cousin of the boss of Chihuahua, Luis Terrazas), a journalist who edited an important newspaper in Chihuahua. He maintained a nonpolitical stance for his periodical until 1905, after which he turned it into a sounding board for complaints against local officials. Until 1907 he supported Porfirista political candidates. When Silvestre became a critic of Enrique Creel, then governor, he found himself harassed and jailed twice. Undoubtedly, Silvestre Terrazas protested at least in part out of a sense of outrage at injustice. But he also felt victimized economically by the system. Creel had, in his capacity as a banker, refused him a loan to expand his printing business. Terrazas would become an important aide to revolutionary Francisco "Pancho" Villa.

The downturn in mining, which began in some areas as early as 1903, left thousands of people unemployed. In 1907 they were joined by thousands more migrant workers thrown out of their jobs in the United States. Relatively privileged in boom times, northern workers suffered all the more during the busts.

Díaz's political arrangements with regional notables were also adversely affected by the depression of 1907 and the drought that accompanied it in some areas. They upset the delicate balance of rewards that were their underpinnings. In two northern states, Sonora and Coahuila, crucial conflicts among notables over economic interests reopened old political wounds. Sonoran notables clashed over scarce labor resources. The federal government, in conjunction with Díaz's Sonoran allies, warred against the Yaqui people after 1900 to oust them from their ancestral lands in the Yaqui River Valley. The government deported captured Yaqui "rebels" to Yucatán, where they became slaves on the henequen plantations. Army officers and local officials received a bounty for each Indian taken as a slave. The mining boom had already created a labor shortage in Sonora. War and deportation deprived Sonoran hacendados, led by José María Maytorena, of the Yaquis who furnished their labor force and struck at the very heart of the state's agriculture. The Maytorenas were one of the notable families who were once influential in state politics and cast aside by the Porfiristas.

Coahuilan notables were hurt by the Díaz government's allocation of water resources in the Comarca de la Laguna region, which included parts of Coahuila and Durango. In Coahuila notables had revolted in 1893, unable to accept the imposition of Díaz ally José María Garza Galan as governor. Among the rebels were members of the Carranza and Madero families, who had lost out during the previous decade in the struggles for political power under Díaz. The rebels succeeded in getting the dictator to abandon his ally and to allow notables to reassert local influence. The uneasy truce endured for fifteen years until 1908, when the Madero family suffered a series of economic setbacks, and Díaz adopted a hard line against the recalcitrant notables. Díaz embittered the Maderos and other local notables when he sided with a foreign company in the allocation of water from the Rio Nazas in the Laguna. The Maderos and other hacendados in the region were already staggering from the declining prices of their commercial crops (guayule and cotton), when hit by the worst drought in more than a decade. In both Sonora and Coahuila old rivalries revived with disputes over economic interests.

There were four types of rural people who rose in revolution in 1910. The first was the "modern" peon of La Laguna in Durango, who resided on the great commercial cotton estates of the region. These peons fought under their hacendados, such as Madero. Most resident peons, however, did not join the revolution. As we have seen, their conditions were quite privileged in areas like Chihuahua. Other residents, the slaves of Yucatán's henequen plantations, for example, were too oppressed to rebel. Many resident peons, imported from afar to work the lands expropriated from local villagers, were isolated from or at odds with the local people.

The second category of rural rebels included the tribal Indians of the north, most important the Yaquis of Sonora, who allied, like the Laguneros (residents of the Laguna), with regional hacendados. The third group was comprised of the residents of landholding villages on the central plateau, typified by the followers of Emiliano Zapata of Morelos. These villagers, beset on all sides by encroaching hacendados, population pressures, and an economic depression that drastically limited their ability to earn income to supplement their shrinking landholdings, were desperate by 1910. The fourth and final category was made up of small landowners, known as rancheros, mostly from the sierra regions like western Chihuahua, who fought to regain lands lost to corrupt politicians and hacendados after the successive railroad booms. All in their own ways fought to establish or reestablish control over their everyday lives. Some fought in vain to return to a past era. Others took up arms to find a place in the new economic order.

The glue that held the multi-class alliance of dissident elites, middle class, and rural people together was the charisma of Francisco I. Madero. Madero was an odd revolutionary. He was the son of one of the richest families in Mexico, whose fortune included vineyards, cotton growing, textiles, cattle, coal, banks, rubber plantations, and foundries in several states. He was small and, as a youth, sickly. Quite early he was smitten by "the religion of spiritualism," which included communication with the dead. Francisco attended school in Paris and at the University of California in Berkeley. In 1893 he returned home to manage one of the family's haciendas and proved himself to be an excellent businessman. Most notably, he treated his employees very well, tending to their illnesses personally, having learned homeopathic medicine, feeding the needy, providing first-rate housing, education, and paying high wages. Sometime in 1903 Francisco, through spiritual communication with his dead brother Raul, determined to save Mexico. The following year he entered politics in opposition to the local regime. Very soon he came to the attention of both Bernardo Reyes, the state political boss, and Porfirio Díaz, who decided to leave him alone for the time being. In 1908 he published a book, *The Presidential Succession of 1910,* which called for a return to the principles of the Constitution of 1857 and the end to one-man rule. The Anti-reelectionist movement began formally in May 1909. Madero financed a tour of Mexico by selling off his assets, and founded new Anti-reelectionist clubs as he traveled, and encountered enormous, cheering crowds, despite unsubtle harassment by the government. In April 1910, the Anti-reelectionist party held a convention. The party selected Madero as its presidential candidate.

Madero was an unlikely revolutionary, but he was ideally suited to bring together a disparate coalition of contradictory interests. His main goal was to oust Díaz, thus ending "boss rule." His principles were those of the Liberals of 1857. Dissident elites saw him correctly as one of them. He and they sought no profound changes, only to establish a new regime with them in charge. The middle class asked for a chance to compete equally. Its members regarded Madero as a reflection of their democratic ideals. Rural people thought Madero a fair man, a benevolent hacendado, who would see to justice in the form of restoring their lands. The coalition, of course, did not outlast either the victory of the revolution or Madero himself, who was murdered in 1913 by conservative military officers.

The events of 1910 and 1911 were remarkable and swift. On June 5, 1910, the government arrested Francisco Madero on charges of sedition. Sixteen days later Díaz was reelected for a six-year term. On July 22 the dictator released his opponent, judging the threat ended. On September 16 Mexico celebrated its Independence centennial. A supremely confident Porfirio Díaz seemed at the height of his power. In October Madero fled the country to the United States. On November 20 he issued the Plan of San Luis Potosí, which proclaimed his rebellion with the motto of "no reelection and the end of boss rule." Díaz was inaugurated on December 1. Scattered uprisings took place in the Chihuahuan sierras that drew thousands of government troops. On February 14, 1911, Madero crossed back over the border to lead the Chihuahuan revolutionaries. Defeat and a slight wound persuaded him to leave military operations to Pascual Orozco, Jr., the guerrilla leader in Chihuahua. In the meantime, the dam broke. Local revolts erupted all over the nation. By April much of the countryside was in rebel hands. On May 11 Orozco, against Madero's orders, captured the border town Ciudad Juárez. Ten days later after intense negotiations Díaz resigned and went into exile. The people elected Madero president on October 15, 1911; he was sworn in on November 6.

EPILOGUE

The thirty-five years of the Porfirian peace crumbled in 1910 and 1911. The Mexican Revolution and nearly three decades of continuous civil wars ensued. The issues over which Mexicans fought were the same as those that had haunted Mexico from its first cry for independence a hundred years before: who was to rule and how were they to rule? Common people struggled, as they had since 1821, to assert influence over the mundane aspects of their lives that the Díaz regime had taken away. The fiercest conflicts from 1910 to 1940 erupted over local autonomy, land, labor organization, and religion, all of which went to the very heart of average Mexicans' material existence and beliefs.

A multi-class alliance of dissident elites, ruined middle class, outraged country people, and unemployed workers united around Francisco I. Madero to oust Porfirio Díaz in 1911, but it quickly disintegrated in the face of widely divergent goals. Revolutionary hacendados clashed with villagers over land. Other elites contested workers over wages and conditions of labor. The middle and lower classes disagreed about the preeminence of private property. (Private property was a crucial tenet of middle class values.) Notables and country people, revolutionaries or not, took advantage of disruptions to reassert local and regional prerogatives.

The Porfiristas briefly restored themselves in 1913, taking advantage of both the disintegrating revolutionary coalition and the resurgent regionalism by murdering Madero, and installing General Victoriano Huerta as president. The revolutionary coalition, however, reconstituted to oppose Huerta. Venustiano Carranza, a Coahuilan notable, Pancho Villa, a bandit-businessman from Durango, and Emiliano Zapata, a villager from the state of Morelos, led three loosely tied revolutionary movements to the defeat of Huerta in 1914. Once again, however, the coalition fell apart and the three factions set upon each other in a bloody civil war lasting three years.

Politically, in many ways, by 1914 it was as if the ninety years of Mexico Independence had not occurred. Within three years after Madero's triumph, the nation was torn asunder. From 1914 to 1917 there was virtually no functioning national government. Politics were once again almost exclusively regionally based. By 1917, Carranza, with crucial assistance from his best general, Sonoran farmer Alvaro Obregón, won. Zapata and Villa waged guerrilla warfare until 1919 and 1920, respectively. (Zapata was assassinated and Villa retired.) Carranza won the civil war because he attracted a significant minority among country people and workers by offering a program of land reform and offering support to nascent labor unions.

The victorious Carranza, who initially represented both dissident elites and the middle class, attempted to restore a strong centralized national government. He refused to respond to the needs of rural people and urban workers, although he had promised reforms. His middle class allies, however, recognized the necessity of compromise with the lower classes. The radical Constitution of 1917 was the middle class's attempt to reach agreement with the common people of the countryside and cities. A strong new revolutionary central government would, according to the new constitution, ensure equity and fairness in everyday life. Villagers would not require control over their local government in order to protect their lands. Industrial workers would rely on the national government to obtain living wages.

Carranza rejected this compromise and, as a result, the middle class, led by Obregón, overthrew him in 1920. Mexico was by then, however, again shattered into regional and local factions, more often than not headed by military officers. Obregón and his middle class allies barely held the nation together. His presidency (1920–24) and that of his successor, another Sonoran, Plutarco Elías Calles (1924–28), were unsteady balancing acts. Obregón and Calles had to make sure they satisfied each interest group—villagers, workers, notables, and generals—just enough to keep them from allying with one or more of the others against them. The Sonorans withstood three major revolts: (Adolfo) de la Huerta (1923–24), Cristero (1926–29), and (Gonzalo) Escobar (1929). Much like in the first decades after Independence, common people were needed by elites (this time the new revolutionary elites) as allies, and as such they could bargain successfully to regain their lost control over everyday life.

The triumphant middle-class revolutionaries were, in actuality, much like the nineteenth-century Liberals, who had sought to instill individual initiative, the merits of private property, and the capitalist work ethic in their fellow Mexicans and to stamp out the influence of the Catholic Church. These revolutionaries also came to advocate, as had the Porfirian Liberals, a strong centralized national government and authoritarian rule within a formal structure of democracy in order to further their goals of economic development.

Calles, who emerged as the dominant caudillo of the Revolution, when a Catholic zealot assassinated Obregón shortly after his reelection as president in 1928, to his credit, did not fall into the same personalist trap as had Porfirio Díaz. Calles set about to construct a powerful national political party that would further the goals of the middle class revolutionaries (some of whom were now actually quite wealthy) without relying on any one leader. Although it took more than a decade, the revolutionary regime established a new Porfiriato, but without its weaknesses (at least until the 1960s).

The revolutionary party, known by three different names from 1929 to 1946—the National Revolutionary Party (PNR), the Mexican Revolutionary Party (PRM), and the Institutionalized Revolutionary Party (PRI)—constructed a new stability with excruciating thoroughness in the 1930s. First, it brought together the regional bosses, ostensibly to divide up the spoils of revolution in an orderly manner. Second, the party captured the loyalty of country people and workers, making them directly beholden to it. This was crucial, because rural dwellers and workers had formed the bases of support of the post-revolutionary regional political bosses, who, in turn, allied with the national regime. As long as the common folk's political allegiance to the revolutionary regime was through the regional bosses, the regime would be constantly in peril. When the bosses had independent popular support, they could oppose the national regime with impunity.

Ironically, land reform and labor unionization were the crucial elements in weaning country people and workers from the regional bosses. Lázaro Cárdenas, who was president from 1934 to 1940, undertook an enormous redistribution of land to rural people. In essence, he returned the lands the haciendas had expropriated from villages during the Díaz era and rewarded other country people with land for their services as soldiers during the Revolution. Independent organizations of country people, which had sprung up in the 1920s, originally free to ally with whomever was most responsive to their interests in times of political factionalism, joined national organizations closely tied to the revolutionary party. In return, these country people received land. Similarly, autonomous labor unions, often locally based, joined national unions also linked to the party. In return, members of these unions received privileged treatment in the form of higher wages and better working conditions. The oil workers' union, for example, which became a bulwark of the PRI, won for its members the highest wages in Mexico. Thus, the acquisition of redistributed land and improved working conditions became instruments of the central government. Country people and urban workers were tied directly to the revolutionary party with no intermediaries. Hence, the regional political bosses lost their independent bases of support.

Meanwhile, the national party gradually eroded regional and local political autonomy through patronage. The depression of the 1930s hit hard at municipal and state government revenues. These entities could only turn to the national government/revolutionary party. By the mid-1940s politics was a monopoly of the national revolutionary party and its local and state branches. The process of centralization, however, never went smoothly.

In some areas religion became the focal point of the protests of country people against revolutionary intrusions into their everyday lives. The Cristero Rebellion (1926–29) shook the Obregón-Calles regime to the core. Country folk fought against government prohibitions against public Catholic religious ceremonies and persecutions of priests. A second series of rebellions from 1934 to 1938 arose over the same issues. Experiments in socialist education during the 1930s also brought violent protests from the countryside.

By 1940 the revolutionary political party had reconstructed the Díaz era (though not with the same allies) system of rewards and punishment. Unlike Díaz, the party had extended the benefits of the system to selected elements of the rural and urban lower classes. Millions of country people received land in the agrarian reforms of the 1930s. Similarly, tens of thousands of workers obtained living wages and better conditions of labor through favorable government regulations and rulings. In return, however, these Mexicans had to surrender a good part of their control over their everyday lives to the national government through the revolutionary political party.

For nearly three decades this tradeoff operated relatively peacefully and successfully. By the late 1960s, the cost of this bargain—inequities, unfairness, corruption, and authoritarianism—had proven too high. Since then protests have periodically shaken the hold of the ruling party. By the mid-1990s, the PRI had lost its monopoly on politics. Nonetheless, Mexico has yet to find an equitable and democratic path to link everyday life and politics.

SELECTED BIBLIOGRAPHY

Alcaraz, Ramón. *The Other Side or Notes for the History of the War between the United States and Mexico.* Trans. Albert C. Ramsey. New York: John Wiley, 1850.

Alonso, Ana María. *Thread of Blood: Colonialism, Revolution, and Gender on Mexico's Northern Frontier.* Tucson: University of Arizona Press, 1995.

Anderson, Rodney D. *Outcasts in Their Own Land: Mexican Industrial Workers, 1906–1911.* DeKalb: Northern Illinois University Press, 1976.

Anna, Timothy E. *Forging Mexico, 1821–1835.* Lincoln: University of Nebraska, 1998.

———. "Inventing Mexico: Provincehood and Nationhood after Independence." *Bulletin of Latin American Research* 15(1996): 7–18.

———. *The Mexican Empire of Iturbide.* Lincoln: University of Nebraska Press, 1990.

Arrom, Silvia M. *The Women of Mexico City, 1790–1857.* Stanford: Stanford University Press, 1985.

Balmori, Diana, Stuart F. Voss, and Miles Wortman. *Notable Family Networks in Latin America.* Chicago: University of Chicago Press, 1984.

Bazant, Jan. *Alienation of Church Wealth in Mexico: Social and Economic Aspects of the Liberal Revolution, 1856–1875.* London: Cambridge University Press, 1971.

Beals, Carleton. *Porfirio Díaz, Dictator of Mexico.* Philadelphia: J. P. Lippincott, 1932.

Beezley, William H. *Judas at the Jockey Club and Other Episodes of Porfirian Mexico.* Lincoln: University of Nebraska Press, 1989.

———, Cheryl E. Martin, and William E. French, eds. *Rituals of Rule, Rituals of Resistance: Public Celebrations and Popular Culture in Mexico.* Wilmington: Scholarly Resources, 1994.

Benjamin, Thomas. *A Rich Land, A Poor People: Politics and Society in Modern Chiapas.* Albuquerque: University of New Mexico Press, 1989.

Berry, Charles R. *The Reform in Oaxaca, 1856–1876: A Microhistory of the Liberal Revolution.* Lincoln: University of Nebraska Press, 1981.

Calderón de la Barca, Frances. *Life in Mexico*. Berkeley: University of California
    Press, 1982.
Callcott, Wilfrid H. *Santa Anna: The Story of an Enigma Who Once Was Mexico*.
    Reprint ed. Hamden, Connecticut: Archon Books, 1964.
Chance, Joseph E., ed. *The Mexican War Journal of Captain Franklin Smith*.
    Jackson: University Press of Mississippi, 1991.
————, ed. *Mexico Under Fire: Being the Diary of Samuel Ryan Curtis,
    1846–1847*. Fort Worth: Texas Christian University Press, 1994.
Chowning, Margaret. "The Contours of the Post-1810 Depression in Mexico:
    A Reappraisal from a Regional Perspective." *Latin American Research
    Review* 27 (1992): 119–50.
Coatsworth, John H. *Growth Against Development: The Economic Impact
    of Railroads in Porfirian Mexico*. DeKalb: Northern Illinois University
    Press, 1981.
————. "Obstacles to Economic Growth in Nineteenth-Century Mexico,"
    American Historical Review 83 (1976): 80–100.
————. "Railroads and the Concentration of Landownership in the Early
    Porfiriato." *Hispanic American Historical Review* 54 (1974): 48–71.
Coerver, Don M. *The Porfirian Interregnum: The Presidency of Manuel González
    of Mexico, 1880–1884*. Fort Worth: The Texas Christian University Press,
    1979.
Corbett, Barbara M. "Republican Hacienda and Federalist Politics: The Making
    of Liberal Oligarchy in San Luis Potosí, 1767–1853." Ph.D. diss., Princeton
    University, 1997.
Cortés Conde, Roberto. *The First Stages of Modernization in Spanish America*.
    New York: Harper & Row, 1974.
Corti, Egon Caesar Count. *Maximilian and Charlotte of Mexico*. Reprint ed.
    New York: Archon Books, 1968.
Cosío Villegas, Daniel, ed. *Historia Moderna de México*. 10 vols. Mexico:
    Editorial Hermes, 1955–1974.
Costeloe, Michael. *The Central Republic in Mexico, 1835–1846*. London: Cam-
    bridge University Press, 1993.
Cotner, Thomas E. *The Military and Political Career of José Joaquín Herrera*.
    Austin: University of Texas Press, 1949.
Crawford, Ann Fears, ed. *The Eagle: The Autobiography of Santa Anna*. Austin:
    State House Press, 1988.
Cross, Harry E. "Living Standards in Rural Nineteenth Century Mexico:
    Zacatecas, 1820–1880." *Journal of Latin American Studies* 10 (1978): 1–19.
Cumberland, Charles C. *Mexican Revolution: Genesis under Madero*. Austin:
    University of Texas Press, 1952.
Dabbs, Jack A. *The French Army in Mexico, 1861–1867: A Study in Military
    Government*. The Hague: Mouton & Co., 1963.

DePalo, William A., Jr. *The Mexican National Army, 1822–1852*. College Station: Texas A&M Press, 1997.

DiTella, Torcuato S. *National Popular Politics in Early Independent Mexico, 1820–1847*. Albuquerque: University of New Mexico Press, 1996.

Ducey, Michael T. "From Village Riot to Regional Rebellion: Social Protests in the Huasteca, Mexico, 1760–1870." Ph.D. diss., University of Chicago, 1992.

Dumond, Don E. *The Machete and the Cross: Campesino Rebellion in Yucatán*. Lincoln: University of Nebraska Press, 1997.

Eisenhower, John S. D. *So Far from God: The U.S. War with Mexico, 1846–1848*. New York: Anchor/Doubleday, 1989.

Falcón, Romana. "Force and the Search for Consent: The Role of the *Jefeturas Políticas* of Coahuila in National State Formation." In *Everyday Forms of State Formation: Revolution and Negotiation of Rule in Modern Mexico*, edited by Gilbert M. Joseph and Daniel Nugent, pp. 107–34. Durham: Duke University Press, 1994.

Fowler, Will. "Dreams of Stability—Mexican Political Thought During the 'Forgotten Years': An Analysis of the Beliefs of the Creole Intelligentsia (1821–1853)." *Bulletin of Latin American Research* 14 (1995):287–312.

———. "The Forgotten Century: Mexico, 1810–1910." *Bulletin of Latin American Research* 15 (1996): 1–6.

French, William E. *A Peaceful and Working People: Manners, Morals, and Class Formation in Northern Mexico*. Albuquerque: University of New Mexico Press, 1996.

Green, Stanley C. *The Mexican Republic: The First Decade, 1823–1832*. Pittsburgh: University of Pittsburgh Press, 1987.

Griswold del Castillo, Richard. *The Treaty of Guadalupe Hidalgo: A Legacy of Conflict*. Norman: University of Oklahoma Press, 1990.

Guardino, Peter F. *Peasants, Politics, and the Formation of Mexico's National State: Guerrero, 1800–1857*. Stanford: Stanford University Press, 1996.

Haber, Stephen H. "Assessing the Obstacles to Industrialization: The Mexican Economy, 1830–1940." *Journal of Latin American Studies* 24 (1992): 1–32.

Haber, Stephen H., ed. *How Latin America Fell Behind: Essays on the Economic Histories of Brazil and Mexico, 1800–1914*. Stanford: Stanford University Press, 1997.

———. *Industry and Underdevelopment: Industrialization of Mexico, 1890–1940*. Stanford: Stanford University Press, 1989.

Hale, Charles A. *Mexican Liberalism in the Age of Mora, 1821–1853*. New Haven: Yale University Press, 1968.

Hamnett, Brian. *Juárez*. New York: Longman, 1994.

Harris, Charles H. III. *A Mexican Family Empire: The Latifundio of the Sánchez Navarro Family, 1765–1867*. Austin: University of Texas Press, 1975.

Johns, Michael. *The City of Mexico in the Age of Díaz.* Austin: University of Texas Press, 1997.

Kandell, Jonathan. *La Capital: The Biography of Mexico City.* New York: Random House, 1988.

Katz, Friedrich. "Labor Conditions on Haciendas in Porfirian Mexico: Some Trends and Tendencies." *Hispanic American Historical Review* 54 (1974): 1–47.

————. *The Secret War in Mexico: Europe, the United States, and the Mexican Revolution.* Chicago: University of Chicago Press, 1981.

Knight, Alan. *The Mexican Revolution.* 2 vols. London: Cambridge University Press, 1984.

Knowlton, Robert J. *Church Property and the Mexican Reform, 1856–1910.* DeKalb: Northern Illinois University Press, 1976.

Krauze, Enrique. *Mexico, Biography of Power: A History of Modern Mexico, 1810–1996.* New York: HarperCollins, 1997.

Mallon, Florencia E. *Peasant and Nation: The Making of Postcolonial Mexico and Peru.* Berkeley: University of California Press, 1995.

Marichal, Carlos. *A Century of Debt Crises in Latin America, From Independence to the Great Depression.* Princeton: Princeton University Press, 1989.

Mayer, Brantz. *Mexico As It Was and Is.* New York: J. Winchester, 1843.

McCaffrey, James M. *Army of Manifest Destiny: The American Soldier in the Mexican War, 1846–1848.* New York: New York University Press, 1992.

McLachlan, Colin M. and William H. Beezley. *El Gran Pueblo: A History of Greater Mexico.* Englewood Cliffs: Prentice-Hall, 1994 (2d ed. 1999).

Meyers, William K. *Forge of Progress, Crucible of Revolt: The Origins of the Mexican Revolution in La Comarca Lagunera, 1880–1911.* Albuquerque: University of New Mexico Press, 1994.

Miller, Simon. "The Mexican Hacienda between the Insurgency and the Revolution: Maize Production and Commercial Triumph on the Temporal." *Journal of Latin American Studies* 16 (1984): 309–36.

Nickel, Herbert. "The Food Supply of Hacienda Laborers in Puebla-Tlaxcala during the Porfiriato: A First Approximation." In *Haciendas, Latifundios y Plantaciones en America Latina,* ed. by Enrique Florescano, pp. 113–59. Mexico: Siglo Veintiuno, 1975.

Ober, Frederick A. *Travels in Mexico and Life among the Mexicans.* Boston: Estes and Lauriat, 1884.

de la Peña, José Enrique. *With Santa Anna in Texas: A Personal Narrative of the Revolution.* Trans. Carmen Perry. College Station: Texas A&M Press, 1975.

Perry, Laurens Ballard. *Juárez and Díaz: Machine Politics in Mexico.* DeKalb: Northern Illinois University Press, 1978.

———— and Stephen R. Niblo. "Recent Additions to Nineteenth Century Mexican Historiography." *Latin American Research Review* 13 (1978): 3–45.

Pitner, Ernst. *Maximilian's Lieutenant: A Personal History of the Mexican Campaign, 1864–7.* Trans. and ed. Gordon Etherington-Smith. Albuquerque: University of New Mexico Press, 1993.

Reed, Nelson. *The Caste War of Yucatán.* Stanford: Stanford University Press, 1964.

Richmond, Douglas W., ed. *Essays on the Mexican War.* College Station: Texas A&M Press, 1986.

Ridley, Jasper. *Maximilian and Juárez.* New York: Ticknor and Fields, 1992.

Rodríguez O., Jaime E., ed. *The Mexican and Mexican American Experience in the Nineteenth Century.* Tempe: Bilingual Press, 1989.

————, ed. *Patterns of Contention in Mexican History.* Wilmington: Scholarly Resources, 1992.

Roeder, Ralph. *Juárez and His Mexico.* New York: Viking Press, 1947.

Ruggeley, Terry. *Yucatán's Maya Peasantry and the Origins of Caste War.* Austin: University of Texas Press, 1996.

Ruiz, Ramón. *Triumphs and Tragedy: A History of the Mexican People.* New York: W.W. Norton and Company, 1992.

Ryan, James W. *Camerone: The French Foreign Legion's Greatest Battle.* Westport: Praeger, 1996.

Salas, Elizabeth. *Soldaderas in the Mexican Military: Myth and History.* Austin: University of Texas Press, 1991.

Samponaro, Frank N. "The Political Role of the Army in Mexico, 1821–1848." Ph.D. diss., State University of New York-Stony Brook, 1974.

Santoni, Pedro. *Mexicans at Arms: Puro Federalists and the Politics of War, 1845–1848.* Fort Worth: Texas Christian University Press, 1996.

Saragoza, Alex M. *The Monterrey Elite and the Mexican State, 1880–1940.* Austin: University of Texas Press, 1988.

Sartorius, Carl. *Mexico about 1850.* Reprint ed. Stuttgart: F. A. Brockhaus, 1961.

Scholes, Walter V. *Mexican Politics during the Juárez Regime, 1855–1872.* Columbia: University of Missouri Press, 1957.

Shaw, Frederick John, Jr. "Poverty and Politics in Mexico City, 1824–1854." Ph.D. diss., University of Florida, 1975.

Siemens, Alfred H. *Between the Summit and the Sea: Central Veracruz in the Nineteenth Century.* Vancouver: University of British Columbia Press, 1990.

Sims, Harold D. *The Expulsion of Mexico's Spaniards, 1821–1836.* Pittsburgh: University of Pittsburgh Press, 1990.

Singletary, Otis A. *The Mexican War.* Chicago: University of Chicago Press, 1960.

Sprague, William F. *Vicente Guerrero: Mexican Liberator.* Chicago: R.R. Donnelly and Sons, 1939.

Stevens, Donald Fithian. *Origins of Instability in Early Republican Mexico.* Durham: Duke University Press, 1991.

Tenenbaum, Barbara. *The Politics of Penury: Debts and Taxes in Mexico, 1821–1856.* Albuquerque: University of New Mexico Press, 1986.

Tutino, John. *From Insurrection to Revolution in Mexico: Social Bases of Agrarian Violence, 1750–1940.* Princeton: Princeton University Press, 1986.

Vanderwood, Paul J. *Disorder and Progress: Bandits, Police and Mexican Development.* Revised ed. Wilmington: SR Books, 1992.

————. *The Power of God against the Guns of Government: Religious Upheaval in Mexico at the Turn of the Nineteenth Century.* Stanford: Stanford University Press, 1998.

Voss, Stuart F. *On the Periphery of Nineteenth Century Mexico: Sonora and Sinaloa, 1810–1877.* Tucson: University of Arizona Press, 1982.

Walker, David W. *Kinship, Business, and Politics: The Martínez del Rio Family in Mexico, 1823–1867.* Austin: University of Texas Press, 1986.

Warren, Richard A. "Vagrants and Citizens: Politics and the Poor in Mexico City, 1808–1836." Ph.D. diss., University of Chicago, 1994.

Weeks, Charles A. *The Juárez Myth in Mexico.* Tuscaloosa: University of Alabama Press, 1987.

Weems, John Edward. *To Conquer a Peace: The War between the United States and Mexico.* College Station: Texas A&M Press, 1974.

Wells, Allen and Gilbert M. Joseph. *Summer of Discontent, Seasons of Upheaval: Elite Politics and Rural Insurgency in Yucatán, 1876–1915.* Stanford: Stanford University Press, 1996.

INDEX

Afro-Mexicans, 37, 125

Agiotistas, 48, 68–69

Agriculture, commercialization of, 8, 153, 169, 184, 193

Aguador (water carrier), 41

Aguardiente, 111

Alameda Park, 200, 202

Alamo, 76

Algonzas, Captain Tomás, 123

Álvarez, Diego, 94

Álvarez, Juan, 10, 49, 57–58, 94, 101–103, 105, 124

American Smelting and Refining Company (ASARCO), 197

Ampudia, General Pedro de, 89

Angostura, Battle of, 80

Annencuilco, Morelos, 111

Anti-clericalism, 7

Anti-reelectionists, 224

Antuñano, Esteban, 70

Apaches, 28, 74–75, 110, 217

Arable land, 64

Arista, General Mariano, 79

Army, 53–54; political threat to González, 212; under Díaz, 218–219

Artisans, 37, 40, 177, 196, 207

Atchison, Topeka, and Santa Fe Railroad, 172

Authoritarianism, liberal, 109

Ayutla, Plan de, 94, 101, 102–103

Bajío, 199

Banco de Avío, 70, 72

Bands, brass, 128

Bandits, 11, 69, 107, 133, 140, 211

Banking, under Díaz, 170, 178

Barreteros (drillers), 34, 195

Batabs, 60

Batopilas, Chihuahua, 175, 196

Bazaine, Marshall Achille, 116, 121

Beals, Carlton, 134, 163

Benefices, 7

Bocas, Hacienda de, 152–153

Booms and Busts, 168, 184, 196

Bosses, local, 190 regional political, 108, 184, 231

Bounty, on scalps, 110

Bourbons, 4

Bourbon reforms, 5, 12

Bravery, 83, 123

Bravo, Nicolás, 46, 58

Budget, 68

Bullfighting, 157

Bureaucracy, 183, 199. See also Middle Class

Bustamante, Anastasio, 18, 21, 46, 47, 48, 53, 57, 59

Cabinet secretaries, 46

Caciques, 29

Calderón de la Barca, Fanny, 17, 23, 35–37, 70

California, gold rush, 110
Calles, Plutarco Elías, 230–231
Camarillas, 193. *See also* Villages
Camino Real, 110
Campeche, 102
Cananea, Sonora, 197; great strike, 207
Cantabria, Michoacan, 188
Cantón, Francisco "Pancho," 216
Capitación, *See* head tax
Capital flight, 62
Capitalist work ethic, 9, 10
Carlota (Charlotte), 112, 114, 117, 119, 120, 122
Carranza, Venustiano, 221, 225, 230
Casta Divina, 180
Castas, 11; upward mobility, 53
Casualties, civil wars, 135; war with the United States, 87
Caudilloism, 3
Centralism, 3, 6, 10, 48, 50
Centralists, 54, 55, 60, 68, 99
Centralization, 185
Cerro Gordo, Battle of, 80
Chalco, 153
Chiapas, 192; economic development, 179
Chihuahua, 96, 110, 123, 177, 182, 197, 215, 221, 226; loss of autonomy, 217–218
Child labor, 40
Children, 42; citizenship, 128; control over, 139
Cholera, 22
Church. *See* Roman Catholic Church
Churubusco, Battle of, 83
Científicos, 12, 220–221
Cinco de Mayo (May 5, 1862), 96–98, 115–116, 125, 128, 163
Cities, 9; secondary, 140–141
Citizenship, 128, 137
Coffee, 153, 179; women's work, 150
Córdoba, Veracruz, 153
Class, tensions, 10
Climate, 64

Clothing, *See* Dress
Coahuila, 25, 27, 32, 103, 221; notables, 225–226
Cockfighting, 156–157
Coercion, as pillar of Díaz regime, 210, 219
Coffee, 191–193
Cofradía(s), 30, 41
Collective landownership, 9, 176
Colonial rule, 4, 5; damaging heritage, 65
Comanches, 27–28, 74–75, 110
Communications, 183; impediment to development, 64
Comonfort, Ignacio, 96, 103, 105, 106, 130
Company Store, 151
Congress, Mexican, 59, 108–109, 129–130, 209; bicameral, 131; under Díaz, 211
Conscription, 82, 136, 163
Conservatism, 6, 48
Conservatives, 7, 19, 56, 58–60, 96, 103, 105–108, 111, 112, 115–116, 123, 127–129, 213–214
Constancia Mejicana, La, 70
Constitution, of 1824, 21, 50, 55; of 1836, 46, 58; 1842, 59. *See also* Organic Bases; of 1857, 98, 100, 104, 106–108, 113, 209; of 1917, 230
Contract Labor, in mines, 195–196
Copper, 174–176
Corn, imports, 185; production, 185–186
Corn and Beans, 142–143
Corn ration, 25, 27, 152
Corpus Christi, 154–155
Corral, Ramón, 215; vice-president, 221
Corruption, 62, 185; under González, 213; under Díaz, 219
Cotaxtla Squadron, 123–124
Country people, politics, 50, 54; rebels, 226; relations among, 133
Courts, 183
Creel, Enrique C., 216, 220, 224–225
Creelman, James, Interview with Porfirio Díaz, 167, 223

Crime, 204
Criminal Code, 1871, 139
Cristero Rebellion, 230, 232
Currency, scarcities, 135–136
Cyanide Process, 175

Daily Routine, 141
Day of the Dead, 155
De la Huerta, Adolfo, rebellion, 230
Debt, international, 108, 115
Debt peonage, 25, 38, 104, 151, 189; abolition of, 120
Democracy, 129
Denver-Rio Grande Railroad, 172
Department Stores, 202, 205
Deportations, Political, 180
Depression, 167, 168; destabilizes politics, 169; of 1907, 183, 187, 210, 221–223, 225
Díaz, José Faustino, 161
Díaz, Luz, 164
Díaz, Porfirio, 6, 8, 12, 97, 109, 120, 124, 130–131, 137, 160, 161–167, 168–173, 182, 185, 198, 208; fall, 221–228; first term, 211–212; ideology, 213–214; political genius, 209–210, 219–221; regime periodization, 209–210; relations with Great Britain, 211 relations with the United States, 211–212; suppressing regionalism, 214–218
Díaz, Porfirio, hijo, 164
Diet, changes in, 186
Diseases, epidemic, 12, 22, 35, 40, 141
Distribution of Wealth, 168, 177
Divorce, 107, 139
Domestic markets, 168, 177; human constraints, 62, 65; railroads, 171
Domestic service, 13, 40, 43, 135–136, 200, 205–206
Double standard, sexual, 14, 139
Draft, See conscription
Drainage Projects, Valley of Mexico, 203
Dress, 144–146

Drinking, 156, 203–204. See also Pulque
Drought, 187, 221
Durango, 25, 27
Duty-free Zone, 211

Earthquakes, 35–36
Economic development, 168; export-led, 183; institutional framework, 62
Economic Downturns, revolts, 210
Economic growth, 182; legislation to enable, 213
Economic legislation, 62
Economy, in wartime, 109–111
Education, 9
Eighteenth century, 4
Elections, 9, 108
Electricity, 175
Elites, 184–185; disdain for lower classes, 185
Entertainment, 154–157, 198
Entrepreneurship, small-scale, 183
Escobar, Gonzalo, rebellion, 230
Export crops, 13
Exports, 174
Expropriation Law, 1859, 133

Families, under Díaz, 217
Federalism, 3, 6, 10, 48, 50, 102, 113, 132; economic implications, 67; Díaz rejects, 216
Federalists, 53, 99
Ferdinand VII, 45
Filisola, General Vicente, 76
Finances, national government, 53–54
Flooding, Mexico City, 35, 203. See also Drainage Projects
Food, 142–144; consumption, 186; Mexico City, 35
Foreign investment, 8, 168, 171, 182–183; under Díaz, 209; under González, 213
Foreign loans, 68, 108
Foreign Relations, Díaz regime, 209

Forey, Marshall Elie Frederic, 116
Franz Joséph of Austria-Hungary, 117, 147
Free trade, 7, 48
France, 96, 115, 120
French Army, 120–121, 125
French Foreign Legion, 123–124
French Intervention, 3, 6, 93, 96, 97, 109,
    113–116, 163, 165, 212; blockade 1838, 59;
    physical destruction, 134
Fueros, 95; military, 53

Gadsden Purchase, *See* Treaty of Mesilla
Gambling, 156–157
Gamboa, Federico, 164
Garza Galán, José Maria, 225
Gender relations, 13; impact of war, 14, 133
Geography, as a constraint to economic
    development, 64–65
Germand Investment, 179
Goliad, Battle of, 76
Gold, 176
Gómez Farías, Valentín, 46, 51, 52, 53, 58
Gómez Pedraza, Manuel, 56
González, General Manuel, 165, 167,
    169–171, 209; presidency, 212–213
González Ortega, Jesus, 97, 108
Governors, under Díaz, 214
Great Britain, 55, 68, 77, 96, 115, 212; invest-
    ment in Mexico, 171
Grito de Dolores, 14, 45, 128, 161
Guadalajara, 5
Guanajuato, 110, 175, 199
Guatemala, 5
Gueletao, 94
Guerrero (state), 163, 221; economic devel-
    opment, 180
Guerrero, Vicente, 18, 21, 45, 55–56, 57, 58
Guerrilla warfare, 163; war with the United
    States, 81–82, 85
Guggenheim family, 175

Guilds, 41
Gutierrez Estrada, Miguel, 114, 116

Hacendados, 5, 23–29, 127–128, 189–190, 192
Hacienda(s), 6, 23–29, 134, 136, 151; in
    crisis, 70–72; relations with villages, 29,
    126–127, 136, 139, 169, 176; working con-
    ditions, 152–153
Hacienda del Maguey, 26–27
Hans, Alberto, 124
Hapsburgs, 4
Head tax, 126
Henequen, 191; transformation of Yucatán,
    188–190
Herrera, José Joaquin de, 46, 60, 77, 78
Hidalgo (state), 182
Hidalgo, Father Miguel, 5, 18, 45, 50, 124
Hidalgo, José Manuel, 114, 116
Hidalgo de Parral, Chihuahua, 196
Hombres de bien, 12, 46, 47, 51, 53, 56, 58,
    59, 100, 101, 129, 185; war with the
    United States, 86
Honor, 139, 187
House of Tiles, 202
Households, single-parent, 135
Housing, Mexico City, 34–35, 201; country
    people 150; farmers, 148; middle class,
    148; wealthy, 147–148
Huerta, General Victoriano, 229
Huntington, Hollis P., 172

Ideology, during the Díaz administration,
    213–214
Immigration, lack of, 65
Independence, 3, 5, 6, 22
Indians, 12, 126–128, 132, 184; dress, 146; no-
    madic, 211; resistance, 74; technology,
    192; work ethic, 31–32
Indian tribute, 67. *See also* Head tax
Indian wars, 138

Infant mortality, 39–40, 42–43

Industrialization, 8, 177–179, 184; delay in development in Mexico City, 41; impact on crafts, 193; and women, 13, 205; work ethic, 140, 177

Institutional development, Díaz administration, 169–171; impediment to economic development, 65–69

International Harvester Corporation, 180

Iturbide, Agustín (Agustín I), 18, 21, 45–46, 50, 56, 67, 112

Iturbidistas, 55

Izábal, Rafael, 215

Jecker and Company, 106

Jefes Políticos, 132, 185; under Díaz, 216–217, 218

Jockey Club, 202

Juárez, Benito, 6, 10, 19, 20, 53, 92, 93–97, 106–109, 112–115, 120, 122, 124, 126, 128–132, 161–162, 165, 176, 185, 210–211

Juchitán, Oaxaca, 163

Juntas patrioticas, 128

Kinship, networks, 184, 198

La Bufa, Battle of, 130

La Laguna, 174

La Noria, Plan de, 130, 165

Labor, Forced, 183

Labor Conditions, 179

Labor scarcity, 33, 151

Labor unions, 10, 206–208; and the revolution, 231–232

Laissez-faire, 7. See also Free trade

Land, as a commodity, 193; expropriations, 187–188

Land tenure systems, 4

Landholding, communal, 127, 134, 137–139, 176; urban, 133. See also Villages

Landholding, Concentration of, 170, 176–177

Landholding, foreign, 137

Law of Colonization (1830), 75–76, 169, 176

Lead, 176

Leopold, King of Belgium, 128

Leperos, 34, 55

Lerdo, Miguel, 108

Lerdo de Tejada, Sebastián, 53, 97, 98, 130–131, 165, 211

Ley Fuga, 210

Ley Juárez, 95, 103

Ley Lerdo, 103, 110, 133

Liberal contradiction, 113

Liberal Party, 220

Liberalism, 6, 48

Liberals, 7, 58, 99–100, 104, 106–109, 113, 126–129, 132, 137–139, 162–163, 210, 213–214, 216, 227; mestizo, 165

Limantour, José Yves, 167, 170, 222; científicos, 220; and railroads, 172, 174

Living Standards, 185–187

Loans, Forced, 135

Local autonomy, 9, 30, 127, 183, 217

Local government, 134

Lone Star Republic, 76

Lower classes, upward mobility, 56; politics, 100

Loyalty, under Díaz, 214

Lozada, Manuel, 100

Lucas, Juan Francisco, 127–128

Luneros, 27

Madero, Evaristo, 215

Madero Family, 221, 225; mining interests, 175

Madero, Francisco I., 14, 190, 224, 226–228, 229

Manga de Clava, Hacienda de, 19

Manhood, 138

Manufacturing, 72, 205
Market, Sunday, 150
Márquez, Leonardo, 106–107, 123
Marriage, 9, 11, 42, 43, 107, 139; age of, 135
Matamoros, Battle of, 123
Maximilian, 93, 97, 98, 112, 114–118, 120–123, 127, 147, 151, 163; beautification of Mexico City, 142; execution of, 123
Maya Indians, 10, 30, 31–32, 60, 102, 189; family life, 32, 189; Texas War, 76. *See also* Yucatán
Mayer, Brantz, 144, 157
Mayo Valley, 215
Mayordomo, 22
Maytorena Family, 222
McLane-Ocampo Treay, 106
Meals, *See* Food
Medical care, war with the United States, 84
Mejía, Tomás, 97, 107, 123
Merchants, 5
Merida, Yucatán, 102
Mestizos, 12, 128, 164–165, 193; dress, 145
Metate, 32
Mexican Central Railroad, 167, 171–172, 177, 187
Mexican National Railway, 167, 171–172, 187
Mexico City, 34–44, 59, 66, 67, 69, 111, 183; living conditions, 12, 141–142, 182, 198–206; war with the United States, 81, 90
Michoacan, 136, 188; economic recovery, 71, 72
Middle classes, 37, 40, 206, 230; expansion, 183, 200; fear of masses, 204; revolution, 224
Mier y Terán, Manuel de, 75
Migration, from countryside to city, 42, 135, 184, 196, 198–200; outward from villages, 188; to the United States, 182, 184
Military, 5, 53–54, 113; as political leaders, 46; leadership, 82

Military Zone Commanders, 214
Militia, 53, 102
Milpa, 23
Miners, 194–198
Mining, 63, 67, 174–176, 178, 182–183, 194–198
Mining camps, 33–34, 194
Mining Code (1884), 167, 170
Miramon, Miguel, 97, 106, 123
Missions, Catholic, 75
Moderados, 7, 56, 100, 103, 105; *See also* Liberals
Molina, Olegario, 180, 216, 220
Molina-Montes Family, 181, 222
Monarchism, 6, 45
Monarchists, 116
Monarchy, 112
Monopolies, 177
Monterrey, economic development, 179, 196; war with the United States, 89
Mordita, La, 219
Morelos(state), 111
Morelos, Father José Maria, 55
Mori, Petrona, 161
Mortality Rates, Mexico City, 203
Mulattoes, 12
Mutualist societies, 10, 206–207

Namiquipa, Chihuahua, 138
Napoleon III, 112, 114–117, 120
National Bank of Mexico, 170
National Guard, 126, 128, 132, 163
Nationhood, sense of, 5
New Spain, 4, 5, 22
Noise, Mexico City, 204
North, working conditions, 182, 190
Northern frontier, 74–75
Notables, 48, 49, 60, 214–218; discontent, 222, 225; revolutionaries, 229
Nutrition, 26

Oaxaca, 94, 95, 130, 137, 161
Oaxaca City, 140
Ober, Frederick, 145
Obrajes (textile factories), 38
Obregón, Alvaro, 230–231
Occupation, United States, 90
Order and Progress, 12
Organic Bases (Bases Orgánicas), 59–60
Orizaba Strike, 208
Orozco, Pascual, hijo, 227
Ortega de Díaz, Delfina

Palm Sunday, 156
Palomas Land and Cattle Company, 177
Pan American Railway, 179
Pan o Palo, 211
Paredes y Arrillaga, Mariano, 68, 79
Parián Riot, 21
Paseo de la Reforma, 200
Paso del Norte (*See also* Ciudad Juárez),
    96, 123, 228
Pastry War, 21, 59
Paternalism, 197; erosion of, 184
Patriarchy, 126
Patrons, 5
Peace negotiations, war with the United
    States, 85–86
Peon(s), 24, 25, 38, 136, 187
Peones acasillados (permanent workers),
    See Resident peons
Pintos, 105
Plateros District (Mexico City), 200–201
Plaza, 140
Plow, 192
Political culture, 5
Politics, 6–13, 46–51
Polk, James K., 77, 78, 87
Police, 204
Political Economy, Porfirian, 169
Poor, the, 12; Mexico City, 39–40; politics,
    50, 56; diet, 144

Population, 22, 37–38; decline, 4; growth,
    10–11, 185, 198–199
Populacho, *See* Leperos
Positivism, 220
Potable water, Mexico City, 35
Presidential Succession of 1910, 227
PNR (National Revolutionary Party, 231
PRI (Party of the Institutionalized Revolu-
    tion), 97
PRM (Mexican Revolutionary Party), 231
Prices, staples, 9, 144, 185–186
Prieto, Guillermo, 55, 57, 106
Private Life, intrusions into under Díaz,
    217
Professionals, 200
Protestantism, 193
Prostitutes, 37
Prostitution, 204
Protectionism, 7, 48
Public lands, Giveaway of, 176–177. *See also*
    Terrenos Baldíos
Puebla, 23, 30, 103, 105, 116, 125, 130; strike,
    207
Puebla Sierra, 127–128, 136
Pueblo, *See* Village
Pulque, 144, 156; consumption, 203–204
Punishment, corporal, 28
Puros, 7, 100, 103, 129. *See also* Liberals

Querétaro, 111, 123, 140

Race, 10–12, 22
Railroads, 165, 171–172–175, 179, 184, 187,
    212; consolidation, 174; economic link-
    ages, 174; political instability, 176; work-
    ing conditions, 182
Rancheros, 150, 192–193, 217; Diet, 144;
    House, 150
Rancho(s), 23, 134
Reform era, the(La Reforma), 3, 6, 7, 98,
    103–106, 183

Reform, Fiscal, 170–171
Reform Laws, 109–110, 121–127, 133–134, 137–139, 182
Regimentation, 184. *See also* Work Ethic
Region, as a determinant of hacienda conditions, 25–26
Regions, 5, 102
Regionalism, 3, 96; and the army, 219
Religion, 130–131; celebrations, 154–155; in the villages, 33; and protests, 232
Republicas de indios, 30
Republicans, 126–127
Republicanism, 6
Resident peons, 24–25, 151–152, 190–191. *See also* Peones Acasillados; vaqueros
Resistance, to land expropriations, 187; to modernity, 9, 10; to oppressive conditions, 31
Restored Republic, 97, 128–131
Revenues, government, 62, 67, 96
Revolution, 3; 1910, 223–228, 229–232
Revolutionary Coalition, 229
Reyes, General Bernardo, 220–223
Riots, urban, 9, 50
Riva Palacio, Mariano, 89
Riva Palacio, Vicente, Home, 147, 180–181
Roman Catholic Church, 9, 31, 58, 59, 66, 100, 104, 107–108, 111, 113, 121, 127, 130–131, 193, 211, 231; as banker, 7–8, 69–70, 89; conciliation with government, 212; expropriations of its land, 110, 137
Romero Rubio de Díaz, Carmen, 162, 164
Romero Rubio, Manuel, 216; científicos, 220
Rurales, 210, 217; myth, 219

Salm-Salm, Princess, 93
San Jacinto, Battle of, 76
San Juan de Ulua, 95
Sánchez Navarro family, 25, 27–28, 89

Sanitation, Mexico City, 35
Santa Anna, Antonio López de, 6, 10, 16–20, 21, 46, 56–60, 95, 98, 101–102, 104, 112, 130, 162; his leg, 18, 60; fiscal policy, 68; Texas, 76, 77; war with the United States, 79–81, 86, 89
San Juanico, Hacienda de, 111
San Marcos, Hacienda de, 111
Schools, Public, 138
Scott, General Winfield, 80, 85, 86, 89
Seamstresses, 136
Seven Laws (Siete Leyes), 58–59
Sharecroppers, 24, 138, 153, 188, 190
Shepherd, Alexander, 175, 197
Shepherds, 26
Sierra Gorda rebellions, 101
Silver, 174–176; decline of, 63–64, 72; mining, 110; recovery, 72–73
Sinaloa, 140
Slash and burn cultivation, 32–33
Slavery, abolition, 62; 104; new forms, 179, 183, 189–190
Smelting, 175
Soldaderas, 125
Soldiers, war with the United States, 82–84; French Intervention, 123–126
Sonora, 110; Triumvirate, 215–216
Spain, 96, 115
Spanish, invasion of Mexico, 1829, 18, 21, 53
Squash, 143
Strikes (labor), 167, 207
Subsidies, Railroads, 171
Subsoil Rights, 170
Suffrage, 14, 50, 54
Surveying Companies, 170

Tabasco, labor conditions, 183
Tacubaya, Plan de, 105
Tampico, 12
Tariffs, 9, 56, 178
Taxes, 9, 30, 31, 126, 135, 183, 185

Taylor, General Zachary, 78–79
Technology, advances in, 133, 175, 184; limitations, 178, 192; mining, 195; rasper, 188
Tehuantepec, Isthmus of, 106, 163
Temporary Workers, 24, 151–152, 191
Tenants, 24, 137, 152–153
Terrazas, Luis, 177, 215–216, 220
Terrazas, Silvestre, 224–225
Terrazas-Creel Family, 181, 222
Terrenos Baldíos (vacant lands), 169
Texas, 6, 58, 74; loss of, 75–77; annexation of by the United States, 21, 77
Textiles, 72
Three Guarantees, 45
Tithe, 7, 58, 69
Tlaxcala, Strikes, 207
Tobacco Industry, 206
Tomochic Rebellion, 167, 218
Torreón, Coahuila, 196
Torres, Luis, 215
Tortillas, 32, 125, 142–143
Transportation, 61, 72, 183. See also Railroads
Treaty of Mesilla, 21, 68, 102
Trial by jury, 104
Tripartite Intervention, 98
Trusts, 181
Tuxtepec, Plan de, 131
Tyler, John, 77

Unemployment, 188, 203
United States, 21, 68, 114; civil war, 115, 120; high wages, 183, 190, 196; investment in Mexico, 171, 174–175; relations with Díaz, 211–212 strategy in war with Mexico, 79; trade with, 73
Unskilled workers, 37
Upper classes, 37, 40; fear of lower classes, 11, 12, 50–51, 101, 204–205
Urrea, General José, 76

Vagrants, 190
Valencia, General Gabriel, 81
Vaqueros, 190; dress, 146
Vecindades, 34, 181
Veracruz, 12, 18, 19, 59, 115, 134, 141; coffee region, 150, 153–154, 191–193; war with the United States, 80, 87
Victoria, Guadalupe, 18, 21, 45, 46, 47, 55, 56, 58, 68
Vidaurri, Santiago, 96, 100, 103
Villa, Pancho, 225, 229–230
Villages, 9, 12, 24, 29–33, 54, 100, 103, 107, 132, 137–139, 151, 180, 192; buying land, 71; expropriation of lands, 111, 126, 127, 182, 188; inter-village rivalries, 136 (See also Haciendas); leadership, 5, 49, 54, 193; under Díaz, 216
Violence, 8

Wages, 39–40, 42, 178, 185–186, 190, 192–198, 207, 232
War, 3, 6, 123–126, 133; impact on politics, 136; impact on women, 14
War of the Reform, 3, 6, 93, 96, 98, 99, 106–108, 112–114
War to the death, 122
War with the United States, 3, 6, 19, 21; 74–90, 109–110, 124–125; psychological effect, 99
Wars of Independence, 4; economic impact, 61–62
Water and Sewerage Systems, 203
Wealth, distribution of, 136, 183, 199, 202
Wife Beating, 139
Women, 3; in coffee regions, 191; in the countryside, 28–29, 32, 33, 150–151; employment, 135–136, 184; heads of households, 43, 135; in henequen region, 191; in manufacturing, 200; in Mexico City, 39–40, 41–42; in war with the United States, 84. See also Domestic Service

Work day, hacienda, 26
Work Ethic, capitalist, 184, 198; culture
    clash, 193
Work place, 184

Yaqui Valley, 215
Yaquis (Yaqui Indians), 75, 180; rebels, 226
Yucatán, 5, 10, 23, 27, 32, 188–190; Caste
    War of, 6, 60, 101–102; economic devel-
    opment, 180; labor conditions, 183, 191;
    notables, 216

Zacatecas, 135, 141
Zapata, Emiliano, 111, 226, 229
Zapotecs, 163
Zaragoza, Ignacio, 124
Zinc, 174
Zocalo, 34
Zuloaga, General Félix, 105